A TIME OF RENEWAL

A TIME OF RENEWAL
*Clusters of Characters, C.P. Snow
and Coups*

Philip Snow

The Radcliffe Press
London · New York

Published in 1998 by
The Radcliffe Press
An imprint of I.B.Tauris & Co Ltd
Victoria House
Bloomsbury Square
London WC1B 4DZ

In the United States of America
and Canada distributed by
St Martin's Press
175 Fifth Avenue
New York
NY 10010

A full CIP record for this book is available from the British Library

A full CIP record for this book is available from the Library of Congress

ISBN 1–86064–149–0
Library of Congress Catalog card number: available

Copy-edited and laser-set by Oxford Publishing Services, Oxford
Printed and bound in Great Britain by WBC Ltd, Bridgend, Mid Glamorgan

For the three generations: my wife Anne and my daughter Stefanie, who have seen the 46 years described in this narrative, and my granddaughter Philippa, who has seen the most recent 16.

Contents

Illustrations

1. Author on change of career, 1952.
2. Humphrey Evans, author's wife and daughter with author at Garden House, Cambridge, 1953.
3. Sir Will Spens, Chairman of Rugby Governing Body.
4. Author, captain of MCC *v.* Rugby, flanked by RES Wyatt and RE Bird, 1955.
5. Ratu Sir Lala Sukuna, Field Marshal Earl Elexander of Tunis, President of MCC, and author, on the presentation of the painting of Albert Park, Suva, for the Imperial War Memorial Gallery at Lord's, 1956.
6. Charles, Pamela and author outside the Bursary, Rugby, 1952.
7. First meeting of the International Cricket Conference, in succession to the Imperial Cricket Conference, at Lord's, 1966.
8. Lord Parker of Waddington presents author to the Queen on Rugby's four-hundredth anniversary, 1967.
9. Stefanie, author and wife listen to a speech by Charles in the Cholmondeley Room at the House of Lords on Stefanie's twenty-first birthday, 1968.
10. Ratu Sir Penaia Ganilau, Adi Lady Laisa, author and wife at Rugby, 1970.
11. Ratu Sir George Cakobau, Adi Lady Lealea, author and wife at Angmering, 1980.
12. Sir Colin Cowdrey introducing author and wife to John Major at 10 Downing Street, 1991.
13. The International Cricket Council at Lords, 1994.
14. Ratu Epeli Nailatikau, author's wife, Ratu Sir Kamisese Mara, Adi Lady Lala Mara, author and Adi Koila Nailarikau at Angmering, 1992.
15. The three generations: author's wife, Anne, their daughter, Stefanie, and granddaughter, Philippa, 1995.
16. The author's granddaughter, Philippa, aged 16, 1995.

Abbreviations

ADC	Aide-de-camp
CBE	Commander of the Order of the British Empire
CH	Companion of Honour
CIE	Companion of the Order of the Indian Emperor
CMG	Companion of the Order of St Michael and St George
CPU	Commonwealth Press Union
CSI	Companion of the Order of the Star of India
DC	District Commissioner
DSO	Companion of the Distinguished Service Order
EE	English Electric
FRS	Fellow of the Royal Society
GC	George Cross
GCB	Knight *or* Dame Grand Cross of the Order of the Bath
GCIE	Knight Grand Commander of the Order of the Indian Empire
GCMG	Knight *or* Dame Grand Cross of the Order of St Michael and St George
GCSI	Knight Grand Commander of the Order of the Star of India
GCVO	Knight *or* Dame Grand Cross of the Royal Victorian Order
HMG	Her *or* His Majesty's Government

Abbreviations

ICC	International Cricket Conference (Council)
ICS	Indian Civil Service
JP	Justice of the Peace
K	knighthood
KBE	Knight Commander of the Order of the British Empire
KCB	Knight Commander of the Order of the Bath
KCMG	Knight Commander of the Order of St Michael and St George
KG	Knight of the Order of the Garter
KT	Knight of the Order of the Thistle
LCJ	Lord Chief Justice
LG	Lady Companion of the Order of the Garter
LT	Lady Companion of the Order of the Thistle
LVO	Lieutenant of the Royal Victorian Order
MBE	Member of the Order of the British Empire
MC	Military Cross
MC	Master of Ceremonies
MCC	Marylebone Cricket Club
MI5	Military Intelligence Secret Service Division
MVO	Member of the Royal Victorian Order
OBE	Officer of the Order of the British Empire
OM	Member of the Order of Merit
RAF	Royal Air Force
RM	Royal Marines
SOE	Special Operations Executive
TLS	*Times Literary Supplement*
VC	Victoria Cross

Glossary of Fijian Words

Adi	title of rank for a woman, Lady
Buli	district head
dalo	root vegetable (taro)
kava	drink prepared from *yaqona* roots (Polynesian)
loloma	love
Ratu	chief, Sir
Roko Tui	Government head of a province
sulu	skirt
tapa	decorative cloth handmade from tree bark
Tui	king
Tui Cakau	King of Cakaudrove
Tui Lau	King of Lau
Tui Noimalu	King of Noimalu
Tui Vitogo	King of Vitogo
Tui Vuda	King of Vuda
Tunku	Prince (Malay)
vakabogidrau	lifting of mourning on hundredth night after a death accompanied by presentation of mats, whale's teeth, *tapa* and other property with feasts
vakataraisulu	permitting the taking off of black mourning clothes accompanied by exchange of property and feasting
Vunivalu	title of high rank
yaka	Fijian species of wood
yaqona	*kava* made from a powdered root of the pepper family

Preface and Acknowledgements

I really included most of what I needed to say by way of a preface in the first of these companion volumes coming out a shade before this one and entitled *The Years of Hope*. Its subtitle, *Cambridge, Colonial Administration in the South Seas, Cricket*, faithfully epitomizes its contents, as does the subtitle for this one, its title harmonizing with the first — both in the style of my elder brother, C. P. Snow, perhaps the leading influence in my life, as was manifest in my *Stranger and Brother: A Portrait of C. P. Snow* (1982 and 1983). This work is partly a sequel to that biography. While sequels to *Gone with the Wind*, *Rebecca* and so on are a vogue currently the darling of publishers and held to be in demand, I have to declare that I don't envisage this being in that position.

After the natural break in 1951, where the first volume concluded, there is a different world in the main commented on in this volume. Themes common to both books are my continued connections with the South Seas right up to the present. As in the first volume, vignettes on aspects of cricket sometimes inclined to be off-beat or not commonly featured these days are again offered. I have tried to make them acceptable to the *non-cognoscenti* of what is admittedly an esoteric game and perhaps none the worse for being so. A new background as compared with the first time is that of Rugby School, a well enough known name over quite a lot of the world. Since it does not reflect any part of its academic side the descriptions offered may come afresh or at least from an unusual angle.

As for the characters, these encompass some of my brother's and my own friends and acquaintances, perhaps providing, as it were, a sort of finite social panorama or frieze from the 1950s to the 1990s — with, of course, some entertaining eccentrics on the periphery.

The coda includes a detached view of two momentous recent *coups d'état* in what has often been described as paradise.

The whole is an account, largely chronological for the sake of theme and narrative flow, of ordinary people, of less than ordinary people and of some extraordinary people. A few are celebrated: many of them are, however, pared down. Some of the ordinary and less ordinary have been more interesting. Inevitably, places go with people: the two together, at least for me, have personality and are, and have been (with health), the most important elements of living.

As mentioned in the preface to the first of this pair of books, these are my last publications, the eighth and ninth, stretching back over nearly half a century.

In rounding off, the pleasant duty remains for me to record my acknowledgements to the many who have helped directly or indirectly with this particular volume. For the previous one I did my best to remember all who assisted with it, but I have to admit that since this and its matching volume were originally all one with a single preface and single list of acknowledgements it has not been simple or an exact science dividing the two in these respects. Therefore, some names which should properly be in that book are in this and vice versa. What I earnestly hope is that in one or the other — some are in both — I have not made the cardinal error of missing in this book any who have in their way helped magnanimously with advice, perspective, wisdom and material. Of course, remaining defects are mine and duly apologized for. All that having been said, I do not cease reflecting or observing, but merely refrain from putting these activities on paper.

Permission from Anthony Powell, CH, CBE, MA, and the Bulgarian Ambassador to the United Kingdom to quote from letters is gratefully acknowledged. Similar acknowledgements are due to the *Daily Telegraph*, London, and *The Times*, London, regarding excerpts. Every effort has been made to trace any copyright holders. Any omissions are regretted and will be included in a following edition. Sources of literary aid are at the end of this work in the bibliography.

Individuals whom I hasten to thank for encouragement and help are my daughter Stefanie and her husband Peter Waine, who believed that I should go on record with this and were instrumental in discovering the right publisher, and for their assistance in so many ways, including ideas for the books' titles; my granddaughter, Philippa, for her inspiring curiosity; my wife, Anne who typed unselfishly seemingly ceaseless drafts in my execrable script of all my previous seven books and was pressed to take hard-earned, reluctant but absolutely deserved retirement before the current books to become a diligent, tireless critic; Joe and Lindsay Buzaglo for generous help; Lindsay again and Linda Mitchell for the practicality of extracting this so patiently from a tangled manuscript and recalcitrant, occasionally quite crazy tapes; over many years the staff of West Sussex County Council's superb library service, notably those of Rustington and Angmering libraries, and in particular there Debra Wilson, ALA, Sandra Seddigh and Margaret Smart; Beverley Barrett, Dorothy Sterling and Janet Plomer; all who contributed consciously or unconsciously to the material such as Charles, Lord Snow of Leicester, CBE, Ph.D.; Lady Snow (née Pamela Hansford Johnson), CBE; E. Eric Snow, FIHVE; Humphrey S. Evans, MRCS, LRCP, BA; Christopher C. Legge, BA; Reginald and Gillian Caten; Noel and Alison McEvoy; W. F. Martin Clemens, CBE, MC, AM, MA; Paul A. C. V. Geraghty, MA, Ph.D.; William Warden; Jane F. V. Roth; Adi Sofia Veisa Mara Pennington-Richards (née Hennings); Martin and Diane Daly (née Carrick); Pamela Hampton (née Langford); Iris Johnson (née May); Professor E. John H. Corner, CBE, FRS, MA; Sir Rex de Charembac Nan Kivell; Sydney A. Spence; John and Margaret Goulding; John F. Hughes; Public Relations Officer, Fiji; *Rugby Advertiser*; *Leicester Evening Mail*; *Coventry Evening Telegraph*; *Leicester Mercury*; HRH Crown Prince Tupouto'a of Tonga; Enid Wise (née Thomson); Raymond Burr; Editha Pease (née Le Hunte); Sir David F. Attenborough, CH, CVO, CBE, FRS, MA; Ratu Sir J. Lala V. Sukuna, KCMG, KBE, BA, *Méd. mil*; Ratu Sir Edward T. T. Cakobau, KBE, MC; Ratu Sir

Preface and Acknowledgements

George K. Cakobau, GCMG, GCVO, OBE, JP, Royal Victorian Chain; Ratu Sir Penaia K. Ganilau, GCMG, KCVO, KBE, DSO; Ratu Sir Kamisese K. T. Mara, GCMG, KBE, MA PC; the Royal Anthropological Institute Library; the British Library; the Libraries of the South Pacific University, Suva, and the University of Hawaii, Honolulu; Walter A. Hadlee, CBE; Kenneth A. Stuart, OBE, LLB; Sir Robert L. Munro, CBE, LLB; Professor Gerald M. D. Howat, MA, M.Litt, Ph.D; Henry G. Button, MA; E. James Coode, OBE, MA; Ian R. Salmond, MA; John A. Lourie, Ph.D., MA, BM, B.Ch., FRCS; Christopher J. Heyes, LLB; Professor Harry E. Maude, OBE, MA; Charles R. H. Nott, CMG, OBE, MA; J. Anne Gittins; June Knox-Mawer; Joseph D. Gibson, CBE; Ratu Josua Toganivalu, CBE, JP; Rt Hon George, 2nd Earl Jellicoe, KBE, DSO, MC, JP, PC, FRS; Rt Hon Malcolm MacDonald, OM, PC; Kenneth V. Rose, CBE, FRSL; Colonel Heinrich R. Amstütz, Swiss Cavalry; Adi Losalini Cakobau Browne; HRH Prince Tunku Imran ibni Tuanku Ja'afar of Malaysia; Setareki Tuinaceva, Principal Archivist, and Margaret Patel, Senior Archivist, National Archives of Fiji; Donald H. W. Dickson, Ph.D., FRIC; Professor 2nd Lord Tedder, MA, Ph.D., D.Sc, FRSE, FRSC; Hugh Massingberd; Sir Patrick H. Dean, GCMG; Lady Patricia Dean; Baron Vaea of Houma; Alec R. Waugh; Anne Griffiths, LVO; Catherine Aldington Guillaume; Commander Andrew C. F. David; Arthur L. Baker, MBE; Fabio y Valls (E. G. Fabio Barraclough); Henry Ehrlich and Marilyn Silverstone of *Look* magazine, USA; Père Patrick Georges Farell O'Reilly and Renée Heyum of the Musée de l'Homme, Paris; Charles Vesely; Peter I. Knight, LLB; Professor Joseph F. Maloney; Anne Seagrim; Peggy Rhodes; Brian V. Davies, MA; Edward A. Jones, BA; Professor Albert J. Schütz, MA, Ph.D. and Lynette Furuhashi of the University of Hawaii; Countess Karin Antonini; Alan Maclean; Sheila Lochhead (née MacDonald); Gordon A. Hutchinson, MA; Daryl Tarte; Richard D. H. Roberts; Kenneth C. Harlow; Jack Trotman, CPM; Douglas Ettridge; R. E. S. Wyatt; B. H. Valentine, MC; Fergus G. A. U. Clunie, B.Sc; Robertson R. Wright, MBE; HE Brigadier Ratu Epeli Nailatikau, LVO, OBE, and Adi Koila Nailatikau; Iradj Bagherzade, chairman of IB Tauris & Co, London; and Lester Crook, Ph.D., the Radcliffe Press's publisher, whose encouragement was vital and whose kindness and willingness to edit a huge manuscript giving it sharpness and shape so expertly was far beyond any bounds of duty; and finally those who by simply genial and general enquiry about progress have kept me well and truly at it.

Angmering
Sussex, England
7 November 1988–7 August 1997

1

Horses in Midstream

In *The Times* and the *Daily Telegraph* were advertisements for the appointment of Second Bursar for the Governing Body of Rugby School, only 20 miles from Leicester. We drove out to glance at the ambit of the school and the town and half-heartedly I put in an application, not caring if it were successful or not. Summoned to an interview, I had the same casual attitude. Six of us sat in Jericho Parlour just outside Jerusalem Chamber, the medieval annexe to Westminster Abbey in which monarchs are dressed ceremonially for coronations in the Abbey proper. Alphabetical was the order of going before the board. At S, last to go in, I had a long wait but no nerves since I had nothing to gain or lose.

Inside the Jerusalem Chamber there were three interviewers: Gerald Steel, deputy chairman of the Governing Body of Rugby School, who had been assistant private secretary to Churchill as First Lord of the Admiralty at the beginning of the First World War and then general manager of British Aluminium Company, presiding, Sir Arthur fforde, Headmaster, and John Churchill Dunkin, Bursar. Steel explained that the latter, two years off retiring age after 24 years as Bursar, was being seconded to set up and run an appeal for a quarter of a million pounds to modernize parts of the school necessarily run down in, and outdated by, the war. I did not say so but I was rather put off, mistakenly, in my ignorance of public schools, by the fact that here was one needing money. Was it advisable to be attached to such an institution? I did not know that almost all other schools were contemplating similar appeals and have done so ever since, practically without break.

The interviewers asked me what my duties in Fiji were. The

1

Secretariat spoke for itself: the versatility required in the multi-farious tasks in districts also appealed to them. It all seemed to go quite well and specially so when Steel remarked that he had seen my picture in the Peterborough column of the *Daily Telegraph* that very day, in a group photograph, as captain of the Fiji cricket team touring New Zealand in 1948. I can't remember why there was this piece in about me: it may have been that I had been negotiating at Lord's for a first tour of a Fijian team to England. Anyway, it seemed an esoteric point no doubt over the other five in the short list unlikely to be in the day's press. As the interview ended, fforde transfixed me with a glittering smile, which gave his eyes a glow and creased his face amiably; I was aware too of a very firm handshake. I thought that he seemed a most pleasant person but I presumed that he had been equally courteous to the other candidates. Going out of the door of Jerusalem Chamber, I turned to say I would welcome any decision quickly because my car was booked to leave with us for Fiji in a fortnight and that I would have to pay tax on it if I stayed, but if I could obtain permission to retain it, it would not then be exported. As I left Jericho Parlour the porter whispered to me: 'You're going to get it.' I had no means of knowing whether he said that to all the other candidates.

No sooner had I returned within the hour to my brother Charles's house at 1 Hyde Park Crescent, where Anne and Stefanie were staying with me, when a telegram arrived offering me the post. All were delighted. It meant a reduction in salary from £1000, which I had just reached in Fiji, to £750, but in Fiji essential articles, having to be imported, were expensive, and this to some extent, but not quite, reduced the differential. It would obviously mean having to go extremely carefully until I advanced on the incremental Rugby scale, where the maximum was £1200.

The benign Plum Warner, on the many occasions when I saw him later, used to claim credit for my appointment. He had been at Rugby as a boy and I had asked him to send in a letter of support for my application form. Later, when I knew Gerald Steel and Arthur fforde I asked them separately if Plum's support had been a factor. They both said that it had no influence on my get-ting onto the short list, which had been caused by there appearing to be a strong case in my statement of versatile experience. Both stated that I had impressed markedly at the interview, and I reflected whether this might not have been due to my not concentrating so hard on wanting the job, for I frankly did not know whether I was for returning to Fiji or remaining back in England.

When the announcement was put by Rugby in *The Times*, there was the unusual fact of a leading article additionally about the appointment. It suggested in an informed manner that the boys of Rugby School could look forward to taro (*dalo*) becoming a staple form of their diet. This was funny but somewhat off the mark as I was not domestic bursar (there was not one) and had nothing to do with food or housekeeping, which were the duties of the 12 housemasters. There had, apparently, been 250 applicants; and I was told later by Dunkin — to whom the word 'gentleman' could be applied unpontifically and who was of the highest integrity and sagacity, if a little remote, designedly so, from the 80 teaching colleagues — that if a former member of the school (he was one himself, as were Steel and fforde) had applied the choice might have been more difficult. As it was, I was given to understand that the last to appear in Jerusalem Chamber was just what they were looking for.

The post was that of Second Bursar, with the promise that if my shape fitted I would be Bursar in two years' time on Dunkin's retirement from the nominal post — which duly happened. What I did not know until later, was that fforde and Dunkin did not get on specially well together. This was largely because fforde, a solicitor knighted for legal services, especially regarding contracts in the war, had been appointed as Headmaster by the Governing Body with a view to turning some of his attention to financial affairs, which were primarily the responsibility, with business and non-teaching administration generally, of the Bursar. Dunkin had quite naturally not been pleased with what he regarded as an unnecessarily tactless announcement about fforde in the press. Although fforde had a first-class legal brain (but oddly a fourth-class degree at Oxford) and had been connected with high finance in his contract work in the war at the air ministry, he was not a specialist in school finances. He never intervened in my work or judgements when, after a fortnight, I took over the full day-to-day duties of the Bursar who retired to his house from which to concentrate purely on launching the appeal. My appointment, like those of Bursar, Headmaster and Medical Officer, was made, and was terminable, by the Governing Body: masters were appointed by the Headmaster and either held office at his pleasure or didn't at his displeasure.

Everything happened so quickly. Our first-class passage on the Orient Line's *Oronsay* via Suez would have been appealing: we had greatly enjoyed our voyage home on that Line's *Orcades* and the Suez Canal route after the Australian ports, Ceylon, Marseilles and Gibraltar. (This time we would have had the rarefied company of the Dukes of Somerset and Montrose and the Marquess of Bute.) But both passage and car had to be cancelled. I put in to government for retaining the car as I might need it for my school duties — a thin case which I expected to have turned down — and was allowed to do so on paying the necessary fees.

I could not find out how to resign from the Fiji government service. No one in the Colonial Office seemed to know: it was apparently extremely unusual. Officers retired from a colony either on medical grounds or straightforwardly after the minimum age of 55; and I had 18 years to serve. It was serious that I had no pension for my 14 years. I sent a telegram to Stoddart, the Colonial Secretary, stating that no one knew what notice was required and expressing regret on not rejoining him and on leaving all my friends in Fiji but explaining that I felt the new post was a suitable opportunity, especially in view of family considerations (which, as a bachelor, he probably would not easily understand). I asked for a cash payment for leave due to me because of the war. This was never given, a decision I still find it hard not to resent.

Within a fortnight, before my resignation was accepted by an absolutely formal telegram in reply, I was attending a meeting of the finance committee of the Governing Body of Rugby School. I sat in at the morning's business, trying to comprehend, without the advantage of seeing any papers in advance, the unfamiliar names of Rugby persons and places from memoranda all drawn up by Dunkin. Presiding was Sir Will Spens, the chairman of both the Governing Body and of its finance committee.

After that finance committee meeting in the morning there was unusually — I never knew such a coincidence of meetings subsequently to happen — a meeting of the full Governing Body in the afternoon. This, as I have said, was the body that had appointed me, just as it had appointed the Headmaster and Medical Officer. Our boss was in all three cases the chairman of the Governing Body. The MO and I were expected to work in close liaison with the Headmaster who appointed the 80 masters, just as I appointed all the 70 or so non-teaching staff. My job and fforde's ran in parallel for all working purposes, although nominally the latter was the head of the school.

To my astonishment, when item 5, 'Report of the Finance Committee', came up on the agenda, the Chairman, Sir Will Spens, said: 'I will ask Mr Snow to report on this morning's business.' I had not been forewarned in the slightest. I had not even taken notes. I thumbed through, as I spoke, the memoranda on various subjects without even knowing that School Field was not a field but the name of a boarding house. In fact, that particular example did not come up but might well have done so. Somehow — and I shall never know how — I reported for half an hour out of my head. I should explain that the usual practice was for the finance committee to report its meeting by a fortnight's advance circulation in print to the Governing Body from a long draft prepared by the Bursar and approved by the Chairman. What I was doing was substituting for that long, precisely-written report.

As the years went on and the feat never had to be repeated because there were always long written reports from the finance committee, I never ceased to wonder how I had managed. At the end Spens simply said, 'Thank you, Mr Snow': he was rarely given to eulogy. After the meeting Gerald Steel, the deputy chairman, who had perhaps been anxious to see how his selection had proved himself, came up and said: 'Allow me.' I did not know what that meant. It turned out to be the Rugbeian form of 'warmest congratulations'. Gerald Steel's cheery rubicund features counterbalanced Spens's grim visage: they were splendidly complementary. Steel could be wittily earthy. I have described Sir Will Spens at some length in the *Dictionary of National Biography*.

I was relieved to learn that Spens had been known to say in his rather straight stilted phraseology that he liked the cut of my jib. It was reassuring, working with such a strong personality, for me to hear from Charles (in a letter of 12 January 1953 from Nethergate House, Clare, Suffolk) that: 'Your friend Graves [Charles, brother of Robert, whom I liked and met frequently at the Savile Club] was playing bridge with Spens the other day who said that you were a great success at Rugby and that they were congratulating themselves on you.' It was typical not to know direct from Spens, who did not believe in showing his hand openly.

Spens was a stern taskmaster. At Eton there was a provost as well as a chairman of the Governing Body: he was resident and could scarcely be ignored. I think that fforde and I both believed that Spens regarded himself as provost, albeit absentee. No chairman of the Rugby Governing Body before or after him took up that role or would have been able to do so: his expertness on educational administration was that he was pre-eminent in his knowledge of detail and could not be challenged, however professional the headmaster or bursar.

There was no greater expert in the country on financial and business administration in schools. Like fforde, I was directly responsible to the Chairman (and to the Governing Body). I was exceptionally lucky in my new boss. Whatever I picked up to help me led eventually to the principal post that a bursar could hold — Chairman for three years (normally two) of the Public (later entitled Independent) Schools' Bursars' Association — was in largest measure due to what I learnt from Spens. Daily, for several years, he would telephone me from the Master's Lodge at Corpus Christi and from his home at Ely, reversing the charge. He could understand instantly every point of detail. He used to try the same tactics for the academic administration of the school, the headmaster's province. But fforde was too sly for this. He would never be in his study, or was said not to be in it but either teaching or on The Close watching games. He was in fact more often than not in his study but his secretary was well trained.

Spens was no oil painting. But the one of him by Sir William Hutchison, President of the Royal Scottish Academy, was the best I have ever seen of anyone I have known. I wonder how many looking at it would guess that his severe looks concealed a sharp susceptibility to female charms. This became evident to us when we were invited to stay with him and Lady Dorothy, daughter of Bishop Selwyn of Melanesia and thereafter Master of the eponymous college in Cambridge, in their retirement in Ely Cathedral Close. His wife, a lively, vigorous person, must have been striking in her youth. She was an entertaining puncturer of his public image. It was the only time one could see him put in perspective. He would self-mockingly wince at her recollection of his falling for the Marchesa Marconi when she and her husband stayed at Corpus Christi Master's Lodge. He could not deny that he was infatuated by her Latin looks.

We had gone to Ely in some trepidation, thinking that his sternness would not dissolve for Stefanie to be able to enjoy the visit. On the contrary, he took a great fancy to her. Petticoat influence was probably the only sort to affect him. His charming daughter-in-law, Lady Katharine Cecelia Howard, daughter of George (later Lord) Howard of Castle Howard and granddaughter of Field Marshal 3rd Lord Methuen and of the 9th Earl of Carlisle, was clearly a favourite as we could well see when she was with us. After knowing him as I did through our close contact, I was always consequently prepared for a public face, however rocklike, being capable of crumbling a little or more under female influence. I was never, after Sir Will Spens (and before him Sir Harry Luke), surprised any longer by the revelations that were to occur of private impulses in public life. This realization put some touching faith in possibilities of human frailty at highest levels. It made anything likely at any time — a happy thought bringing increased interest to everyday life. I should emphasize that Will Spens's pleasing susceptibility was an Achilles heel with nothing but the most respectable connotations. His brother, Patrick (whom I met in New York), the last European to hold the supremely elevated position of Chief Justice of India, became 1st Lord Spens.

Perhaps my one failure on my Governing Body début was in the ears of a governor with a head more like a skull than I had seen on anyone alive, The Very Reverend A. C. Don, Dean of Westminster, who called out from the end of the long table: 'Would Mr Snow please speak up?' He himself had the gravelly voice that would reverberate easily in Westminster Abbey, a Royal Peculiar of which he was virtually the bishop. Outside in the Jericho Parlour where preachers would vest themselves was a placard of advice amounting to a command about projecting one's voice in the Abbey. His plea used to be repeated in his time as a governor in the Jerusalem Parlour, quite a capacious room: it was here in front of the vast fireplace where Henry IV had been brought to die. Although too fundamentally ecclesiastical for me to feel totally at home in it, Jerusalem Chamber's history and the fact that here was where I had been appointed made it very acceptable to me and it was always a welcome interlude (in fact proceedings never halted) when the porter who had forecast my appointment brought in tea and crusty, luxuriantly buttered bread. Magnificent to eat just as long as one was not suddenly called upon to speak with a mouthful.

The governors were a distinguished collection. It was rather like having a dozen or more Fiji governors and colonial secretaries to experience all in one room at the same time. As I came to be able to observe their variety, and after first wondering how men with such different careers could apply themselves to governing a specialist institution like a well-known school, I concluded that their contributions and individual presence were valuable. They infused breadth of empiricism into what could be an inbred society. Their depth of dimension brought a healthy objectivity into decisions. Policy was the wiser for their polyglot career backgrounds, even if, and perhaps because, some of them had been boys at the school.

They included Sir William Dugdale, 1st Baronet, an Etonian owner of the same home/part-castle site since the days of the Domesday Book and a governor from 1922, who was always first to be present but was deaf to anything except bellowed communication: he died in 1965 aged 93 and his grandson, Harry, married a daughter of Ratu Sir Kamisese Mara (President of Fiji) in 1991, an unexpected Anglo–South Sea Islands link — and a republic–royal court one as Harry's mother is lady-in waiting to the Queen.

Others of distinction were Sir Patrick Dean (he asked me to call him Pat), a governor since 1939 (and Chairman from 1973 to 1984), Deputy Under-Secretary of State for Foreign Affairs who later became the United Kingdom Permanent Representative at the United Nations (where he was to welcome me 12 years later) and finally Ambassador to America; and J. P. L. Thomas, 1st Viscount Cilcennin of Hereford, First Lord of the Admiralty from 1951 to 1956 and Lord Lieutenant of Herefordshire — like Dean, one of my future chairmen. Also, Major Sir Harold Bibby, 1st Baronet, chairman of the Bibby Line, a director of the Suez Canal Company, and last chairman of Martin's Bank before it lost its identity. Governor from 1932 to 1967, he was the Lord Chancellor's representative on the Governing Body and a holder of the DSO, but surprisingly insisted on prefixing his name with his First World War rank.

Sir Harry Ricardo, a distinguished marine engineer, quiet, silver-moustached and benevolent, was the Royal Society's representative. Sir Robert Watson-Watt, self-declared discoverer of radar and an enemy of Charles's (he had just succeeded on the Governing Body Sir Henry Tizard, a friend of Charles's) represented London University but lasted briefly, overlapping me by only a year, to be succeeded by Sir Harrie Massey, an eminent Australian scientist. There were also C. P. Evers, a genial retired housemaster who gave me, as did other governors, useful advice; and Colonel Terence Maxwell (like Bibby, he insisted on being addressed by military rank, although he had been more of a political than a military colonel in the Second World War). He was the son-in-law of a former chairman of the Governing Body, Sir Austen Chamberlain, nephew of the two Chamberlains who had bought Naitauba island in the Lau archipelago of Fiji.

Appointed at the uniquely early age of 30 in 1935, Terence Maxwell was considered by some to have become a governor through nepotism. Competent and articulate, he was a constant contender for the chairmanship of the Governing Body (he was on it for 38 years to 1973), he was deputy head of a multiplicity of other institutions such as the Australia and New Zealand Bank and computer companies of which, with his early grasp of a measure of prominence and by his energy and directness of approach to targets, he could have been expected to have the top positions but never did. He was the strongest figure of all apart from Spens who nevertheless deferred to him a good deal and, as

9

deputy chairman of the finance committee and governor in charge
of investments, very much a man with whom I had to deal
regularly and, I am glad to say, thoroughly amicably.

With Arthur fforde, he was among the select few whom on leaving I would do so with a springy step. On the other hand, he was
alone in that company as one whom I would visit with a soupçon
of *frisson*. His could be a commanding presence. After a meeting
with the leading Fijian chief, Ratu Sir Lala Sukuna (see *The Years
of Hope*), Terence Maxwell told me that he had not come across a
more impressive figure: through his social connections he must
have met many eminent ones. Ratu Sukuna reciprocated a feeling
of respect in describing in turn that meeting to me. It is slightly
puzzling that Terence never received an honour, close as his
relations were with leaders of his father-in-law's party and close as
his ear was to the Westminster and City floors for so long.

He was a firm supporter of mine, as was Diana, Austen Chamberlain's daughter, a considerate, organizing wife of ability: she
was a leader in London's high society life (referred to in published
diaries) and had her father's distinguished looks. When she gave a
dinner party, even for as few as four including themselves, there
would still be place names including 'Diana' and 'Terence' and
match holders, these similarly inscribed. Terence Maxwell could
be disliked inevitably by some for his ambitiousness and
fearlessness in speaking up on all issues. What he said and the
forthright manner in which he said it was not always music to a
headmaster's ears: he had no experience, it was opined, for taking
attitudes in things academic. But he had valuable wide perspec-
tives from the City world which mitigated against too insular an
outlook in academia.

His forte was of course financial acumen, helping to keep this
institution buoyant and the parents confident that steady hands
were keeping costs down while at the same time offering the best
facilities. He was specially watchful in this respect for any expan-
sionist tendencies under Parkinson's law, attempting duplication
from top to bottom through departments with proliferation of
deputies and assistants, so damaging to the aim of not cutting into
savings carefully made in other directions. In his long term of
office, he was instrumental in keeping increases in parents' fees

below inflationary rises while helping to implement improvements in structures and conditions for personnel. His worth for the maintenance of Rugby's position in the forefront among the prime leaders in the country's schools was never really recognized. Perhaps I saw it as clearly as anyone over nearly a quarter of a century in not easy times.

There were one or two who were not prominent on the Governing Body although holding distinguished posts outside it — Sir Sam Brown, head of the solicitors, Linklaters & Paines, after gaining a knighthood for attaining distinction in the Ministry of Aircraft Production in the war (he quaintly insisted on his name being referred to orally and recorded verbally as Sam), most gentlemanly but not forceful; T. S. R. Boase, Master of Magdalen, Oxford, rather soft; and J. T. Christie, Principal of Jesus, Oxford, rather vapid.

As Lord Lieutenant of Warwickshire from 1939 to 1968, Lord Willoughby de Broke was an ex-officio governor but he never attended, although he did come to meetings in my office with the land agent for the management of the estates surrounding the school. The 20th Baron could hardly have been less than the essence of a country landowner: he died in 1986. In the Battle of Britain (July–October 1940) as a squadron leader he had the vital job at headquarters of directing his squadrons on a gigantic map of southern England. Anthony Cave Brown in his *Bodyguard of Lies* likened him to a croupier attending a roulette board as he disposed the air force from square to square over the territory being vitally fought for, the interceptions under command of Air Marshal Dowding rolling back Goering's effort for Hitler to invade England once the skies were clear.

Lord Dowding was a very different personality from Lord Willoughby: a morose spiritualist but a dedicated winner which again goes to show that it takes all sorts. I do not think that he would have been riveting to meet as an individual: perhaps that was the reason why he was under-rewarded. Lord Willoughby de Broke was distinctive in all his manners and, like Harold Macmillan and Margaret Thatcher, had slanting eyes. He told me once when he was driving me about the Rugby estate that he was a great lover of France, thinking always of it. So much so in fact that

11

he drove me down a series of long twisting two-way country lanes entirely on the wrong side, the while lauding the French way of life, its food and its drink. He had not been drinking. Who was I to point out to the Lord Lieutenant that he should be driving on the left-hand side? I liked Lord Willoughby. He made the two royal visits to the school, which he had to attend as Lord Lieutenant of Warwickshire and in which I had to be a key participating organizer, a relaxed pleasure. No one could have been a more natural sovereign's representative in a county than he in appearance and deed.

Those then were the men I worked directly under in my first years at Rugby, although principally a cabal (that never met) of Spens, Maxwell and Willoughby de Broke. I did not find the Rugby work much different from that of the Fiji Secretariat with the occasional touch of district experience — unpredictable daily, interspersed with variety. I was also registrar of all candidates for the school from birth to age 13. Most of the 80 teaching staff I had to deal with frequently: their housing and other prerequisites came under my direction. The masters — particularly those elevated to housemasterships by sometimes mysterious reasoning — included of course some eccentrics, but not to anything like the extent of my South Sea Islands friends. More of the exotic air of the hothouse was needed for growth of individuality.

Finance came into my work prominently and it had been the work in Section F in the Fiji Secretariat that I had liked least. I simply had to penetrate this natural block. It was at first hard going but after a year or so when I had covered an annual timetable it became automatic. I had the advantage of a character from former days, Harry Samuel Gay, a militant anti-drinking, anti-smoking Baptist with a late discovered predisposition, well concealed, to the ladies, who had started in 1914 in a humble school job to become a clerk to the first full-time bursar, Dunkin, in 1927. He did not show any obstructiveness to my appointment as a much younger man, although he had applied for it himself. Indeed, he gave me the most patient help for which I was eternally grateful: it simply must be recorded in these reminiscences. He could be maddeningly slow but he never let me down in 25 years.

Rugby's intricate accounting was described by the auditors as about as individualistic a system as could be devised. I conformed to it, not feeling qualified to change it, particularly when Maxwell had been associated with it for so long, in fact since Austen Chamberlain became Chairman of the Governing Body in 1932, having given up being Foreign Secretary in 1929. It was a regret of mine that I never knew Chamberlain: he was well before me, with an Archbishop of Canterbury, William Temple, and a few years of Spens in that post after him. I have mentioned that Dunkin and fforde did not work well together; nor did Spens and Dunkin. The latter was not an adaptable man but extremely competent and dedicated, not sufficiently self-propelling although he made his mark in becoming for two years Chairman of the Public Schools' Bursars' Association. He had become an inspector of taxes after having been a boy at Rugby and after spending the First World War in the Middle East. He died aged 62 in 1957, 30 years after becoming Bursar. Highly generous in his help to me, he was a man of more magnanimity than a successor could expect from a predecessor and also towards those who did not give him his proper recognition.

The school buildings were mostly in red and yellow and black brick, almost flippantly designed by William Butterfield, architect also of Keble College, Oxford. The architecture was mid-Victorian at its most blatant, and to John Betjeman's positive delight. Not so to Rupert Brooke's. As a boy at Rugby and son of a housemaster, Brooke saw more of it and complained that it gave him pink-eye through so much exposure to its fancy brickwork. Butterfield's creations apart, the very first buildings replacing the original farm and before Butterfield's time were distinguished in late Georgian castellated style. They were of Rutland stone; they survive in this imposing style.

One of my first acts, on the pretext that it would be part of the Coronation embellishment which included floodlighting of the Georgian block, was to have the plain stone heraldic shields and crests above two main gateways gilded and coloured appropriately. Since they had been constructed they had remained merely part of the stonework colour. I had seen the effect that I now created on some gateways of Cambridge and Oxford colleges, which had similarly tumbled late — after the Second World

War — to the idea of the more pleasing appearance that the original architects had envisaged. 'Ostentatious', commented acidly a very queer, barnacled, garrulous, bachelor housemaster who had barely left the school boy and man. This bothered me not at all: he was not a man to my taste. I had ignored more serious criticisms in my Fiji innovations. The Rugby townspeople unanimously approved. The time came when no one could imagine when the devices had ever been ungilded and unheralded.

Having been put up for the MCC in 1946 by Plum Warner who persuaded R. H. Twining, a Middlesex player and later a president of MCC, to second me, I had been anxious during my leave in 1951 to play the ten qualifying matches that could enable me not to have to wait years for election. By playing successfully in those matches one could be given priority and immediate election. When I still thought that I was going to return to Fiji after leave in 1951, I explained to Lord's that I wished to play my matches in the one season instead of spreading them, as was customary, over two seasons. They agreed in the circumstances. In my first match, batting at No.1, I was bowled first ball — for the first time ever. What was worse I never saw the ball. In my second match on another ground — I was bowled first ball. And I did not see that ball either. Meanwhile, in between qualifying matches I was accumulating runs comfortably for other teams. In my third match for the MCC, again at No.1 (there was a different captain and manager for each match), I should have been run out for 0. My partner and I were in a muddle. I was stranded near his end. Cover point threw the ball to the wrong end where we both were and I scrambled home to the other end just in time. I went on to make 90 and drew some relief. There were still some seven matches to go and I did reasonably in them.

At the end of his ten, Trevor Howard-Smith, the film actor under the name Trevor Howard, not at all a bad bat and a good cover fielder who had been playing in some of the matches with me and performing dismally, was very depressed. He desperately wanted to be a member. Outside films, cricket was his life. It was a hot day at Loughton in Essex. I scored about 30 and was out. He was to bat at No. 7 and asked if he could borrow my Fiji cap. With this he made his highest score, 48. I had a letter from him:

14

Horses in Midstream

Dear Philip,

Just to let you know that I have made it. All thanks to you.

Yours,
Trevor,
Fiji and MCC

I would often come across him at Lord's, sometimes with his friend, Keith Miller, the Australian test player. He had a predisposition for the company of heavy drinkers like Errol Flynn and Robert Mitchum: for him, drinking came second after his passion for cricket. He had wanted while at Clifton to be a professional but he was some way off that standard.

At Lord's, Trevor would not be readily recognized behind his dark glasses. His features roughened and he had a pockmarked face. Never did he have the looks of Ronald Colman, David Niven or Stewart Granger: had he possessed finer features, with his greater ability as an actor, he would have been in the first half-dozen film names in the world, whereas he was a little lower down the scale. With his predilection for heavy drinking, he could not be relied upon for stage appearances that attract official honours from which, like James Mason for a similar reason, he missed out: hence the attachment of his career early on almost exclusively to films and television. When I first met him he had made a name in *Brief Encounter*, *The Third Man*, *The Golden Salamander*, *Odette*, and *An Outcast of the Islands*.

As it was, and despite having to be chauffeured everywhere after a long deprivation of his driving licence, Trevor was a millionaire three times over when he died. He had lived in an unpretentious cottage adjacent to the all-essential village pub next to the studios in England. In essence, a gruffly cordial man without pretences and ego, he abhorred having to act with Marlon Brando, the epitome of pretentiousness and egotism, in *Mutiny on the Bounty*, despite the South Sea Islands location which he soaked up. When he had finished with Brando in Tahiti, I arranged for him to be looked after in Fiji.

15

Word went round among qualifiers for the MCC that there were managers of teams to avoid as being more disposed to put in adverse reports. One of these was Lieutenant Colonel Hon. Gerald French, the peppery younger brother of Field Marshal Sir John French who became Earl of Ypres. He was a former minor county player for Devon, deputy governor of Dartmoor prison and governor of Newcastle prison. I regarded him as a challenge and applied to play for him. There was an age gap but he took to me and I was able to return the compliment by running to accept something he seemed uneasy about — a high catch closer to him at mid-on than to me at mid-off. He did not call 'yours', and I was aware of the risk if I had poached. To my relief, he was intensely gratified and I understood that I had met his standards. My acquaintance with him made me feel that those who described him as peppery must have led more circumscribed existences than most. He was interested in my Fiji jobs, rather different from those of most of the candidates who played for him and ran the risk of a black ball. Other managers played under included Reverend Tom Killick, the Middlesex and England batsman who died early while playing cricket, and Tom Pearce, the Essex captain: they were conventionally affable. Like Trevor, I was duly elected but the process had had its misgivings and trials.

I always managed to make runs for the Authors versus Publishers, although it meant abstaining from the wine at the lunch in the marquee where the speeches were a main part of the day. In 1952, Marshal of the RAF Lord Tedder proposed the toast to literature. As an onlooker the previous year, he had spotted my Fiji blazer and had told me how he had started his life there as a cadet in 1914. I said, to his astonishment, that I knew that he had been in Lautoka for a year before resigning to serve in the British forces in the First World War. He struck me as unassuming and highly perceptive. The reply to that toast was by the slight, impecunious and three times married but literary enough figure, Edmund Blunden, who would have participated in every annual match but for his University of Hong Kong professorship.

The toast to cricket was proposed by Lady Violet Bonham-Carter, later Baroness Asquith, daughter of H. H. Asquith (Earl of Oxford and Asquith and prime minister), who showed a knowledge of the subject which was beyond that of some of the literary figures actually playing in the match. With her hatchet-shaped head and an ugly mouth for her vigorous public speaking, she seemed a masculine figure to me in every way and her cricket aspect came therefore as less of a surprise. The quality of her speech was in no way surpassed by Ian Peebles in his reply for the participants who that year included Chester Wilmot, the Australian broadcaster (soon to die prematurely in an air crash and now forgotten, although celebrated in his time), and Lieutenant Colonel J. W. A. Stephenson, the Essex all-rounder whose exuberance in all departments (not least fielding, especially to his own bowling) was a spectacle in itself, making him a spirited performer of the highest, certainly test, standard. Leicestershire was reported as being only marginally less supine than in 1946 and, having played in first-class matches in New Zealand, I was unimpressed by the set-up and disinterested. It was at the bottom of the county table.

A. W. E. Winlaw, the master in charge of cricket at Rugby School, was not a great performer but an enthusiast. With fforde's encouragement, he immediately asked me if I would help him and the Lancashire bowler, Frank Booth, the school professional and groundsman, in coaching the XI. I had only a few yards to walk to the nets from the Bursary on the boundary of The Close. Rugby Town promptly enlisted me to play for it on Saturday afternoons: it was one of the six strongest batting teams in the Midlands. I was an undistinguished accomplice in the club's record batting partnership of 230 for 0 declared from after lunch to before tea with Morris Burton. On declaration, Burton was 177 not out, myself 47 not out. He had forearms like the legs of a grand piano and made tenure of the crease at the opposite end and the bowler's existence a fearful hazard with the low, sizzling power of his straight drives. Rugby Town never played the school on its own fine ground but every year on The Close, a ground on which I never found it easy to bat. The row of lofty lime trees at one end darkened the view of the ball. So, if given the chance, I made use of that end to bowl from, flighting the ball well up into the arboreal gloom.

My location for working could hardly have been more congenial.

The Bursary was 100 yards away from the headmaster's study and separated by the verdancy of The Close: it gave us both breathing air. I was again on an island. It was indeed The Island. Reputed to be one of a chain of mounds for the Romans to signal to each other if Welsh invaders menaced their construction of Watling Street (now the A5 passing three miles from Rugby), it had been surrounded by a moat. I straightaway did some research and the following was affixed to the Bursary on a notice pointing to the tree-covered knoll:

THE ISLAND

The grass mound situated to the right is known as THE ISLAND. It has been concerned in three distinct phases of history, separated from first to last by perhaps as much as 2000 years.

1. ANCIENT

It is believed by some authorities to be a tumulus or ancient barrow of the early British period and to have had two uses, first as a burial place for a chieftain of the tribe of the Dobuni, and, secondly, as a military vantage point for the tribe. In this neighbourhood there is a series of tumuli, probably used for intercommunicating purposes as beacons or other prominent means of conveying intelligence. Before enclosures, hedges and buildings changed the appearance of the country it was possible to see from one tumulus to another.

Another opinion is that THE ISLAND was the mound of one of the many small Norman castles.

2. MEDIAEVAL

The land to the left on the other side of THE ISLAND belonged to the monks of the great Cistercian abbey of Pipewell in Northamptonshire from the twelfth century to the dissolution of monasteries in the sixteenth century. A moat about 20 feet wide surrounding the mound was constructed by the monks: it held clear limpid water from gravel springs and the monks fished in it for their staple diet. There was a wooden drawbridge with a spiked gate in the centre crossing the moat where the Old Pavilion now stands.

Part of The Bursary stands on the site of the moat.

3. MODERN

In 1797, during the French revolutionary war, THE ISLAND was the scene of the last stand during the great rebellion when the boys burnt their desks and the Headmaster's books on The Close while the Headmaster locked himself into his study. When soldiers and horse dealers carrying whips arrived to put down the mutiny, the insurgents retreated to THE ISLAND, raising the drawbridge as they were surrounded. While the Riot Act was read to the boys, followed by a demand that they surrender, the soldiers waded through the moat, took the rebels in the rear, captured them and led them to the Headmaster. Many were instantly expelled; the remainder were dealt with in other ways. The leading rebel later became Sir Willoughby Cotton. The moat was filled in 50 years afterwards.

THE ISLAND is listed under the Ancient Monuments Act and is protected as a monument of national importance.

I found later that the French Revolution had a knock-on, epidemic effect on some other early-founded schools but with no long-standing results.

The BBC asked me to give talks for its *Calling the Islands* programme. This I did regularly for as long as it continued. All sorts of subjects were requested. These included the Test Match between England and South Africa at the Oval in 1951 when I happened to have my binoculars on Len Hutton for a moment that had no precedent in international cricket. Hutton had mishit an off-break of Athol Rowan to leg, the ball had gone in the air and, in his anxiety to prevent it landing on his wicket, his bat in a second movement (I don't think he was merely following through his shot) knocked the descending ball out of the hands of Russell Endean, the wicketkeeper waiting for what was a catch. Hutton himself had turned with the mis-hook till he was almost facing his wicket when he noticed that the ball was likely to come down on to it. As you will know, it is permissible for a batsman to hit the ball twice or kick the ball away (but not handle it) if by so doing he can stop it from going on to his wicket. Hutton presumably did not notice that the wicketkeeper was diving for a possible catch. So he hit the ball away as it descended. The frustrated wicketkeeper appealed for some method of dismissal — a pause for a moment that seemed an infinity to the watching 30,000. Then the umpire, Dai Davies, having consulted his colleague, Frank Chester, gave Hutton out. No one was quite sure of the reason until the other umpire called, for those who could hear, to the scoring box: 'For obstructing the field'. The last case of a first-class cricketer being dismissed under the law, which, by the way, requires 'wilful obstruction' was 50 years ago in a county match. It had never before occurred in a test match. Hutton told his biographer, Gerald Howat, that he never intended to prevent the wicketkeeper taking the catch.

Ironically, Endean himself entered the list of curious dismissals. Batting for South Africa against England five years later, he was given out 'handled the ball'.

The BBC had given me a seat in a separate part of the Oval for that test against South Africa. Only C. B. Fry was there. We sat together and alone for the five days. Of classic looks and frame, classics scholar, holder of the world long-jump record for 21 years, soccer player for England, captain of England at cricket but never a selector or president of MCC, dominated by a formidable wife but offered the Kingdom of Albania, he was a conversationalist *extraordinaire*. Rather frail, recuperating from an illness and therefore unable to do his regular reporting for the *Evening Standard*, he talked nonstop. Most of what he said was new to me. For a while afterwards I remembered some of Charles Fry's reminiscences and views, but I made no note of them — very remiss of me: I thought that I could keep them in my head. It would have been a valuable record of a spontaneous monologue.

As it is, I cannot remember a word except that his friend, Ranjit-singhji, featured large and often. What did surprise me was that when A. L. Hosie, who used to play a lot for Hampshire while on leave as a jute merchant in India, came up to speak to him, Fry did not know him, although Hampshire had been a team for which he himself had played — in a slightly earlier era. Hosie, whom I knew from playing against Stragglers of Asia for either Christ's or the Cambridge Crusaders, was naturally taken aback and disappointed.

I was able to know the South Africans a little. John Arlott, who had glowingly reviewed my *Cricket in the Fiji Islands* in *Wisden*, had taken me as a guest, and later proposed me as a member, of the Cricket Writers' Club at its dinner for the team at the Press Club. Those whom I met, including S. J. Pegler, the manager who had been a test player and then a district commissioner in Nyasaland for 25 years, Jack Cheetham, who was to prove himself a charismatic, dynamic captain with a real flair for the job, the Rowan brothers, G. M. Fullerton and Endean, were very pleasant and genuinely wanted to know about Fijian cricket. This was before attitudes on racial matters in South Africa hardened but I am sure that the 1951 South African team would have liked Fijians. Sir Hubert Ashton, the former Cambridge, Essex and England player, was the principal speaker: he was without affectation in any way, full of sense and good humour. I was to know him at later functions and meetings when we were on the joint committee of the Governing Bodies' Association together.

I came to know John Arlott well, visiting his house and meeting his first wife, Dawn (I was also to know Valerie, his secretary and second wife, who died early of cancer, and his third wife, Patricia). One lunch time at Arlott's favourite nearby pub in Highgate there was a distinguished-looking, bearded man and a St Bernard dog with him when I joined Arlott. I was introduced, but the name Tim White meant nothing to me. He had been a master at a public school, White told me, and was surprised that I enjoyed Rugby. He seemed to have many strong dislikes and pronounced opinions, but he had a far from petulant countenance. Later, when I asked Arlott what White did, John replied that he wrote under the name T. H. White. This still made no impact on me. I have never found him readable, but he had an impressive, if rather overbearing, face. Terence Hanbury White could apparently be a hectoring personality. A misogynist, he exiled himself with the bottle to Alderney, to the fastnesses of which Arlott himself elected to retire at the end of his career of broadcasting almost exclusively on cricket and poetry.

John in any setting, not least in his long residence among his priceless books and his preferential Spanish wines at The Old Sun, Alresford, Hampshire (the cellar space of this former pub was a magnet for him), was one of the most vivid personalities I ever knew. Overwhelmed by a son of his first marriage being killed on a motorcycle, he ever after wore a black tie. The lugubriousness — almost signifying a sourness atypical of his magnanimity — which I do not think I have witnessed to the same degree in anyone as young or middle-aged — affected his once handsome features. He had the most bottomless capacity for drinking wine I have experienced. Generous in his attitudes, he seemed sometimes to be unable to discern the more technical subtleties in cricketers.

Invited on occasion to sit with him in his tiny commentating box up steep, open stairs, I would be intrigued that the only *aide-mémoire* he had for his day-long broadcasts was the bare scorecard of the match. Absolutely no notes or even a pen.

Other subjects among my talks broadcast to the Pacific Islands included the Wroth Silver Ceremony, which took place on one of the Duke of Buccleuch's fields near Rugby at dawn (of uncertain origin in medieval times), the opening of the Imperial War Memorial at Lord's, where I met for the first time Prince Philip who was about to visit Fiji, reviews of Pacific books, Christmas Day in Fiji, Bradman's forty-fifth birthday and the visit of the Queen and Prince Philip to Fiji and Tonga. It was very undemanding and brought in a useful six guineas a time. They were recordings, apart from one 'live' broadcast for the Home Programme's Travel and Adventure Series for half an hour on a Sunday morning after too heavy a drinking session at the Savile Club the night before, which dehydrated me almost to the point of collapse. It was unfortunately only after the 'live' programme that I was taken to the duty officer's room for a courtesy, and totally restoring, gin and tonic.

Horses in Midstream

It was on visits to Broadcasting House that I came to know Sir Arthur Grimble in the course of his famous self-deprecating talks later to be published as *A Pattern of Islands*. I have described him at length in the *Dictionary of National Biography*.

When the British Phosphate Commission was sued by Banabans in the late 1970s for underpayments of royalties for excavated guano going back to Grimble's time on Ocean Island as resident commissioner of the Gilbert and Ellice Islands, I could never accept the accusations made against him (in the longest civil action in a British court) that he was selfish, malevolent, unjust and desperately driven by ambition. These were all out of character with the Grimble I knew. It is amusing that an administrator of St Lucia who came under Grimble's governorship of the Windward Islands from 1942 to 1948, Edward Twining (later Lord Twining of Tanganyika and Godalming), an ex-army officer, inflated with self-importance, should have considered that Grimble 'was not', according to Twining's biographer, 'lacking in a sense of his own importance'. Twining described Grimble as 'a tall, thin man who was rather fond of the ladies', much given to correcting and re-correcting prose but charming, lazy, quiet, sensitive and gentle, who thought that he had not had his true desserts. That was a working colleague's view.

It has to be emphasized to readers of *A Pattern of Islands* that it is full of hyperbole deliberately encouraged by John Murray, his publisher. When Grimble showed Murray a first draft, possibilities were seen in it — but not of the best-seller it was to become. Murray gave Grimble an advance and advice to exile himself in Italy for six months, exaggerating, imagining, polishing, all of which was done at the expense of sheer blood, sweat and tears on the part of Grimble. *A Pattern of Islands* reads so smoothly that anyone not knowing of its writing, as I did, in the background direct from Murray (Grimble himself never divulged his difficulties with it) would believe it to be an entirely effortless product. He was helped of course by writing of 40 years before about islanders who, not knowing English, would never read it and be in a position to question its accuracy. Grimble ended his official career as Governor of the Seychelles and Windward Islands.

Rivalling Grimble for best-selling success would be Robert Louis

Stevenson — and *Tales of the South Pacific* by James Michener, which was also full of hyperbole. One could never have envisaged the making of two stories of that book's eighteen into the perennially, phenomenally successful musical *South Pacific*, solely through the music and songs of Richard Rodgers and Oscar Hammerstein II (most unusually, Hammerstein wrote the words first and then Rodgers composed the music: moreover, they could not abide each other). In utter contrast with Grimble, Michener, a textbook editor in New York before the war and during it a publications officer, was a rather dull Quaker whom I had met as he passed through Fiji after the remarkable transformation of his couple of short stories from mediocrity. Luck, that undeniable element in life (my brother Charles so strongly believed in it), was bountiful for Michener.

So, with those BBC contacts, making myself part of Rugby did not involve separation from the Pacific. I began to feel that we might be having the most of both worlds. I was in England and the Pacific was coming to it. The great joy is that this has continued to be the good fortune for Anne and me from the time of leaving it. As will be shown, the association has continued to flow and flow. From the very start visitors arrived — the first, Alfred Wendt, a Catholic of German-Samoan descent who had been in my Fiji cricket team touring New Zealand in 1948. Another was Inspector Jaoji (George) Suguturaga, the sergeant major under me when I was in charge of the police on Taveuni island in Fiji. He came in full uniform, dark blue tunic, scarlet cummerbund and white scalloped *sulu* (knee-length skirt) and sandals. On The Close he and I were rounding the clump of trees on The Island when we passed Arthur fforde and a man who caught hold of Jaoji's arm and exclaimed: 'From Fiji, I am sure.' Jaoji's reply was: 'Yes, but how do you place me so correctly, Sir?' The answer was: 'Well, you see, I met Sukuna last week and he was also wearing a skirt which I took to be the national costume of Fiji.' Fforde introduced his companion as Sir Anthony Bevir, formerly of the Colonial Office, private secretary to Churchill from 1940 to 1945 and at that particular time appointments secretary to the Prime Minister.

Then Ratu Sir Lala Sukuna, the most eminent Fijian in the colony's history, came himself to Rugby for the day. He left behind in the train a gold handled umbrella he had purchased to take back to Adi Lady Maraia. We could never trace it. It had a racing scorecard and pencil incorporated in the frame. Not that Ratu Sukuna was a racing man; it was to have been a novelty in Fiji. We asked the ffordes to lunch with him. Both were Oxford men and got on famously, although I later knew fforde to have moods when his sociability could be unpredictable.

Yet another Pacific visitor was Aisea (Isaiah) Tikoilau, brother of Sefanaia Sukanaivalu, who had died gaining the VC, and son of the coconut crab expert. He had come from his very remote Lau island of Yacata in the Fiji group (I had been Provincial Commissioner of the Lau archipelago of 50 islands) for a celebration of Victoria Cross winners or nearest relatives. He knew no English, had to be brought to Rugby by Theo Hansen (who had been on the *Orcades* with me) and returned by me to Ian (later Sir) Thomson, who was attached from Fiji to the Colonial Office in London.

Aisea's tempo never adjusted to that of England. He kept an elaborate diary of his every movement, though time taken over compiling it rather restricted any movements to record at all. But, nevertheless, it was most commendable and really unusual for a Fijian. Immediately after dinner he would retire for the night to write up his diary which was eventually published in the Fijian vernacular journal. We had to catch an early morning train for me to get to a meeting in time and to put him into safe hands in London. It proved impossible to hurry him up at breakfast. It was like mentally pushing a malfunctioning steamroller up a 1 in 6 hill. Clutching an apple, Aisea was whisked down in my car to the station, where we caught the train a minute before it drew out for London.

Although there was so much that was new about life in England and work at Rugby, these visits inevitably brought back affectionate memories of the Pacific — I would have been heartless if it had not been so. I must have commented on it to Charles because on 22 February 1952 he wrote from 1 Hyde Park Crescent, W2: 'I think you will soon get over your nostalgia. I felt the same when I finally broke with Cambridge in 1945, but I scarcely had an hour's regret.' My immersion in Fiji had been for about as long as his in Christ's but I had known so many more people and places in that

25

time. When there were soundings of Charles by his friends after some of the college had recoiled from the first impact of *The Masters* as to whether he would contemplate the mastership for himself on its becoming vacant, he would say that it would be far too claustrophobic and inhibiting for him. His wife Pam, for her part, used to tell me emphatically that she could never entertain the idea of living in the lodge of any college.

Taking Dunkin's advice, I joined the Public Schools' Bursars' Association. I was the youngest bursar by far. Most were retired army, navy or air force officers of about brigadier, rear admiral or air vice-marshal rank and retired top Indian civil service officers, for whom reorientation would have been more difficult at 50 plus than for me at 37. My age had been one of the factors I had taken into account for changing horses in midstream when I did. I felt that I was at my most adaptable then. Further, I anticipated wrongly that the Colonial Service almost everywhere would fold up more rapidly than was in fact the case. It seemed to me that it would follow quite soon after the end of the Indian civil service in 1947 and that, like the effect of the ICS floodgate, there would be a considerable log jam competing for general administrative jobs back in England. As it happened, African colonies did not terminate the British connection until the 1960s (Ghana in 1957, but Nigeria in 1960, Tanzania in 1961, Sierra Leone in 1961, Uganda in 1962, Kenya in 1963, and The Gambia in 1965). Fiji's independence was to be as late as 1970, when I would have anyway been just at the retiring age of 55.

Meanwhile, our effects — all our possessions other than clothes brought with us and a few pieces of furniture acquired in Rugby —left uninsurable in the government stores on the edge of Walu Bay in Suva, had to be sent for, as I could now afford their freight. In 1953 there had been a hurricane, earthquake (the only one on that scale ever in Fiji) and tidal wave, which brought down the corrugated iron roof and sides of the stores. Many of our crates were all smashed in, their contents floating about on the sea water. Friends helped to repack them, but a few items were lost, not least my stock of a score of whales' teeth (then worth £5 each) for ceremonies and requests, which could of course not be exported. However, I would like to have arranged for their redistribution among Fijians of my choice and also to have known who filched them. By great fortune only about a dozen of my old books were submerged. Dried out, they bear stains of a memorable event and, rebound, are museum pieces and totally readable. They included irreplaceable ones bought before the war or sent to me during it: after the Blitz they could never have been come across again.

The Bursars' Association was a very encouraging body to which to belong: it reassured me that I was not in professional isolation and I made friends straight away with the bursars of schools as nearly comparable to Rugby in status and size as to make exchange of information mutually valuable. It was an association that brought professional expertness to the advantage not only of the schools but of clients, enabling fees paid by parents to be lower than they would have been if we had not exchanged secrets and mutually devised means that reduced liabilities for taxation, rates and other overheads. I was impressed by the quality of my colleagues enough to hope that I might get as far as being on its committee some years ahead. The secretary, David Sherwood, Bursar of Badminton School and a qualified accountant, was extremely able. Like James Mason, he had the courage to be a conscientious objector in the war. I never knew why he did not advance to a position more comparable with his worth and his analytical eye. He was secretary for 22 years, very lively and stimulating. He had the same small, grey, close-trimmed moustache and narrow, sloping shoulders as Julien Cahn. Too often those who are the subjects of name-dropping are given fulsome eulogies. David Sherwood's was not a name much dropped. Too seldom does the opportunity occur for a few words to be made public about the many who miss out on eminence but nevertheless had outstanding gifts. Sometimes in their way they are intrinsically greater than those attaining public celebrity. To everyone's detriment, they do not find their proper setting and consequently hardly ever receive the right share of acknowledgement.

I was thankful for my experience with varied degrees of crustiness among the odd government official, planter, commercial and occasional other person in Fiji when having to deal with one or two senior housemasters whose whole lives had been at Rugby, sometimes even as having been boys there. Most of them had led remarkably insular lives, as might be expected or required of their vocations. For them, Rugby was their oyster, if a rather salty one. They recognized in me a person with a quite individual past and no preconceived ideas or prejudices. That I had myself been a boy at a day grammar school in no way came up, although at first I thought it might. Some of the staff had themselves been to grammar schools. In the total of 700 boys there were 60 day boys, some of them with all or half of their fees paid from the Founder's London Estate. Though it was not thought of at the time, I would have been in favour of half of the total being girls, as much as an element contributing to an extra humanizing of, and sophisticating for, the school. (The first three were admitted in my last term: I would have liked more earlier.)

The 12 housemasters were given allowances with which to feed, clean and administer their houses, including the private sides. Up to a short while before I arrived at Rugby they were independent and could make profits from fees by being frugal (I'm not saying that they did, but there was the potential for them) in how they sustained the boys. Less than a third of them did not like the Governing Body taking over control in Dunkin's last years under Spens's quite determined direction. Taking over that sensitive position without having been told of it in advance, I was on unpopular ground until new housemasters, not experiencing any previous system, gradually replaced the two or three die-hards.

I strictly controlled the allowances: it was then possible to divert savings from housemasters' personal pockets to capital expenditure for the benefit of the school. They learnt not to exacerbate delicate bursarial budgeting by overspending. For the first time, and throughout my time, losses to the school did not occur. Profits were not allowed to be made and any excess of income over expenditure was transferred to cover costs of capital improvements. Commensurate with their considerable responsibility in which they were, however, helped by tutors also receiving some favours, housemasters had free living for themselves and their families all the year round, including the 16 weeks of holidays, a considerable monetary and tax-free benefit for their residential service occupation as compared with those unlucky enough not to

be selected for housemasterships by the headmaster, whose personal prerogative it was to choose them.

Of the dozen housemasters, only one was obstreperously dis-
putatious and culpably extravagant at school expense, and another
recalcitrant. A couple of others were still muttering but soon
complied with the abolition of the archaic financial independence
in which Spens was a pioneer among the leading schools where
similar scurrilous, shell-backed, reactionary housemasters resisted
change. Eventually, the new system permeated all for the benefit of
fee-paying parents. The obstreperous, turgid, last-stand housemaster, whose superciliousness was near to caricature, who had
been arrogant towards the ineffably polite Dunkin and who went
above himself once too often, offensive to the Headmaster and
Governing Body and was got rid of. Spens had not been governor
designate of east Britain and proxy for the king in the event of
German invasion for nothing. One or two entrenched housemasters living in the outdated past and standing in the way of
economic buoyancy of the school in difficult financial times were
no deterrent to him. He guaranteed Rugby's stature tersely and
firmly. It was a much respected school among the other half-dozen
at the top.

It was fforde's task to control the beaks, as they were known.
The teaching profession, not only in Rugby but generally, never
forgave him or Spens for the appointment of a non-schoolmaster
to one of the top school posts in the country. He had his share of
difficulty in steering them in exceptional circumstances. The
Colonial Administrative Service professionals had also not liked
rare appointments to governorships of outsiders such as even that of
the Duke of Windsor to the Bahamas. That of fforde into a teaching
world plum was perhaps even more isolated. Himself a man of
remarkable range of disposition — moving from highs to lows and
up again — one was never quite sure what his mood was going to
be. He could be quickly but undisguisedly lugubrious and
uncommunicative. But when he was on top of his form — his
mood could switch for the better in a flash — fforde was
scintillating. One knew that if he greeted one with quotations from
Dante in medieval Italian, the quality of which I could not begin
to assess, or *The Hunting of the Snark*, for at least the first five

29

minutes fforde was really released and overflowing. His lined face would soften with a remarkable, age-lowering, brilliant smile.

He would sometimes select awkward moments to be mischievous and to tantalize. At the end of a talk on the South Sea Islands, which the Rugby Rotary Club invited me to give, fforde, asked by the club to give the vote of thanks, after the usual politenesses enquired: 'I would like to conclude by asking Mr Snow if he has found the local sharks as voracious as those which he has so illuminatingly described.' It was a measure of his popularity — man to man: the ffordes did no entertaining — in the town that this dig at local suppliers to the school and their fellow Rotarians sitting at the table should have fallen about in mirth. So much so that there was no need to try and find a reply. There are those in the town — but they plainly do not necessarily have the best vantage point for judgement — who still regard him as *the* headmaster since the war. Just as it was rather surprising that this unclubbable man should have joined the Rotary Club at all; he was no stuffed shirt.

At Governing Body meetings fforde spoke little — and very quietly, too much so for The Very Reverend A. C. Don, who would boom out: 'I am sorry that I cannot hear the Headmaster.' (In his time the Dean of Westminster had been known to prompt audibly almost all the preachers in the Abbey.) But fforde never scintillated or raised a laugh there. Spens's brooding chairmanship seemed to inhibit him: he was after all Spens's protégé for the position.

Where he could be relied upon to raise laughs was in the unlikely ambience of the sermons that the headmasters were expected to make each term in chapel. A religious enough man (his Christmas cards were of verse composed by him in overwhelming Christian mysteriousness), he would unashamedly lead the congregation into bursts of loud laughter.

Hindi (he was fluent but ungrammatical from having been born in India: his form of it was Hindustani) was something which fforde and I could share. The surprise when he and I were walking on The Close and came on a handful of cavorting town children must have been considerable. Finding it hard to suppress his laughter, fforde called out in Hindustani for them to go away,

30

while they had much the same demand from me. They had no reason to expect anything but English from us — perhaps they thought we were calling out in a European language. The oriental effort was no doubt lost on them. But fforde had found the occasion irresistible to his eclectic mood. His wife, Alison, granddaughter of Sir Alexander Macmillan who was co-founder of the eponymous publishing firm, was a majestic counterfoil, blending common sense with a dry appreciation of Arthur's unorthodoxies. Both were loyal friends of mine.

A dinner to which I took Charles made an impression on him. The Cricket Writers' Club were entertaining the 1953 Australian team at Skinners' Hall, and Charles sat next to me with John Arlott opposite. Lord Justice Birkett, one of the judges at the trial of Nazis at Nuremberg, proposed the toast to the Australian team. It was a smoothly electric *tour de force*. Not only was there the voice — of a mellifluence Charles and I agreed we had never heard the like — but the absolutely liquid flow of words, beautifully composed and delivered with no visible mnemonics of any kind and with a kind of controlled effervescence, if that is not a contradiction in terms. Charles thought it the best piece of oratory of the many instances he had known. Lindsay Hassett, the Australian captain, had to follow. The utter contrast of his spontaneous, really comical pawkiness provided just the right mixture. One could not have had a better example of after-dinner entertainment, when so much of it is forced and scarcely bearable. Lindsay had looked after us when the *Orcades* had called at Melbourne. A true Anglophile, his deadpan humour kept us amused all day up and down the Dandenongs (it was impossible to discern whether he was pulling our legs over that name) and back to dinner as our guest on the liner, where he climbed into my bunk and, sloping his trilby over his eyes, said dreamily: 'Wake me up in London.'

I hoped to have another performance by Birkett (not this time able to be shared by Charles). At the Authors versus Publishers match in 1954, Birkett was in the chair for the lunch as President of the National Book League but to my disappointment — for purposes of seeing whether he could perform without repetition — he merely introduced, supremely mellifluously of course, the speakers. These were Lieutenant General Sir Ian Jacob (son of

Field Marshal Sir Claud Jacob but in no way seeming military), Director General of the BBC, whom I was to meet later at a Bursars' Association dinner, proposing the toasts to cricket and literature, replied to soberly (it was lunch time, although that was no reliable yardstick) by Gilbert Harding for literature and by Walter Hamilton, Headmaster of Westminster School (of whom more later), with dry wit for cricket.

A party given by Billy (later Sir William) Collins, chairman of William Collins, the publishers, for a new book by Neville Cardus (I expected an imposing person: Cardus could hardly have been plainer or less distinguished — quite featureless) had led to my being invited to play for Authors versus Publishers in annual matches at Vincent Square, the splendid Westminster School ground in the middle of London. On one occasion, the Authors' batting order was (1) Sir Leonard Hutton (England), (2) J. H. W. Fingleton (Australia), (3) A. R. Morris (Australia), (4) Philip Snow (Fiji), (5) D. R. Jardine (England, captain), (6) P. G. H. Fender (England), (7) I. A. R. Peebles (England), (8) Alec Waugh, (9) Edmund Blunden, (10) Paul Gallico and (11) Laurence Meynell.

Douglas Jardine could not have been a more pleasant captain. His relationship with the Australians, Jack Fingleton (who had played in the 'body-line' series) and Arthur Morris, was cordial in the extreme. Had he mellowed since 1932/3? Or was he always of the same character but exacerbated by the unfunny Australian crowds and inspired entirely by the thoroughly comprehensible motive of subduing Bradman's run-getting prolificacy? He, in his mid-fifties (he was to die in 1958), and I had a profitable partnership against which Billy Collins, no mean medium swing bowler, toiled enthusiastically and in vain with Mark (later Lord) Bonham-Carter behind the wicket encouraging the head of his firm.

Hutton was entirely unassuming and had retained Yorkshire sounds in his voice in contrast with Compton's absence of London nuances, which I had noticed in Fiji. I could later recognize Moravian strains in him, illuminated by his biographer, Gerald Howat.

Fender, in his sixties, bowled with sustained vigour and commendable concentration on dismissing the opposition. He certainly looked Jewish, but his biographer, Richard Streeton, states that he disclaimed that origin. Ian Peebles, one of whose eyes had been damaged in the Café de Paris bombing in London, also wheeled away at a quicker pace than I remember from playing against him before the war in Sir Julien Cahn's XI.

Alec Waugh, younger brother of Evelyn and in no way comparable with him — Alec was a veritable gentleman, affable and with dignity and a far better writer (I realize that this is a controversial assessment: I hold it strongly) — in a partnership with me, defended stoutly but has gone into print lamenting that I made him run threes and even a five on the huge Westminster ground, one of the largest I have played on and where the boundaries could have profitably been pulled in several yards. He puffed but cooperated in my reaching a 50 to match Jardine's. Alec was fundamentally balanced and sensible. I would see him in the Savile Club where we would both stay on occasion. Later I was to share his deep affection for Nice and gave him letters of introduction to friends in Fiji through which he passed. He was himself a friend of quality to whom I took greatly.

Blunden, in his fifties, was fearfully frail but kept wicket as gallantly as his First World War MC in the trenches could have guaranteed.

Jardine, a surprisingly large man, not only tall but big boned, was much larger than he appeared from pictures, although I had seen him playing in the 1930s. He and I were photographed going out to bat together but I doubted if it would be published noticeably. To my acute embarrassment, as I was supposed to be at a meeting, it appeared brazenly in *The Times*. At about the same period, when I was again supposed to be at a mythical meeting, it came to my knowledge that John Arlott, as television commentator, had the camera swivelled round on me sitting in front of the Lord's pavilion while stating, for no doubt a singularly limited amount of public interest, 'That is Philip Snow, who captained the Fiji team touring New Zealand not long ago and is the author of a top-class book on cricket in Fiji.'

I had come across Gilbert Harding in the Savile where Charles had secured temporary membership for me (not a club man, I did not make it permanent). A puffy, lachrymose figure, Harding, after starting life in a workhouse orphanage, was one of the most celebrated persons in the country, having made his name for studied rudeness — then new to the public's television eye — in *What's My Line?* I tended to avoid both him and his friend Harold Nicholson. On the other hand, Sir Ralph Richardson, who said to me over a urinal wall, 'Intelligent men make the best drivers: I'm a chronically bad driver,' before going to mount his heavy motorcycle parked outside the club was very entertaining to know. So too was the writer Sir Edmund Montague Compton Mackenzie (originally Edmund Montague Compton), one of the most prolific of all writers — 96 books (but this gregarious man was left far behind by the 72 million words, the equivalent of 1000 novels, of the reclusive Charles St John Hamilton, alias Frank Richards of *Magnet* and *Gem*). A couple of the Savile's devotees were eminent and I struck up a rapport with them. Daniel Macmillan, the owner of that eponymous publishing firm, was the avuncular older brother of Harold who apparently idolized him. Charles Graves was brother of the flamboyant and erratic Robert.

Reflecting on the Savile and Arlott connects both in my memory. When on leave from Fiji in 1946, Sir Pelham Warner had invited Ratu Sir Edward Cakobau and me to play for his team (see *The Years of Hope*). I had written articles for his *Cricketer*. He was one of the most attractive figures I was to know. Both he and the assistant editor, Arthur Langford, as self-effacing and charming as Ted Cakobau himself, were enchanted by Ted. It was the beginning of lifelong friendships. Taking Plum Warner to the Savile in 1951 for dinner with Charles, I found him in never less than brightest form. Walking afterwards between us towards Grosvenor Square, he linked his arm (a typical habit) in each of ours and asked: 'What do you make of this man, Arlott, we are hearing so much of? I don't mind any lack of playing credentials, though he may have those, but I can't get used to his custom of referring on the wireless to everyone by their Christian name.' Warner was the first whom I heard comment on this habit, which from then on rapidly extended to all the commentators and inter-viewers, a procedure attributable to Arlott and jarringly overdone, most of all since television came in.

There was some excuse for my attending each year for about 20 years a Lord's test match in a box of the school fees' insurance specialists, Holmwood, Back & Manson, at which Bryan Valentine was the host. It was odd that, as a boy at Repton with H. W. Austin, the Davis Cup tennis player, Valentine was regarded as the better tennis player and Austin superior at cricket. I came to know friends of Valentine — G. E. C. Wood, the England and Kent wicketkeeper who had founded The Googlies, an itinerant club to which I was elected a member, and Leslie Ames, also England and Kent wicketkeeper. Both were very genial, Wood in a moustached, benign manner, Ames with dark, black eyes shining from his deep, sallow, almost Romany countenance, a cultured professional with all the experience of taking the ferocious bowling of Larwood and Voce in the 'body-line' (more properly, 'leg theory') series.

Valentine was, in expert judgement, the man who should have been captain of the England team touring Australia in 1946 instead of the enigmatic Hammond, who, had lost his touch at the end of the war, and was in disastrous social form. Although wounded in the war, when he gained the MC, Valentine was a man of remarkable resilience and, as I came to know him well, a markedly shrewd judge of cricket — and an astute one of insurance because it has to be stated, to thwart the cynics, that a lot of business was got through while watching the matches to the benefit of parents, schools and of course the company. Succeeding him, Colin Ingleby-Mackenzie, of quick-fire wit and as skilful a captain of Hampshire as Valentine had been of Kent, was to carry on the same gifted mixture of conviviality and ungrating shrewdness. Colin was elected President of the MCC in 1996. They were entertaining personalities. Constant annual meetings at Lord's (some termly at Rugby) with them were indeed a justifiable occupation of one's professional time.

When I was sitting in front of the pavilion at Lord's one day in 1953, Ronnie Aird, the MCC Secretary, who knew me from negotiating in 1951 for the first Fiji cricket team to visit England, asked me if I was doing anything for lunch. He said that Sir Donald Bradman was here, that it was his forty-fifth birthday and that he (Aird) would be delighted if I would join in a small party in the clock tower box. Aird sat me next to Bradman whom I thought most congenial. Bradman's accent was only partially Australian but his handshake wholly so, causing the usual unconcealable wince. When he started eating I saw how small his hands were. I knew that his feet were small: his boots were hung up in the pavilion showcase. But for so marvellous a cover fielder to have such small hands surprised me greatly. He remembered contemplatively the occasion in Fiji when a Fijian, whom he described in a book as Ratu Edward Cakobau (too sophisticated for such an action), but who was in fact the fast left-hand bowler, later accidentally electrocuted, Amenayasi Turaga, went up to him. Feeling Bradman's biceps, the hugely muscular Fijian shook his head, politely marvelling that the best batsman in the world had such normal (to Fijians subnormal) arms.

I was so taken up with Bradman that I do not recall any of the dozen or so present except the 6th Earl of Rosebery, Lord Lieutenant of Midlothian and former Secretary of State for Scotland who had captained Surrey as Lord Dalmeny. He fiddled about after lunch under the table and, thinking that I could help him over something that he had dropped, to my consternation I saw him drawing out of his sock, from alongside a range of half a dozen others, one fat Havana cigar. I knew that he was a millionaire (these days presumably a billionaire) and was incredulous that he did not offer some around, although seeing where their repository was I'm glad that he did not. Would the aroma of Havanas have submerged a suspicion of sock? This was my first meeting with a man of his wealth (Sir Julien Cahn apart). Later meetings with millionaires (I except John Paul Getty II of course from these generalizations) confirmed my conviction that they could be in the smallest of matters the most miserly of men — hence accounting no doubt for their cupidity in amassing their fortunes. I never subsequently came across one (Cahn and Paul Getty again excepted) who was not penny-wise and it never ceased to jolt me. I should say straight away that it did not go with being Jewish (Rosebery was of that faith) because I met some most generous Jewish persons of utmost wealth. I was to benefit, not personally but for Fiji's cricket, from the philanthropy of two of the richest men, who happened to be non-Jewish, in the world: but that can await its proper place in the narrative.

Soon, John Dunkin retired from Rugby and, having run the appeal, he passed it over to me in 1954: the aim of a quarter of a million pounds was attained in 1959. This was quite a load on my normal work but gave me the pleasure of yet more journeys to London, which always exhilarated me as I came to know it more intimately. We would sometimes meet in the First Lord of the Admiralty's imposing room overlooking the Horse Guards Parade. J. P. L. Thomas (later Viscount Cilcennin of Hereford), on the appeal committee and our host as First Lord of the Admiralty, had been an MP for many years. He had been a favourite of Churchill's and bore some resemblance to Mountbatten with whom he was close, particularly when the latter was First Sea Lord. They both had the same long, thin, dolichocephalic head and rather aquiline features looking nobly on the world. Jim Thomas was, I believe, much the more genial and generally popular of the two. It was puzzling that so impressive looking a person had never married.

One of my first experiences on taking over the appeal was to receive from the 2nd Marquess of Reading (son of the 1st Marquess, Rufus Isaacs, the only Jew to be Viceroy of India) a Rugby School appeal covenant for £1 a year for seven years. Following it rapidly next day was a letter asking me to substitute for it a covenant for 10s. a year for seven years and saying that he had inadvertently paid more than he intended for his old school.

At first our accommodation in Rugby — an attic flat above a master for two terms — had been awful. We wondered whatever we had done in changing from the relative splendour, or at least spaciousness, of our official residences in Fiji. My first term had been on my own in the Crescent Hotel as the intended flat over a master's in a horizontal conversion of a house was not to be ready for a year. It was at the Crescent Hotel, smelling of kerosene-tainted polish, where the crusty, aged Mrs Wilmot had been the owner, that Air Chief Marshal Sir Hugh Dowding, whose pre-eminence in the recently concluded victory of the Battle of Britain when he was air officer commanding Fighter Command before retiring in 1942, had to stay (other hotels were commandeered for military purposes) during the war. He had signed the hotel register, but plainly Mrs Wilmot was not impressed. Owners of hotels had to be asked if baths could be had. When Dowding requested one, she snapped: 'Certainly not. Don't you know there's a war on?'

As Bursar, I purchased for the school, opposite the Crescent Hotel, a fine, spacious early Victorian villa, Horton House, which had been lived in for 43 years by William Sharp, MD, FRS, physician and surgeon, the designer of it who had introduced science teaching to the school. The house was for conversion but this time into two vertical flats. The first school occupant of the half with the handsome high galleried landings over two sides of the hall, the castellated bay window and corniced, Adam fireplace in the drawing room leading through a French door on to an elegant lawn where there was a cedar of Lebanon at least 150 years old, had left the staff unexpectedly early after moving into it. I put in an application to the housing committee (of which I was secretary but of course was absent for this decision) in 1955 and, to our lasting delight, it was allocated to us. We never wanted to leave it, as my seniority increased, and didn't until retirement two decades later. To us it was the best house owned by the school. It had been the first in Rugby to be lit by electricity.

Horton House, 6 Hillmorton Road (Charles was to name a character in his novels Lord Hillmorton, based on his friend, Harold Macmillan) was to be the destination of a series of visitors, some of whom stayed with us. Of Pacific names already mentioned in the first of these two volumes, Ratu Waka Vosailagi, clerk at Naduruloulou in my second phase there, came from a course in England. His was the highest rank in Nasigatoka. With him was Raman N. Nair, the first Indian to be a district officer: he later became the first High Commissioner for Fiji in Australia. Waka had brought some *yaqona* and, borrowing my largest mixing bowl presented to me in Lau, proceeded to squat behind it and strained the *kava* through muslin, while, to our great surprise, Nair sat cross-legged (I had never seen an Indian do this) at the side, bringing the half coconut bowl to me and clapping his hands as he sank to his haunches. It was the first *yaqona* ceremony that we were given in Rugby. Always, visitors from Fiji brought the sort of gift that they would customarily present in Fiji — a bottle of liquor, *yaqona* (already pounded into a powder), a fan, *tapa* (bark cloth), handing it over crouched down with the clapping of hands. Even chiefs like Ratu Edward Cakobau would never think of a visit without a token gift. Exceptions were the visits of Ratu Sir

Lala Sukuna, although if I were returning visits to him in London I would always take a bottle of the hard stuff.

Jonati Mavoa, later to be acting Prime Minister and to die as a minister from a fall downstairs in Suva, was a Lauan of the *crème de la crème* in the Fiji Secretariat. He came from a course at Ruskin College, Oxford. When I met the Oxford train at the station no one got off before it was whistled away. Then, as the train gathered speed, a door opened dramatically and out flew Jonati at alarming and dangerous velocity but marvellously — just — keeping his balance. A slow moving, slow speaking, inhibited man, he had fallen asleep and had seen the Rugby sign-board only as the train was practically away from the platform. After he died, his widow, Bale, later became the fourth wife of Ratu Sir Penaia Ganilau, the last Governor General and first President of Fiji. A more communicative, totally extroverted Fijian, Major Jesoni Takala, was training as a district officer and was later to be an assistant high commissioner in London. He came with a Sarawaki, Zairuddin, who, on returning to his country as a district officer soon afterwards, was killed by tribesmen's blowgun darts.

Ulaiasi Vosabalavu, the former leader of the Fijians in the Secretariat but now in retirement, came by surprise one day to say — instead of telephoning — that he could not come, as arranged, the next week as he was going to the continent. He, in turn, was in no way surprised that we were conveniently in for his unexpected call. This incident never failed to amuse Ratu Edward — 'Typically Vosa.' We had told Old Man Vosa, a sprightly, half-spectacled Fijian of the old school, that we were about to go to Paris. In case his route was through there, we gave him a piece of paper containing our address in Passy and the time of our being there. In Paris, returning to the flat late one night, we were told by the concierge that a black man (he was bronze) with glasses had called and was surprised and disappointed that we were out. How he managed, knowing no French, to trace us at all remained a mystery. The only explanation seemed to be that his unconcerned joviality would get him anywhere. His unshakeable euphoria and that of so many of his race was one of the strongest evocations of the South Sea Islands. The recollection of their good humour was always a salutary influence on oneself if anything was inclined to be awry.

Immediately after Vosa, came Wal and Dorothy Warden, our planter friends from Taveuni who had been on leave when we left that island. They had been on the same ship coming over and taught Vosa card tricks, none of which worked when he demonstrated them to us, a fact that did not attenuate his enthusiasm for repeating efforts that always ended in failure. His spectacles would be discarded, the cards would be peered at within an inch of his nose. The bewilderment of the hapless entertainer changed eventually to a mirth that would exceed that even of his audience.

We now confidently believed we were having the best of two worlds — England, with all its conveniences and refreshing change of character after life on islands, and friends from Fiji with whom to reminisce and to show off the local sights — a tour of the school where rugby football (which had its adherents in Fiji, where every forward seemed to be a three-quarter and vice versa) had been started in 1823, as well as visits to neighbouring Stratford-upon-Avon country and Warwick Castle.

Humphrey Evans, one of our closest friends in Fiji, visited us often. He mock-disdainfully dubbed Horton House 'The Deanery'. We once converged with him on Clare where he applied his indefatigable photographic skill, contriving with a long cord and remote control to include himself in the pictures. He was not in the country when the pin-up love of his life, with whom he corresponded regularly and tirelessly from Fiji, Dorothy Tutin, was in *Romeo and Juliet* at Stratford-upon-Avon. Anne and I took Stefanie to it. Afterwards, I wrote a note to Dorothy and asked the stage doorman to give it to her. It said that we were Humphrey's closest friends. Back came a reply that she would see us in half an hour. The doorman had explained that after the final scene she always lay flat out, arms and legs dangling over a bed, in her dressing room for that period to secure utter relaxation. Humphrey had never met her. She was interested to know what we thought of him. Bottles were opened and in came Geraldine McEwen, herself not unlike Dorothy Tutin in pertness and voice, and Richard Johnson. Stefanie was duly impressed, as were we.

The theatre is accorded more than its fair share of official honours when one considers the plaudits the profession secures on the stage, like sportsmen on the field (there should at least be retirement before that happens). But why Dorothy Tutin is not a Dame (compare Dame Wendy Hiller) and why Trevor Howard received nothing and James Mason only a CBE remains a mystery (compare Sir Michael Hordern, Sir Michael Redgrave, Sir Stanley Baker, Sir Donald Wolfit, Sir Felix Aylmer, Sir John Gielgud, Sir Derek Jacobi, Sir Terence Rattigan, Sir Noel Coward and Sir Ian McKellan). Perhaps James Mason found that his pacifism in the war counted against him. Olivier was overdone with a peerage. It raises the whole question of, among others, the proportion of unacknowledged doctors and scientific experts — like authors — scantily honoured, underpaid and not even having the compensation of living relatively unsolitary existences.

A visitor who attracted much attention, just as Jaoji Suguturaga had soon after our arrival in Rugby and for the same reason, was another bushy haired Fijian inspector, Uraia Moku, in police uniform which has been described before, stopping the local population in their tracks. Some took a lot of convincing, at least those who observed from the rear, that so much hair and the wearing of skirts did not mean that this figure was an Amazon.

Richard Aldington tended to write to Charles utterly out of the blue. In a revelatory excerpt of 9 August 1954 from Les Rosiers, Ancien Chemin de Castelnau, Montpelier, he wrote that: 'As a small child during the South African war when I heard talk of the Empire I used to lie in bed and wonder if ... the great Empire would ever end. I have alas lived to see it and wish I hadn't. It was a mistake to return from France in 1919.' The imperial affection, nostalgia of the profoundest depths, linked to a death wish, was hardly to be expected in so radical and iconoclastic a thinker. It did not reduce my admiration for this good friend.

In 1954 my father died in his eighty-sixth year. Anne, Stefanie and I had been going to see him, travelling every Sunday by car the 40 miles from Rugby to Leicester and back, trying to compensate for the many years that we had not managed to see him while we were abroad. He had never been ill in his life and had been the ultimate in independence for all of it — except for his dependence on the organ and piano. On his way to the organ at St Mary de

Castro, two miles into the city from Richmond Road, and with a status rivalled only by the cathedral (to which it was regarded by some as superior), he had slipped on ice in the dark, fractured his collar bone and was not found in the iced-up gutter until some while later. This had shaken him, and the vicar had to tell us, after his determined resumption, that at times his playing of the organ was a little behind the tempo of the service. It was heartbreaking to advise him to retire because it was clear that it would deprive him of his last remaining interest in life. He had spent 55 years at three churches, 23 of them at St Mary de Castro. The lodger in the top part of the house, who shared the downstairs kitchen, suspected very early one morning that father was ill: he found that he had died in his sleep. Father had refused to live either with us or my brother Eric, as this would have meant separation from the organ. There could not have been a more conscientious, kindly, gentler man.

Charles described father's death in *The Sleep of Reason* and considered it 'his best single piece of writing'. It was done from the lodger's account that Eric and I gave him. Charles was in Canada and could not attend the funeral, which for me was so moving that I could not bear to be in the front of the small assembly at the burial. Comical he was and seemed at times, despite or because of his sturdy independence, also tragic, almost Chaplinesque. I was glad that Stefanie just knew him: she had reached the age of seven when he died and had seen him once a week since our return in 1951. No. 40 Richmond Road, where all four sons had been born, was left by mother (father as a bankrupt twice could not own it and the eldest brother, Harold, had died 25 years earlier) to Charles, who now passed it to Eric and me. We sold it for £400. It was almost beyond habitation but its demolition five years later has left a raw gap in Richmond Road to this day (marked by a Leicester City Council blue plaque as the birthplace of Lord (C. P.) Snow). The vacuum is the only one in the street. Charles had written from Toronto on 24 October 1954:

> I was very sad to hear of father's death. But I believe he would have been pleased to die so easily: I don't think life had any more meaning for him: and I find it a curious kind

of comfort to see how one can slip out of life. .... I think of appointing myself as Governor-General after Massey, with you as Chief Adjutant.

Then he wrote from London on 29 March 1955: 'I think it is reasonable that I shouldn't take a share of the estate. If so, however, I don't see why I should pay any of the expenses. Does that strike you as fair?' The estate was in fact the £400 less solicitors' expenses over the sale.

Charles and his wife, the petite writer, Pamela Hansford Johnson, pretty with black hair and porcelain blue eyes, had met us on the *Orcades* at Tilbury Docks. Pam had been divorced from her Australian husband, Neil Stewart, and briefly engaged to marry Dylan Thomas, only for them to decide otherwise in the registry office. Pam's mother described Thomas to me as 'a drunken slob'. Charles and Pam had moved from the leased 1 Hyde Park Crescent, London, to Nethergate House, Clare, in Suffolk, a Jacobean building of arresting beauty, to accommodate Pam's mother and her own two children shortly before their son, Philip (after me) Charles Hansford, was to be born.

A year later Charles, Pam and family moved to 199 Cromwell Road, London, from Clare, about which he wrote on 23 May 1956 from the Civil Service Commission in Old Burlington Street, London: 'I will take £3250 for an immediate sale (I paid just over £6000).' This was when I thought I had a buyer for him. Nethergate House had five large bedrooms and became for a while a restaurant.

The move back to London coincided with his rather depressing book, *Homecomings*, but the new address alongside an increasingly busy road brought them pleasure. It was a block of flats, Cromwell Mansions. Above them was Baroness Marie (Mourie) Budberg, who did not conceal that she had been Maxim Gorky's and H. G. Wells's mistress. She epitomized the Slavonic *grande dame*, larger than life, corpulent yet commanding in an otherwise unimperious way. She had blue hair and was meretriciously bejewelled when Pam and Charles took me to meet her. Her life had been less than ordinary. First married to a Russian diplomat who was shot by the Bolsheviks, she then married Baron von

Budberg, divorcing him a year later. Her salon, said to be London's last literary one, included Olivier and Vivien Leigh, Priestley, Joseph Conrad, and Wells of course. She was chief reader and film adviser for Sir Alexander Korda, the Hungarian naturalized as British, and a translator. Until she died in 1974, her 'at homes' at Cromwell Road were five times a week from 6.00 to 7.30, where there was so much alcohol and cigarette smoking that I was concerned for the fire risk to the lower flat. On the ground-floor level, where Charles and Pam lived, there was a bus stop immediately outside. As Charles and Pam were both on television a lot now — *Brains Trust* programmes, simulated 'dinners' with Bob Boothby as host at what were in fact lunches — people in buses could be seen to recognize, and point out, both of them sitting unconcernedly in the drawing room with the curtains always undrawn.

Ever vigilant for advancing me, Charles had written to me from Nethergate House on 11 July 1956:

> In *The Times* of today there is an advertisement for Secretary General of the Commonwealth (formerly Empire) Press Union. ...
> This is the job that Arnot Robertson's husband has held for a long time (nearly 30 years): it is worth your looking at. You could perhaps get a K out of it — he did, and he is a man of about one-tenth of your capacity.

Charles and I had long known Arnot Robertson, the novelist, but I had not met her husband, Sir Henry Ernest Turner, who died in 1961. I prevaricated, thinking about the travelling involved. Charles then wrote, on 24 July 1956, from the Scientific Branch of the Civil Service Commission in London: 'God forbid I should press the CPU on you. It *would* mean some flying. The only things in favour are (a) a good salary (b) a probable K.' I took it no further.

On election this same year as the youngest to hold office as President of the Old Newtonians' Association, I took Bert Howard as my guest to the dinner. R. L. S. Ager, the former Headmaster, was present as of right and it gave me pleasure to have an opportunity to go some way towards redressing the wrong at De

Montfort Hall in 1946 when I had reserved all my praise for Bert (I gave him some on this occasion) but this time was able to make the right noises about Ager. There would have been few, if any, of the audience nine years earlier present, but at least Bert and Ager were there and I felt that the latter was now given by me, as publicly as I could, the proper place that he had in my estimation.

I had not been long at Rugby before Diana Rait-Kerr, curator of Lord's museum and library, who had been written to by John Masefield for information, passed the Poet Laureate on to me. He was thinking of writing about the Australian Aboriginal cricket team touring England in the previous century and Diana, whose father, a former secretary of MCC, had been at Rugby, thought I could help him with information about indigenous Fijian skills with weapons which the Aboriginals used to display on exhibitions between the cricket. The armoury was in fact dissimilar. Masefield asked me to meet him at his house, which was tucked away near the Thames at Abingdon. Quite unpoetic in appearance and manner, he showed that he had his feet on the ground and seemed to have no time for dilettante poets who were over-aesthetic. His background had been so far removed from that type: it had been a struggle and a fiercely masculine one, and he could not abide foppishness. That emerged strongly in a man whose realism and warm common sense appealed to me. His only son had been killed in the war after leaving Rugby but he was no sentimentalist and yet wholesomely human.

In 1955 I had revived the MCC versus Rugby Town fixture, which had expired in 1913 when Sir Arthur Conan Doyle, a distinctly useful player, was captain of the MCC. For the occasion, henceforward an annual one, I had persuaded R. E. S. Wyatt, the England, Warwickshire and Worcestershire all-rounder to play, together with R. E. Bird, the Worcestershire captain, Billy (later Sir William) Collins, Mark (later Lord) Bonham-Carter, Sir Charles McLeod, 3rd Baronet, Hon. F. H. M. Fitz Roy Newdegate, later 3rd Viscount Daventry and as Lord Lieutenant of Warwickshire to be governor of Rugby School, together with B. W. Quaife, the Worcestershire wicketkeeper and son of W. G. Quaife of England and Warwickshire. J. R. Burnet, Yorkshire's captain, also played.

Wyatt was aged 54 and in little or no practice. Having difficulty in getting Rugby Town out, I prevailed on him to bowl. Very reluctantly he did — and swung the ball vastly, so much so that I kept him on for an hour while he collected five wickets. I also had to get him to help me in batting: with him I reached 50 odd and we almost made a win out of a drawn, large scoring match. But, ever after, Bob would balefully look at me when we met, accusing me of killing him on his last appearance on the field, every minute of which, in his deadpan way, he had enjoyed.

I was to be very surprised when Billy Collins, who so often used to get me to play in his matches of authors (he always hoped to have a book from me) versus his firm, later had a consuming affair in Kenya with Joy Adamson, the celebrated Austrian tamer of Elsa the lioness and eccentric promoter of conservation for the World Wildlife Fund (who was murdered by a possibly maltreated servant). Billy was always a diverting, dashing personality with his bright, amused brown eyes under ambitiously roaming eyebrows. But I never expected that range of unorthodoxy. He certainly entered into the spirit and soul of possibly his most famous author.

In 1956 there came the chance for me to play under F. R. Brown's captaincy of MCC versus Rugby School. I took to Brown immediately. He is a captain I could have played for 100 per cent: he was a master of the almost intangible, delicate art of leading, indubitably given to only a few and I could well understand how, with his inferior team in Australia in 1950/1, he was recognized as one of the very best captains England had produced. All the same, he might have tilted the 1950/1 series in Australia England's way had he not declined to take Bill Edrich, the well-known tearaway character on and off the field.

I, of course, had had an earlier challenge in Ratu Sir George Cakobau when I captained Fiji on the first-class tour of New Zealand in 1948, and in the first of these two volumes I have explained how I dealt with it to mutual ease of mind. Plum Warner told me that when he was captain of the England team to tour Australia he had insisted on Len Braund, like Edrich in temperament and in intemperance, being selected. He said: 'I told the selectors that I would guarantee to have Braund sober on the field. Not only did I do so, but he enjoyed the tour to the full and was a match winner. Brown should have taken the challenge over Edrich similarly.'

In Brown there was an honesty, an absolutely firm intention to win by every lawful strategy, an unflagging energy and enormous strength physically and mentally, a quite magnetic charisma. Unsubtle in appearance and seeming to be dominated by raw brawn, underneath that slightly off-putting exterior Freddie Brown was a man, one instinctively felt and soon learnt, of charm and, most importantly, natural command.

On 6 December 1956, Charles wrote:

> With some uncertainty I have just accepted a K. It will (if we all survive) be in the New Year's Honours: I didn't want you to see it first in the paper. It is being given for my official career, which pleases me. These things are of course nothing but a nuisance to a writer: it will do me a slight but perceptible amount of harm. However, there are inducements on the other side. People who compare me with Trollope perhaps ought to realize that I've gone much further in the public service than he ever did.
>
> This is naturally secret. It is death if these things get out.

When I asked if it was to be a KBE or Knight Bachelor and whether a peerage would not be far distant, also if he would like a rest and stay with us, he replied on 17 December: 'Normally we'd like to come but we shall be moving into the new flat and must be on the spot here. I've never had more maddening minor things to do. Kt. Bach. The House of Lords has in fact been canvassed, though only tenuously, by some of the Labour people.'

It was from Cromwell Road that Charles, accompanied by Pam and me, went to Buckingham Palace for his accolade, an occasion described by me in *Stranger and Brother*. I never speculated that I would follow, in infinitely humbler rank, those footsteps in the Palace 22 years later.

Also in 1956, after I had been Bursar for four years, I was elected to the committee of the Public Schools' Bursars' Association. This was in record time: no one had made it anywhere near as quickly. But I did not think that it would lead me further beyond the three-year span as there were one or two bursars in their late forties (I was 41) and early fifties ahead of me in their time at leading schools. But, in 1959, the favourite for the position of vice-chairman, which led inexorably to the top post, the Bursar of Winchester, in his late forties, resigned suddenly and I was put up to replace him. I could hardly believe my luck — the youngest vice-chairman ever by far, similarly so when I became Chairman after three years in 1962.

About this time I met in Rugby E. W. Dawson, a schoolboy hero of mine on the Leicestershire county ground at Aylestone Road. He was one of the most handsome men of his time, deeply tanned, with the blackest hair and wearing a Cambridge sweater. How ineffably handsome were many of those in the group pictures of the Oxford and Cambridge cricket teams of the late 1920s and early 1930s. Some consolation perhaps for the noble-looking generation destroyed in the First World War. Dawson had captained Cambridge, Leicestershire and played for England in South Africa. He was now connected with Outward Bound and a master had arranged for a talk from him within the school. When I saw his name I asked John Dewes, who had played for Cambridge, Middlesex and England and was now master in charge of school cricket, if he knew that Dawson was coming. John Dewes will forgive my remembering that he had not heard of Dawson, even though he was in the era of no more than 30 years earlier. Well, in 30 years there would be many who played for Cambridge. Anyway, I arranged for Dewes to come with him to the house after the talk: Eddie Dawson was as charming as he seemed to me from afar those 30 years earlier. I was pleased to meet him yet again in 1970 at Leicestershire's new ground, Grace Road, when paintings of Dawson's two great professionals and my boyhood idols, Ewart Astill and George Geary, were unveiled. It is interesting that one's heroes of early youth would tend to be provincial rather than national, even though there were such paragons as Sutcliffe, Hobbs, Tate, Larwood, Chapman, Hendren, Verity, Ames, Hammond, Woolley and Leyland in the England teams of that era.

In 1957, John Arlott and I were invited by Ronnie Aird to address all the county cricket secretaries assembled in the Long Room at Lord's. John, a friend since his review in the 1950 *Wisden* of my *Cricket in the Fiji Islands*, had been as keen as I was to have the first Fijian cricket team tour England. He had tried numerous sources for the considerable financial help required. Following up one such, he had taken me to meet Jack Hylton, the 1930s band leader who was now an impresario with great wealth, near Savile Row. Hylton, who kept us waiting for an hour (to John's distinct displeasure) while he was alone in his room dominated by a grand piano, was clearly attracted by the novelty of bare feet, skirts and heads of hair but could not be persuaded to take the final step. He left his room, boarded his chauffeured, open Rolls-Royce, took an apple out of his pocket and was driven off through the West End munching away in full public view. Not a man of taste, we concluded, in our chagrin.

The most important possibility was to arouse interest in the counties themselves. First, John spoke, then I, in a hurry as I had to catch a train back for an urgent meeting in Rugby. But we had done enough to convince all, including the at first incredulous Wilf Wooller (secretary of Glamorgan) and T. E. Bailey (secretary of Essex) that here was a chance of entertainment on the field for spectators and no loss of money for the clubs. It was agreed that the gate money would be divided: the way was clear for a tour in 1959 embracing fixtures with MCC at Lord's, the bottom half of the counties, the top half-dozen minor counties and the universities.

As a bolt out of the blue, there appeared soon after a statement by the egregious J. W. Gosling, the ill-fitting manager of the 1948 Fiji tour of New Zealand, that for any tour of England the team would only have three or four Fijians, who would be wearing trousers, close cut hair and rubber shoes, a number of Indians and the rest part-Europeans. I could not believe that there had been this transmogrification in so short a time since the comparatively successful, nearly all-Fijian 1954 tour of New Zealand. Where had the Indian cricketers suddenly come from? There was only one qualified to be in the top 22 in my time and there was no one selected for the following touring team in 1954. Why the change of Fijians' appearance and so few of them likely to be chosen? John and I agreed that there was nothing to be done in the time left but to arrange with the MCC to call the whole thing off. It was of course a *canard* by the Anglophobe Gosling who would not have been allowed to accompany the team after his 1948 tour defects. He himself went to live in Australia shortly afterwards. Eventually, with him out of the way, I succeeded in arranging for Fiji teams to come to England; they were not as expert as in 1948 and 1954, but competent, picturesque and almost wholly Fijian — only a single (but proficient) Indian.

Ratu Sir Lala Sukuna's wife, Maraia, had died in 1956. In reply to my condolences, Ratu Sukuna wrote from Rairaiwaqa, Suva, Fiji on 26 October 1956:

> I very much appreciate your sympathy and kind words on the passing of Maraia whose friend you were and whom she greatly liked. I am alone now at 'Rairaiwaqa' going through the funeral obsequies; the *Vakabogidrau* takes place on the 10th November and the *Vakataraisulu* at Lakeba in May next. All these ceremonies are performed with the best of intentions but they do pull one down, when one is so greatly distressed. However, I am greatly supported by expressions of sympathy and sincere friendly feelings from old friends. I am hoping to see you again in the not too distant future: also Anne and Adi Vuikaba.* Please give my sincere *loloma*s to them.

Ratu Sukuna himself died two years later on his way to England with his young wife, Adi Maca Liku, on board ship in the Indian Ocean. They had been due to stay with us. I was deeply shocked when Kingsley Roth telephoned from Cambridge to tell me.

During his visit, in memory of Lady Maraia, Sukuna had planned to present furniture made from Fiji's fine timber, *yaka*, for a room in the Royal Commonwealth Society's headquarters in London. This was ultimately carried out in the presence of the 9th Earl De La Warr, chairman of the Society's council and formerly Lord Privy Seal, President of the Board of Education and Postmaster-General, Sir Alan Burns, chairman of the Society's library committee who had met Ratu Sukuna at the founding of

---

* Vuikaba is Stefanie to whom he had given in 1947 the name of his favourite sister. *Adi* is Fijian for Lady, the counterpart of the male *Ratu* (Chief).

the United Nations in 1946 and was a former governor of British Honduras and the Gold Coast, past governors of Fiji, Lord Milverton and Sir Alexander Grantham, and the current governor, Sir Kenneth Maddocks, whom I had met before — he seemed particularly congenial and was to write an all too brief account of his Colonial Service career neatly entitled *Of No Fixed Abode*. Sir Harry Luke, whom I was pleased to meet again, made the presentation on Sukuna's behalf. Giving a résumé of Ratu Sukuna's career and emphasizing that he held a French VC, Luke graciously said that he 'was not only easily the most eminent Fijian of his generation but also probably much the most versatile man ever to have come out of a small island, not only in the Pacific but in any other ocean. Indeed I think he was one of the most remarkable men ever produced by the colonial empire'. Of Sukuna's diaries as District Commissioner, Lau (the post in which I succeeded him in 1940 — he asked me to call him Jo, a privilege accorded to perhaps only half a dozen Europeans and, of course, to no Fijian). Luke said:

> He wrote them, I thought, like Conrad; the same command of language and of every nuance of the language, vivid, terse, descriptive — it was a delight to read — so much so that I think one of the things we must regret about him is that he never wrote an autobiography. To anyone not knowing him, and not having seen him, merely to hear him speak it would never occur that he was a member of another race.

Although neither of them ever got on well with each other, Luke's magnanimous speech epitomized here some of the outstanding qualities in Sukuna. If the Permanent Under Secretary of State for the Colonies or the Secretary of State himself had been imaginative round about 1948 (when Sukuna was 60) the opportunity to have a native as the first governor of any colony in the empire should have been taken. Ratu Sir Lala Sukuna should have succeeded Grantham. It would have been the finest historical gesture for Fiji and the proper reward for Sukuna.

On his last visit to England in 1956, I had shown Sir Lala, who created quite a stir in his Savile Row tailored *sulu* and highly polished sandals, a cricket match on The Close at Rugby. The only Abyssinian player ever of any note, John Asfaw, son of the Emperor's Lord Great Chamberlain, was batting for the school, stylishly and effectively. Sukuna was intrigued and insisted on meeting him.

It was on this visit too to England that he presented on behalf of the Fiji Cricket Association a painting of Albert Park. I had commissioned this on their behalf as a contribution to the magnificent Imperial War Memorial at Lord's, where the picture is striking among those of the many main grounds all over the world. I had drawn what I thought should be the view represented, showing the Government Buildings and the Grand Pacific Hotel, with Joske's Thumb ruggedly erect among the mountains across the Suva lagoon. The artist, Alfred Stone, followed my sketch faithfully; the picture can be seen on the jacket cover of *The Years of Hope*.

I had not been warned before the presentation that Sukuna had had a stroke in Fiji. Meeting him the day before at the Royal Commonwealth Society, where he always stayed when alone in London, and drinking with him I had noticed nothing. But early on in his speech presenting the picture at Lord's, in front of the President of the MCC, officials and members of the Australian and MCC teams, which were playing, his mind began to wander and he was not anything like his most imposing, succinct self. His command of English nevertheless still impressed those hearing him for the first time, but I was disappointed because he meandered on about Samoan women playing on Albert Park when he could have given some history of near first-class encounters on the Park, such as against Trumper, Noble, Sobers, Ramadhin, and actual first-class Fiji matches in New Zealand.

Field Marshal Earl Alexander of Tunis was President of the MCC. He made a most gracious speech of acceptance, astonishing me by quoting from my *Cricket in the Fiji Islands*, which Ronnie Aird must have given him as homework beforehand. I was deeply impressed by Alexander who made Sukuna and me his guests in his presidential box for the whole of the match, which fascinated Sukuna on whom Neil Harvey, the Australian left-hander, made a strong impression. Countess Alexander was equally pleasant. I doubt if I've ever met a more charming couple in whose presence one felt dignity, utter composure, genuine interest and tangible yet unostentatious style. Sukuna and I felt that we had got to know Alexander quite well in those full days together. Alexander exuded taciturnity — no wonder he had been given the task of extrication from Dunkirk, the command of southern Britain after it, when the threat of invasion was at its peak, the steadying up in Burma and, probably mistakenly, the Italian campaign.

Humbly catching a bus on the Edgeware Road back to the Cumberland Hotel, to where he had moved, Sukuna told me on it that Alexander was a chief of the type Fijians would follow anywhere. I never heard him say that of anyone else in all our conversations over the years. Now Ratu Sir Lala Sukuna had died. He was a man Europeans would follow anywhere. I was always sorry that it never proved quite possible for Charles to know Jo Sukuna, though he stayed with us in Rugby in 1956 when he was photographed in our garden doing his habitual rolling of pungent Fiji tobacco in banana leaves as the Fijians' form of cigar. Charles was to meet, however, the nearest equivalents to Sukuna in Ratu Sir Edward Cakobau, Ratu Sir George Cakobau and Ratu Sir Kamisese Mara. But not Ratu Sir Penaia Ganilau.

Another war leader, whom I was to meet soon after the fascinating days with Alexander, was Marshal of the RAF Viscount Portal of Hungerford. When Aird introduced me to him we talked for quite a while. It was difficult not to be overwhelmed by his beak of a nose, the most protruding I have ever encountered. That overcome, it was easy to understand how his manner gained him so much admiration and friendship when competition for the top war posts was stiff. He may have lacked Alexander's handsome style but they both had the simplicity of manner that is perhaps the greatest attribute of a successful leader.

In 1957 Arthur fforde, who had not been very well (Alison had asked me to keep an eye on him on visits to London for meetings), was offered, after nine years at Rugby, the chairmanship of the BBC. This caused some disbelief, close to derision, in his critics' quarters in Rugby, for fforde had been irrevocably against television and never watched it himself, while disapproving of others' attachment to it. He caught up with me circling Caldecott's Piece, the second large ground fringing the school buildings and in its own right the envy of many a school that it and The Close could both be part of the hereditament. Trying to reach a decision, he was anxious to elicit a view about accepting it should his health hold out. We walked round the ground three or four times, he with his minute steps and furrowed brow but clearly, I felt, with his mind made up in the right direction. He was pleased to have a change but, being without specific experience and subject as he was to temperamental vagaries, he was exposing himself to potential criticism from a wide world, not for the first time.

Charles told me he had been embarrassed at a BBC dinner soon after fforde's appointment, for he was sitting next to a drunk Gilbert Harding who started talking loudly nonstop to all around him when he decided that fforde's speech had gone on for long enough. If fforde had been at his best, even Harding could scarce have refrained from conceding gruff amusement. Apparently, fforde had been treading too carefully for a Harding hoping for gaffes.

His successor at Rugby was Walter Hamilton. He had been Headmaster of Westminster and was a professional schoolmaster. Unlike fforde, he had not been at Rugby as a boy. I was at the formal interview that the Governing Body — simply going through the official motions — gave him before appointment: in fact, I fetched him to the Jerusalem Chamber from Westminster School next door. He was calmness itself. For him, it was almost a sideways move: he wanted it for his young family as a change from London. There was no rival.

He settled in as though he had been resident for ages. Jane was eye-fixingly attractive — and shy with it — as the wife in her early thirties of a man who had been a confirmed bachelor to the age of 43. Her cornflower blue eyes were highlighted by the pink of her cheeks. She quickly made herself at home in her self-effacing way.

The sage installed, the kingmaker, Will Spens, thought it opportune for himself to retire in 1959, at the age of 75, after virtually 30 years on the Governing Body. He had with characteristic confidence and precision told me long before that he would retire at that age. He did not believe in anyone going on longer unless circumstances were quite exceptional. It was certainly a safe time. The appeal I had been running was almost, despite the Marquess of Reading's reduction of annual covenant by 10s., at its target.

There was a personable successor to Spens available with whom Hamilton and I would work happily. This was Jim Cilcennin, whom we have met briefly when he was First Lord of the Admiralty. As J. P. L. Thomas, he had been given a peerage after having been an MP since he was 28. He had started as assistant private secretary to Baldwin, been parliamentary private secretary to the secretaries of state for the dominions, colonies and foreign affairs, financial secretary to the Admiralty and finally himself First Lord of the Admiralty. Jim Thomas, as he had been, had the professional charm of a politician. All his life had been in politics, without being either suave or pusillanimous, and he had never put a foot wrong. Tall, his dark hair changing to grey, with bright smiling brown eyes and eyelashes that could not be missed, slim and with a limp from the sciatica he attributed to the hammock-shaped mattresses of the boarding house of his youth at Rugby, he was beautifully mannered. Both Hamilton and I worked most harmoniously with him. For the former, it was a relief not to have a chairman like Spens hovering about, even at the end of a tele-phone. Lord Cilcennin (pronounced Kilkennin) gave me my first of many meals in later years that I was to have at the House of Lords. It was lunch, which did not come up to my expectations. Apparently, peers did not like to spend too much of their daily allowance but, even so, it was subsidized by government. I was struck unfavourably by the antiquatedness, over-familiarity and Londonness of the waitresses. I thought the Commons, where Jonati Mavoa took me as his guest while he was on a course as clerk to the Legislative Council, Fiji, worse still. Cilcennin seemed popular with all his fellow peers, including an ex-miner, whom he introduced to me and whose absence of aitches was as con-spicuous as his humble friendliness.

Jim Cilcennin was on a later occasion to give me a superior meal, cooked by himself in his bachelor flat. He was a particularly close friend of Anthony Eden and of Mountbatten. He told me that he could think of no nicer end to his working life than, because he was a kinsman of the Earl of Warwick, the absentee owner in Switzerland, to take over the imposing Warwick Castle. But he said: 'I could never afford it. Even the peacocks would starve.'

A disappointment was to meet Lieutenant-General Sir John

Glubb (Pasha). His chinless appearance did not fit the position of prestige he had attained; there must have been something about him but in the short meeting it eluded me. After all, Field Marshal Lord Plumer of Messines had a most unimpressive face, but was probably one of the most successful of the First World War leaders and more humanitarian by the standards of that war compared with the handsome but doubtfully successful Field Marshal Earl Haig, apparently impervious (but with probably no alternative) to mortality and casualty rates.

It gave me pleasure to be among a handful of people invited to Lord's for the opening of the Warner stand. There was no match on and Plum walked, with Bernard, 16th Duke of Norfolk, President of the MCC, across the corner of the ground. He recalled that it was the spot where his first boundary for Rugby at Lord's had gone: it was next to where the new stand now made a graceful curve. The Duke ushered him to where the score of Plum's selected friends were waiting. It was all very informal and Plum was touched, introducing us to the Duke, whom none of us had met but were struck, at least I was, with the unmistakable feeling that here was a character and a half. One of the neatest stories in cricket lore, involving his name, is unfortunately not printable here.

Pam and Charles, after Pam had done work in 1957 on my *Bronze and Clay*, leaving the descriptive passages untouched, and after their return from Malta (Charles had agreed to serve on the University of Malta Royal Commission for four years), put pressure on Anne, Stefanie and me to go to Le Coq-sur-Mer in Belgium for a holiday with them. But first a vignette of Malta, contained in a letter from Pam of 8 July 1957 written from the Hotel Phoenicia:

> As Charles says, this isn't a country, it is an experience. We shall have to restrain ourselves from writing a novel about the melodramatic goings on here and gorgeous personalities, from the ferocious to the dotty or they won't ask us to replace Laycock [the Governor]! This is more priest-ridden than any Catholic country I've ever known. It is a constant

battle royal between the excellent but peppery Mintoff* and the minute and awful Archbishop. .... It is sometimes beautiful — dusty yellow like Greece in sapphire and jade seas and sometimes resembling nothing so much as a bomb site. Which it is. We have met pretty well everyone, and some people *too* often.

On 5 September 1957, Pam wrote on a postcard: 'Coq-sur-Mer would be a splendid family place for *all* of us one year, madly cheap, beautiful food, miles and miles of wonderful sand. There is really nothing to do in the evenings out of season and one should come earlier.' And Charles the same day had written to me from the Hotel Bristol, Coq-sur-Mer, saying that 'Le Coq is visually grotesque — Walt Disney architecture — but the sands are splendid.' Then, on 17 September 1957, Pam wrote from 199 Cromwell Road that they were 'wondering whether we could all go in a party next year say from Monday August 11th–Monday August 25th. We are even wondering whether Bert and Cecil [the Howard brothers] would like to come. We'd then have a party of eleven. .... PS If you brought the car over ... trips to Bruges, Ghent and Brussels. .... Love to you all and Brandy naturally, Pam.' Brandy was our Gordon Setter.

If anything, we wanted more variety than Belgium was likely to supply. We also knew of their rather finicky taste in food, and chauffeuring the car would not have been practicable with nine (or more) of us, if the Howards were there including Andrew, Lindsay and young Philip. It did not seem very enticing, except for their company, which would have been further illuminating, if perhaps inevitably repetitive in range of subjects more aligned to me than to Anne or Stefanie. I felt ungrateful when both had been so helpful with *Bronze and Clay* (tentatively retitled *The Edge of the World*) but what I had seen in 1951 driving through Belgium had not been sufficiently attractive. They expressed themselves very sad that we would not fall in with the Le Coq idea.

But at the beginning of 1958 they went to America for two months, Charles as Regent's Professor at the University of Cali-

---

* Dominic Mintoff, the Prime Minister, was a fan of Charles's writing.

fornia, Berkeley, having asked me to spend every Sunday with young Philip, who had had to be left behind in London for that time, to see that he was all right. As it turned out, he was in the charge of a veritable dragon of a nanny whom I had to moderate. They had always arranged for me to look after Philip — and, if I could, his half-brother, Andrew, now a scientist married in Australia, and half-sister, Lindsay (now the second wife of 4th Lord Avebury, a Buddhist widely known as Eric Lubbock and for his major surprise in becoming Liberal MP for Orpington and for his public declaration of the bequest of his body to the Battersea Dogs' Home) if anything happened to them both. I therefore felt a little better about my indebtedness to them.

Pam wrote to me from the Cunard Line's RMS *Queen Elizabeth* on 21 March 1958, saying 'Charles is on his way to becoming a Great Man in certain circles in US. He has made a tremendous impression, and is so good at it that I feel only a cross between Cleopatra and Boadicea could be a fit helpmate for him.' This was on her way back, leaving Charles in California for another month. In a postcard from London on 10 April, she wrote that 'C has had an awful adventure trapped in a snowbound train in the Sierra Nevada for thirty-six hours!'

Every year up to the end of the 1960s we used to go *en famille* to France where Stefanie soon became our interpreter and acquired an ease with the country which was to be so helpful for her in her future career. I had fallen in love with Nice and Paris when I had returned through those cities after having driven in 1951 over the Alps to pick up Charles and Pam from Venice. They are my favourite urban locations of all that I've seen in the world.

In 1959 Ratu Edward Cakobau had stayed with us, diffusing charm effortlessly over everyone he met. I never knew him fail to exude it. Only once did he seem to be different — in a late night discussion about Ratu Sukuna whom he thought had tended to suppress him somewhat in his career by insisting on his being an economic development officer when he would have been happier in his other capacity as a commissioner. He was unusually serious and frustrated. This was to recur when, I suspect, he thought he was going to miss out on being the first Fijian Governor General.

The Cricket Writers' Club, of which I was a member, invited me to compose a profile on Bula for publication in *Cricket Heroes*. I was in the company of Arlott, Cardus, Jim Swanton, Peebles and Bill Bowes: Bula's name was among those of Hendren, Leyland, Hobbs, Tate, Verity, Wooller, May and Fry. It looked incongruous but my chapter was picked out by reviewers for its unusual content and style. I sent a copy to Bula but his English would not have been up to understanding it.

I was staggered to hear over the wireless one lunch time in 1960 the announcement of Viscount Cilcennin's death: he was only 56. I telephoned his secretary who confirmed that he had died dictating a letter to me. We used to exchange letters about three times a week. It was thought that his daily injection against his sciatic complaint had been cumulatively too strong. I told Hamilton immediately: he was incredulous. It had been so short a term of office. Gerald Steel, deputy chairman for so many years, was the obvious person to succeed. This he did gracefully and comfortably. After we had agreed the agenda for meetings, Gerald Steel and I both enjoyed the lunches at Brooks's Club (one that I might have been tempted to join were I in any sense a club man), centred on potted shrimps, for me an absolute delicacy.

He, Hamilton and I represented Rugby at the Chairman's memorial service in St Martin-in-the-Fields attended by Macmillan and Mountbatten — in full regalia, taking one back to his reign as Viceroy of India — among a mass of celebrities.

Despite the shock of Cilcennin's death, I was experiencing a sense of comfort, of wellbeing and euphoria. There was a permanence, if I wanted, of tenure in a congenial atmosphere: far away were the uprootings every year or so between districts and head-quarters in Fiji but, on the other hand, there were seemingly no ladders to climb, for better or worse. Complacency could set in if one were not pinching oneself to its dangers. But there was something to be said for a spell at least of serenity unshaken by ambition. The horses had been changed in midstream without too much misgiving, maladroitness or wetting of feet — a tribute, I felt, to the horses of the Colonial Service in the South Sea Islands and of Rugby School rather than to any equine skill on my part.

2

Flirting with Change and Fraternal Involvements

My Rugby predecessor, Dunkin, had told me: 'Don't be like me. I have stayed at Rugby for 24 years. I should have moved and I recommend that you do not repeat my mistake, as you otherwise might because of your relative youth on appointment.' Although I could reasonably have had some residue of restlessness from the extreme mobility of Colonial Service life, I did not actively seek a move from rock-like Rugby; but approaches were made to me from Winchester, where the Bursar had suddenly left. I went to see what it was like but was instantly put off by the fact that it was about half the size of Rugby and therefore claustrophobic. (I was disposed, even at Rugby, to thinking in terms of wider spaces as in the Pacific.) The feeling was reinforced by the bursary and the headmaster's office being next door to each other, whereas at Rugby they were separated by the length of The Close, a few minutes' walk that was in no way administratively inconvenient (although fundamentally independent, we could regularly call on each other or telephone), but psychologically essential for me with my background in so many solitary parts of Fiji where I had become used to having to take action alone.

Verisimilitude prevailed at Harrow, where I was invited to succeed Brigadier John Knott (ex-Sudan), who was particularly keen to see me accept. He was the chairman of the Bursars' Association from whom I was to take over in that capacity.

In both cases, the houses offered were much inferior to Horton House, 6 Hillmorton Road, Rugby — I was most unlikely ever to find anything better in a school. Or in a university, which could not tempt me as a married person because the perquisite of free bachelor rooms within college still meant that I would have to purchase a house — certainly so in Cambridge or Oxford. These circumstances, as well as disinterestedness, prevented my moving. It would have required a great increase in salary to have compensated. Harrow would have been a move sideways, if that: academically it was less accomplished than Rugby and again was smaller. No school could in fact have been upwards. Eton was larger, but a closed shop. Anyway, Peter Proby was about my age and was to stay there almost as long as I did in Rugby before he inherited his father's baronetcy.

Invited by New College, Oxford, I did have a look at it, staying overnight with the Warden, Sir William Hayter. The college was very condensed. It gave off the same slight sense of suffocation as Christ's. The fellows were on parade for me to see and for them to see me. I instantly found the intense, nervy, quicksilver, precious presences of Lord David Cecil and A. J. Ayer didactic, unworldly and unattractive. Not even the latter's well-known atheism seemed to help his feet to be on the ground. Some of their colleagues were equally ethereal. I was surprised that Hayter, with his experience as ambassador to Russia from 1953 to 1957, was obviously finding the atmosphere tolerable, even congenial. There was too a very close Winchester connection: its bursar was automatically a fellow of New College. On return to Rugby, I declared my disinterest and was never in the least drawn to bursarship in the male-enclosed claustrophobic air of a university, except one college, to which I will refer in a moment.

I would have had to think deeply about deserting Rugby, which had made us so welcome. If, from a genial collection of 80 or so teaching staff, I had to pick out one for his permanent state of benevolence, it would be Norman Hughes, a modern languages teacher and former housemaster. His vigour, wit and conviviality were remarkable. When, years later, machine-minded staff trying to be ahead of their times despite my warning that I had seen American language laboratories left derelict in 1964 because technical staff could not be obtained to keep them going, arranged for the opening of the first language laboratory at Rugby, James Hunt, the wise second master sitting next to me, whispered: 'I would

sooner have one Norman Hughes than a dozen of these things.' It
was an easy society into which to fit.

In any case, now I was, as vice-chairman and then Chairman of
the Bursars' Association, meeting a number of new persons whose
names had become known to me by virtue of those posts, and
through my being on the Joint Committee of the Governors of
Boys' and Girls' Schools, Headmasters, Headmistresses, Bursars
and Medical Officers. Will Spens had been a prominent chairman
of that committee and he believed strongly in its usefulness.
Walter Hamilton, as chairman of the Headmasters' Conference,
was one of the three representatives of the headmasters and I, as
vice-chairman/Chairman of the Bursars' Association with John
Knott and David Sherwood, of the bursars. Hamilton and I used
to exchange glances in meetings which too frequently implanted
un-Spens-like doubts on its efficacy. We were about 18 in all but
two or three tended to do all the talking out of the fronts of their
heads: their pretentiousness defied credulity. Hamilton, who
epitomized sagacity and experience, only spoke when provoked
and even then he let off the supremely orotund monopolizer, Sir
Griffith Williams, former deputy secretary, Ministry of Education,
and a school governors' representative, followed by Sir Desmond
Lee, Headmaster of Winchester, and other school governors, Sir
William Cleary, a deputy secretary in the Ministry of Education,
Sir William Cash, a director of companies, and Sir Harold Howitt,
a leading accountant on multiple national committees regarded as
one of the government's three wise men (I forget who the other
two were: so much for their impact and what they were supposed
to be wise about).

One who had had a wealth of experience, if not in the educational field, seldom spoke. He looked orientally inscrutable. His
fame, outside his MC and bar and three First World War wounds,
was indeed oriental. Lieutenant General Sir Thomas Hutton was a
governor's representative: he had been general officer commanding in Burma until relieved under Wavell's judgement in desperate
circumstances by Alexander and was retired at the age of 54. The
inarticulate but intelligent Wavell probably made the right move,
though he himself never succeeded in capturing Churchill's way-
ward approval. When Hutton did speak, he did so laconically, to

the point, but rather sadly and with a fixed oriental seriousness. I think he was always reflecting on having been so hard done by in Burma, where Wavell had failed to back the battle decisions of Hutton who had saved the Burma Army in its prolonged retreat. It was later judged that Hutton's foresight could not have been better, but recognition years after the campaign was begrudgingly given and then not by government.

A strikingly contrasting presence was that of Dame Diana Reader Harris, who, as Headmistress of Sherborne Girls' School, was one of the three representative headmistresses. Her handsomeness was fascinating to watch when the tedium of endless monologues — it could seldom be considered debate — became too heavy. I expected a greater future for her than that of acquiring a dame's status. She should, I suppose, have been in politics but I intuitively felt she was too intelligent and unimpassioned for that emotional outlet. Her fine looks, stateliness and dignity would have made a magnetic impression in wider fields than those in which she was seen.

As chairman of the bursars for three years — for 1962, 1963 and 1964 — I had to make three long opening addresses printed in the association's annual report. These did not worry me, despite the mischievous follow-up speaking position David Sherwood, as secretary, elected to occupy. He would delight the audiences with his noteless, unconventional contributions and sometimes alarming sense of fun, mostly at the expense of the retired rear admirals, brigadiers and air vice-marshals. There were too few colonial and Indian civil servants to form a target. Among the bursars were a couple who had been knighted, Sir Alister Ransford of dignified mien, Bursar of Loretto, who had been Mint Master of HM's Mint, Bombay, and Sir Kerr Bovell, Bursar of Worksop, a warm personality, who had been Inspector General of Police, Nigeria. Sherwood was a match for anyone on the joint committee, which, as secretary of the Bursars' Association, he was unique in attending perennially. No other association's secretary (headmasters, headmistresses and so forth) qualified for perpetual attendance (God help them) except the secretary of the Governing Bodies' Association, which is what John Knott had turned to on retiring from Harrow.

Charles had at the end of the 1950s been especially busy. *The*

Conscience of the Rich, so long delayed, had at last come out. It had had to wait for the death in his nineties of Frank Cohen, a principal, patriarchal character and father of a Jewish friend of Charles's, Dick Cohen, who was in turn a cousin of Sir Andrew Cohen, Governor of Uganda, and his sister, Catherine Hunt, who had married a Gentile, James Hunt, my friend as second master and housemaster at Rugby.

Charles had delivered the Rede Lecture at Cambridge. Entitled 'The Two Cultures and the Scientific Revolution', it remains one of his lasting claims to fame. Seldom a week goes by, even now, without my hearing or seeing a reference to his leading part in facing up to this dichotomy where little progress has been made in the mental gap. In 1993 there was an incomprehensible, uncomprehending television programme over three nights on the subject, invoking his name repeatedly. I, for one, subscribed in practice to his theory that the gap between the arts and sciences had been unbridgeable. I had — and still have — not the faintest idea what the second (or any other for that matter) law of thermodynamics is about and, although my life has brought me into touch not unusually and not infrequently with men of very different kinds, there were often instances of lack of comprehension on my part and on others' parts of respective cultures. Charles's name has thereafter been linked irretrievably with 'the two cultures'.

At this time he wrote to Lionel Trilling, the American author, that 'The only Club I really like is the Savile. But the older I get the less I like all-male societies.' Club life never seduced me: it seemed made for bachelors and misogynists. I spent my time more profitably in the Royal Anthropological Institute, the British Library and unacademic parts of London.

Very much now in the public eye, Charles was President of the Library Association and gave the Godkin Lectures at Harvard. *Science and Government* was largely on the conflict between Sir Henry Tizard, chairman of the Aeronautical Research Committee from 1933 to 1943 (who had been the representative of the Royal Society on Rugby's Governing Body just before my appointment and was the essence of normality), and Viscount Cherwell (F. A. Lindemann), the wildly eccentric and egocentric scientist adviser of Prime Minister Churchill from 1940 to 1945 and Paymaster-

General. One simply could not read a paper in that period without seeing Charles's name mentioned in some capacity, notably 'the two cultures' and 'Tizard versus Lindemann'.

Anne and I were at the opening of the new Alderman Newton's Girls' School, which had moved out of the centre of Leicester and away from the boys' school. Charles had been asked to open it and referred, not quite correctly, to Anne as head girl having ultimately married me as head boy. Anne had left before reaching prefectorial status, but then only one or two of the staff were there from her time and they probably did not notice the promotion. A commemorative plaque marks the occasion at which Charles made a graceful speech mentioned in my *Stranger and Brother*. He was in a pleasing television programme, *Return to Cambridge*, which showed him ambling along, with commentary apparently to himself, among university sights such as the Cam, which in truth he never saw much of in his time. The Christ's settings were well done.

I met two wartime figures of different calibre. Lieutenant General A. E. Percival, who, as general officer commanding Malaya, had surrendered to the Japanese in Singapore, returned to his school. One could well understand why he had not made much impression in Malaya. His features, with protruding teeth, were far from prepossessing: they belied his DSO and bar and MC in the First World War. He seemed to have no compensatory charisma for his appearance and he didn't come over as one to shape up to the most exacting responsibilities facing him. But history has shown that no one was likely to have been able to rescue the position what with the scarcity of aeroplanes and warships, even given that there was, at first, distinct numerical preponderance of British military forces over the invaders on the ground.

Marshal of the RAF Sir John Slessor, Commander-in-Chief of the coastal command and commander-in-chief of RAF Mediterranean and Middle East, whom I had met at a bursars' dinner, was a more obviously pugnacious and outspoken type of leader: he would have been better suited to the dire circumstances of 1942 in the Far East had he had anything to command there.

There could hardly have been two such contrasting types of wartime commanders for me to have met within a month of each other.

Meanwhile, Charles had cajoled me to put in for the bursarship of the new, as yet unbuilt, Churchill College, Cambridge, in which he was taking an important founding part. This gave me perforce the opportunity to meet further distinguished academic figures. A friend of Charles's was Sir John Cockcroft, who was moving from being in charge of the United Kingdom Atomic Energy Research Establishment at Harwell to being the first Master (from 1959 to his death in 1967). Cockcroft asked Anne and me to have lunch with him and his wife at Harwell. I was surprised by the top surface of the grand piano being taken up with all Cockcroft's profuse awards and decorations, including the OM and Nobel prize. The display did not seem to fit in with so unostentatious a nature.

In a letter of 29 January 1959, Charles had warned me that 'If John Cockcroft raises the point that he asked me to go with him to Churchill, tell him that you know I had taken it very seriously. I think this will please him.' The point did not arise. After lunch, Cockcroft, in his concentrated but friendly and not too obtrusively Yorkshire manner, asked me all about myself. We seemed to get on well. I could certainly have worked with him and would have liked to have been in on the creation of an absolutely new college — the first at Cambridge since Selwyn's foundation in 1882. Charles reported that Cockcroft wanted me rather than the only other nominee, a major general, who was, however, sponsored by Christopher Soames, Churchill's son-in-law.

I was asked to the Master's Lodge at Christ's to meet the other trustees on the selection committee (Charles was one but was of course not present). There cannot often have been such a crystallization in five persons of three masters of colleges, three OMs, three Nobel prize winners (not necessarily the same persons). Lord Adrian, Master of Trinity, Vice-Chancellor of Cambridge and Nobel prize winner in medicine, was at the head of the table and Brian Downs, Master of Christ's and a retired vice-chancellor (reported by Charles to be well disposed to me), was present. He had been a tutor in my time at Christ's but was surprisingly never an outstanding character in Charles's Cambridge novels, although a long-standing friend of his, dying only recently in his nineties. Other selectors present, with Cockcroft of course, were Lord Todd, Nobel prize winner in chemistry and later the Master of

Christ's, Patrick Blackett, OM and Nobel prize winner in physics, judged by Pam to be the most handsome of all men in his cragginess. Then there was Noel (later Lord) Annan, Provost of King's. Ubiquitous where he sensed power for making appointments, his head seemed to look metallic or even hostile. He was, I felt, not in the same class as the other selectors. From memory, I think that the remaining trustees were Churchill himself, Lord Knollys, a former governor of Bermuda and then chairman of Vickers, Lieutenant General Lord Weeks, Lord Godber, former Secretary of State for War and Minister of Labour, and Lord Tedder. Lord Weeks and Lord Tedder were said to be well disposed to me. Churchill regularly presided over the trustees in person at his house, 28 Hyde Park Gate, exactly opposite what was later to become the office of the Fiji High Commission/Embassy.

On 12 March 1959, Charles wrote to say that 'Just by sensing the atmosphere I gathered that Cockcroft wants you and Annan is running someone else' and then, in a postscript, added 'I have the very strong impression that Annan thought that he had it in the bag for his candidate until you appeared on the scene.' There was an equality of votes on the selection committee; Cockcroft had not been able to vote. So the matter had been referred to Churchill, the Visitor, who naturally opted for his son-in-law's nominee. At least I had the distinction of having been deprived directly of a better job by Churchill in person.

History has shown that I was in good company at a far more exalted level than mine — the illustrious names of Field Marshal Sir Claude Auchinleck, Lieutenant General Sir Thomas Hutton and General Sir Neil Ritchie. Churchill also disposed of Field Marshal Earl Wavell pretty fiercely but eventually conceded the viceroyalty of India, the peak of appointments. Churchill certainly chose some extraordinary friends and advisers — the erratic Lindemann, the indiscreet Moran, the odd Bracken, the saturnine Beaverbrook, the unbalanced Admiral of the Fleet Lord Fisher, the exhibitionistic Onassis. Some were obviously court jesters. To one of them, 1st Earl Birkenhead, can be attributed one of the neatest of quips: 'Mr Churchill is easily satisfied with the best.'

In a humble way I was not totally dissatisfied with the outcome at Churchill College. Only that appointment because of its unique nature could have drawn me away from Rugby. Charles told me that when as an Extraordinary Fellow he came to know the Bursar and to like him, Major General J. R. C. Hamilton, who was nine years older than me, considerately asked Charles to convey his condolences to me — a nice gesture from the competitor.

This was a time when Charles was being bombarded with requests for details about his way of life. *Time and Tide* wanted to know his routine. He replied:

1. I write with a pen in an inconveniently illegible long-hand.
2. My favourite time for writing is 10 a.m. to 2.00 or 3.00 p.m., without lunch. When writing a novel I normally like to work regularly.
3. I have an office and also a study. At various times I have written in all sorts of places. If pressed I think I could still write almost anywhere.

To the question 'How do you find inspiration?', he answered 'I don't think I can give a short and meaningful answer.' He also wrote to Leslie Cross in Milwaukee who described him as a big, somewhat cherubic man, amiable with an explosive chuckle:

Although I always keep at it I can't write easily. I write with — well, not quite *great* difficulty but *some* difficulty. But I try to keep going. I'm not the sort of chap who spends a morning striking out a comma and substituting a semi-colon. ... I make it a practice to read a good many news-papers from a good many places.

At this time, in 1960, my close friend, Kingsley Roth, died at only 57. His *Fijian Way of Life* was sadly his only major publication. No doubt had he lived, there would have been further important anthropological and historical works, although he was punctilious in not publishing until he had crossed all his ts. Kingsley was a restrained, thoughtful, kind person of real gifts: he made signal contributions in his 30 years' service for the colony he loved and for the standards of which he was a scrupulous guardian. He and his wife, Jane, were among the most loyal of my friends. Jane took over as honorary curator of the splendid Pacific collection of the Cambridge University Museum of Archaeology and Ethnology. Kingsley would have been delighted to know that she continued his erudition with her excellent editing, helped by Steven Hooper, of the fascinating *Fiji Journal of Baron Anatole von Hügel 1875–1877*.

Major Rowland Bowen was never more than an acquaintance of mine. He was so much given to caustic public correspondence or acerbic observations on the telephone that to keep one's distance spelt wisdom. In the library at Lord's I had come across this very different and strikingly strong personality, unlike anyone whom I had known or was to know. He was remarkable, indeed sensational for one with so steely an intellect. Bowen had been in MI5 and was now founder and editor of the *Cricket Quarterly*, a severe organ of disestablishmentarianism. He was later to write the authoritative *Cricket: A History of its Growth and Development*. A trenchant critic, he had praised my *Cricket in the Fiji Islands* as fascinating and extremely rewarding for followers of the game.

One of my more peculiar telephone encounters was when he rang to implore me to lead a *coup d'état* with a former Lord Mayor of London, Sir Bernard Waley-Cohen, 1st Baronet, to overthrow what Bowen regarded as the iniquitous MCC 'nepotic committee election' (in fact a nomination) system. He said that he had a judge (not named by him) also lined up. I could never have worked with Waley-Cohen under any circumstances. His unwholesome, ferocious countenance had put me off totally when I had once encountered it. He was always in the news as a fanatical stag hunter, no less than as a president of the Devon and Somerset Staghounds. Bowen was motivated by a vendetta against Billy (or Cathie, as he insisted on referring in print to Stewart Cathie) Griffith, the MCC Secretary. As his telephone call went on and on remorselessly, I stopped Bowen in his tracks by saying that I was an absolute non-starter and that I had nothing against Billy Griffith or the MCC. Indeed, quite the opposite was my position. MCC had generously made me an honorary life member, almost certainly arranged by Griffith, an honour I enormously appreciated. How could he have thought of me, I asked Bowen. He ignored the question and put down the telephone brusquely. Had he either been drinking (he sounded sober) or affected by the moon? His habits were not known to me, so I could not think how my name arose in his erratic mind. I mention this because it was part of his swings between inspiration and lunacy. It was one of the odder telephone episodes in my life. Not only brilliantly incisive, Bowen's views were the epitome of originality, worthy of adoption but sometimes also off-balance. He was self destructive, literally. It was said that a defective eye was the result of a compass thrust into it by himself and when he tried to sever a leg with a penknife (as reported on the front pages of the national papers) he revealed he had an irresistible urge to see how much pain and disability he could self-inflict. Men scarcely come any stranger this side of him. He was not a man to cross or to have been allied with.

In 1959 John Corner succeeded Sir Harry Ricardo, another FRS, as the Royal Society's representative on Rugby's Governing Body. Professor of botany, he was at Cambridge, for which university the representative was now Reverend Meredith Dewey, like Corner, a Rugbeian. Dewey seldom spoke at meetings but was a stronger individual than he was given credit for. Dewey was quietly connected to an aristocratic family and, staying overnight once with us at Rugby when the weather turned hostile, he put aside his taciturnity and merged comfortably into our household. John Corner led Royal Society expeditions, including one to the Solomon Islands, by Pacific standards almost neighbouring the Fiji archipelago, as a result of which he and I became friendly. Staying with us, he was persuaded to tell, apparently rarely and then most reluctantly, of his unique experiences as assistant director in the gardens department of the Straits Settlements from 1929 to 1945.

When the Japanese invaded he did his best to give himself up: no Japanese came for him, an unusual disinterest. The Governor, Sir Shenton Thomas, just before his internment, sent a note via Corner requesting that the Japanese should preserve the scientific collections at the Museum and Botanical Gardens in Singapore: he told Corner to stay there. Eventually, the Japanese came across Corner and allowed him to continue his research, which aroused the interest of a Japanese marquis of scientific repute and consuming curiosity who was appointed Civil Governor of Malaya. This coincidence was Corner's salvation, for he was a dedicated scientist and would surely have pined away if he had been deprived of the Gardens and if they had been allowed to revert to bush. Some Europeans in Singapore, interned and maltreated, hearing of his apparent freedom and not knowing the circumstances, naturally thought that Corner must be a quisling, or at least a collaborator. He saw out the war, virtually confined to, but having to watch his step in, his beloved Gardens, and published in 1981 perhaps the most unexpected account — and a very gripping one — of anyone involved in the war with the Japanese. It is entitled *The Marquis* after his Japanese protector. It almost succeeds in instilling a little faith in the Japanese, at least in their genuinely cultural pursuits. I am glad to have been one, after struggling past his modesty, to have pressed for his singular story to be widely known to Japanophobes like me. I only wish there had been a marquis or two to give the same consideration for captive human stock as for flora.

The year 1961 was when the Queen Mother expressed a wish to come to the school after opening the new Rugby town hall. Walter Hamilton, who had received her once at Westminster, and I were the organizers. I was able to bring in a certain amount of colonial protocol, although I had never had to deal with a royal visit as such. We had everything as ready as could be when, less than a fortnight before, the Queen Mother broke her ankle. We assumed that the visit would have to be put off. Not so. The Queen Mother had the ankle put into plaster and merely asked that the programme be adapted to cut out climbing stairs and for the use of a wheelchair. The head boy of the school was appointed to push her about up specially constructed ramps. She arrived on time, stepped on the red carpet, met half a dozen of us — Gerald Steel, the Hamiltons, the Hunts, Anne and myself, the senior master, the senior housemaster and his wife — and was then conducted round a shortened route by Hamilton, myself and the head boy. We had tea on the lawn. I arranged for a stool on which to rest the royal ankle: the Queen Mother had asked for this, almost her only specific request. Her china-cornflower blue eyes were soft and

71

gracious, her teeth disappointingly discoloured and uneven when her smile broadened. Her private secretary, then and until his recent death, Lieutenant-Colonel Sir Martin Gilliat, told me that everything had gone off excellently. The Queen Mother also thanked me warmly for making her visit so comfortable. I would like to have responded with a remark about her courage and forbearance when she could so easily have put off the occasion. But one is trained to listen to, rather than to address, royalty. The more's the pity because it would break some of the tedium no doubt for royal personages.

In 1962 Will Spens died aged 80 in his retirement home in the Close of Ely Cathedral. He had not been to everyone's liking. But we worked well together, tough as he was. He knew that I was to be the Chairman of the Bursars' Association from 1962 for at least a couple of years (with only one precedent of it for three years) and told Lady Dorothy, as she informed me in reply to my letter of condolence, that he considered me the best bursar he had known in a lifetime of contact with them. That was one of the highest compliments which, coming from that source, I could have received. I think that he had forgotten in his generalization that his own son was for a time domestic bursar of Corpus Christi, college of father and son.

At the Bursars' Association dinner in 1962 (as at the Cricket Writers' Club dinner for the South Africans in 1951, when Dudley Nourse, their captain, replied to Ashton's toast to cricket), I saw a lot of Sir Hubert Ashton, the bursars' guest of honour, whose common sense was striking. Of three first-class playing brothers, he had been the most prominent, close to England standard. It was the third after-dinner speech I had heard him make because at the Cricket Writers' Club dinner for the Australians in 1961, when Lord Justice Birkett and Richie Benaud (the Australia captain who knew his job as no one has in the last half century or more, with the exception of Bradman) made speeches of high quality, Ashton was the other speaker. I sat between Eric and Arthur Langford: Charles could not be present at the dinner. Bill Bowes was chairman, an accomplished one: he had always looked an amateur, while being a professional, on the field.

There was a modicum of light relief this year, which was otherwise to be one of real trauma for Charles and which, although front-page news in the national press, is now little or imperfectly remembered by the public. Charles was a little put out that I had not told him of my selection for the Midlands panel of the BBC programme, *What Do You Know?* (*Brain of Britain*, a designation for the programme I disliked: I think that it was shame about that egotistical title which put me off letting Charles know in advance). I had been persuaded to enter it and did well at the audition.

With some confidence as a result, I turned up at the Playhouse Theatre, Northumberland Avenue, at its corner with the Embankment. Franklin Engleman, very professional, timing himself to the precise second from long experience, was the chairman. We had a pre-run of the panel on the stage while the theatre was empty and I answered not only questions put to me but those with which the other three could not deal. We adjourned for half an hour while the theatre filled. Engleman had reminded us that it was 'entertainment' and that we should be light-hearted if opportunity allowed. It was exceedingly foggy outside where I went for air: the Thames was invisible beyond the Embankment wall across the road. On return and soon after the performance began, the other two before me answered their questions. The first one to me, which I now forget, was sticky. Remembering Engleman's homily, I said brightly: 'On this very foggy night, I haven't the foggiest.' To my surprise the audience failed to appreciate the joke (as I thought it to be). Engleman glared and the questions passed along without my attempting a disconcerting repetition. Although I managed to answer most of the remaining questions, the only woman participant, a civil servant, answered all of hers. I tied for second place with a police sergeant. A tie was an unprecedented occurrence putting the producer, his eye on the clock, in a stage dilemma. It was decided to have a sudden death question. I knew the answer but was just beaten to it by the sergeant who, with the woman, went through to the next round when they were both eliminated. Third I was but fourth, a customs inspector, had failed to answer any. He too had of course been auditioned and done well. The questions did not run right for him and I greatly sympathized with his unprecedented nil score. Of course, I had overlooked in my joke that the programme was being recorded. When it was broadcast months later on a gloriously bright summer day, fog was in no one's mind and there must have been some mystification among those listening. I know that I could have sunk through the floor as I heard the misfiring yet again.

The retina of Charles's left eye became detached. This was particularly alarming for someone who lived for reading. It was operated on, but on 28 April 1962 Pam wrote to say that 'The op has failed after all our hopes and the left eye is a goner. C. being very philosophical.' Nevertheless, he travelled in a black eye patch (and huge black handkerchief astride his head for holding the patch) to St Andrew's University, there to be installed as Rector in succession to Lord (Bob) Boothby of Buchan and Rattray Head. He broke the journey with us at Rugby. St Andrew's received him sympathetically. He would normally have been given a rector's bumping about in rumbustious fashion not well suited to anyone of his age and condition. His address *On Magnanimity* could not have been improved upon, prepared as it had been before an attempted character assassination by the paranoiac F. R. Leavis trying to scrape up some publicity for himself, in this instance via Charles's *The Two Cultures*. *On Magnanimity* ranks with Charles's best writing. Then he sailed to America for four honorary degrees and again there for the play of *The Affair* on Broadway.

Charles's physical setback had naturally caused him to think profoundly. He wrote from the English Electric Company on the Strand, London on 25 July 1962:

You may remember Anne Seagrim. I was always very fond of her and after she left the Windsors' ménage we took up again — in, of course, the most concealed kind of way. No one — except now you — knows anything at all about it. It has been a great support and joy for me and has made a big difference to my life. It is likely to go on, just like this, for a long time. I have already made provision for her in my will, and shall have another look at that when I know how much I'm likely to be worth. She bears a situation which is easy for me but inevitably at times far less very well. But the thing she is finding increasingly a horror is to be cut off from news when I happen to be ill. So I am really asking you to be a channel of information. If I can't communicate with her (which is of course the case if I can't get outside the flat) I should like her to be able to telephone you. Further, if I happened to be taken seriously ill or die suddenly, she would rather hear it from you than see it in the newspapers. Will you take on this job? . . . I know you won't let any of this slip, by a gesture, to anyone at all.

This was how it was to be. I had to do it before the year was over. I never met Anne Seagrim since seeing her in 1946 on leave and never communicated, except in what immediately follows and on Charles's death, until 1980. The reference to the Windsors was to the fact that she had been private secretary to the Duke (she was later private secretary to Field Marshal Earl Alexander). Unusually, she had two cousins, one awarded a VC and the other a GC. With Pam and my mother, she was the third principal female influence in his life, as I mentioned in *Stranger and Brother*.

Towards the end of the year Charles's retina trouble recurred. The second operation on the detached retina was overwhelmed by a happening during the surgery. *The Times* and the *Daily Telegraph* carried on their front pages the laconic announcement that Sir Charles Snow had suffered cardiac arrest while under anaesthetic for an operation on his eye but was being treated successfully. I saw him at Moorfields Hospital in a setting of gloom, curtains drawn, with a bandage over his eye. He was highly philosophical, repeating his henceforward well-known dictum that he had been over to the other side and that there was nothing there. It was the only light relief that could be brought to a disaster resulting in death for three minutes. He told me that if it had occurred in America a heart surgeon would have had to be called under that country's regulations to get the heart going again. Ethics and practice there would never have allowed the eye surgeon to make the incision and manipulate the heart. But in America or anywhere else there would have been no time for the emergency. Lorimer Fison saved his life but the eye operation had to be stopped and Charles would of course never countenance its repetition.

Perhaps the best first-hand account is that of Charles to Mrs Lionel Trilling on 19 December 1962:

I shan't ever be able to read with the bad eye again but they have given me back a good deal of useful sight. That is, if I suddenly went blind in the right eye I could walk around quite comfortably with the other. This is a bigger insurance than I should have thought before this happened. During the operation I had a somewhat overdramatic time.

They were just stitching up the eye — this is of course quite a delicate but quite minor operation — when my heart stopped. They had to slice me open and get it going again. This didn't matter to me but it was very hard on Pamela. They told me a couple of hours later and I confess that I had a sense of psychological vertigo. There were no after effects of any kind whatever.

To the end of his life vision in the eye was extremely limited. It was pathetic to see him lift his glasses and put his eyes right down on to the paper for anything specially small. And marvellous that he got through as much reading as he did, for instance in tackling conscientiously as many as half a dozen books for review every week in the last decade of his life. The year 1962 was, as I have said in *Stranger and Brother*, a dramatic one for Charles. That was an understatement, contrasting it with the trend of his previous three years.

The year had started for me with Gerald Steel at the age of 78 retiring as Chairman of the Rugby Governing Body. I had suggested to Hamilton that the Governing Body could not possibly do better than appoint Lord Parker of Waddington, the Lord Chief Justice of England (he always insisted on emphasizing 'of England' to differentiate himself from chief justices of other parts of the UK). Hubert Parker was first known to me when he was Mr Justice Parker and a trustee of the Rugby School War Memorial Funds from 1914 to 1918 and from 1939 to 1945, of which I was concurrently, with bursar and many other jobs, a trustee and secretary. I had found his quiet, solid personality a most congenial one with which to work. The stature that he could bring to the chairmanship was apodictic.

Lord Parker was a little unwilling to take over the post as he had only recently taken on the full load of the LCJ's work. It was the best appointment that could have been made. My part in it was never known, except by Hamilton, and I am proud of it. Son of a judge, also styled Lord Parker of Waddington, he brought real eminence and stateliness to the post and also proved a most conscientious chairman. He was approachability itself. I could call on him (when he was not sitting on the bench in the Royal Courts of Justice) to discuss matters and to go over the agenda and my numerous memoranda. Before seeing me, he would have done his homework on them, busy as he always was, with, I took it to be, the simplest of ease. His mind picked out of course the essentials and technicalities infallibly.

Of course, as an expert all his life in that field, academic administration was second nature to a man like Spens. It had, however, been interesting to see how Cilcennin, with his different career background, was able to pick up the fundamentals of Governing Body meetings. Steel had been so long number two to Spens that they presented no difficulties to him. For Parker, with a judicial lifetime behind him, his training also made the administration a task without strain. The facts soaked in as receptively as into a cerebral sponge. I found the experience of going over the papers with four such different personalities in itself educative.

I had quietly prevailed on Hamilton to help in ensuring that the Chairman of the Governing Body and not the deputy chairman of the Governing Body must continue to take the chair at the finance committee meetings. It was vitally important that the Governing Body should know the workings of the finance committee inside out. So Lord Parker and I would go together in a taxi from the Royal Courts of Justice to Lombard Street and the superbly furnished boardroom of the now extinct Martin's Bank. We convened there because Major Sir Harold Bibby was chairman of the bank and always arranged a splendid lunch with glistening silver on the long gleaming table after our finance meetings.

Parker had friendly, very rich brown eyes (how many of the persons I had worked with had eyes of that warm kind), indicating a sense of humour that was nevertheless seldom exhibited. He always had a mysterious bright red drink on his capacious desk, which was laden with files and briefs. It looked like non-fizzy Cherryade and I never saw him sip it. I believe that it was

medicinal. It later became clear that he avoided social life as much
as he could, although to try to opt out of Buckingham Palace state
banquets was, I think, beyond his powers, lofty though he was in
official precedence (or perhaps because of that). His wife, a
diminutive Kentucky lady, was a charity organizer and probably
socially inclined.

As he died soon after retirement as LCJ in 1970, I think that his
health must have been less than robust for some time. He tucked
himself away up an ungravelled track in Dorset as soon as he
retired, but sadly survived so short a time there in his solitude. He
had told me that he disliked public speaking, so probably avoided
many of the Inns of Court dinners that a LCJ would be expected
to attend and speak at. For him, Speech Day at Rugby was no
sinecure, I suspect, though he carried off the occasions with
tremendous dignity and splendid composure.

He would come into his rooms, at the Royal Courts, where I
would sometimes be waiting, bewigged and in his scarlet robes.
He always seemed glad to discard them. I do not think he enjoyed
the trappings of office or any publicity. However he could not
evade it at times – such as when he gave the spy, George Blake
(George Behar, the son of an Egyptian Jew, who after escaping
from a Nazi concentration camp during the Dutch Resistance
became a Royal Navy sublieutenant and joined the SOE and
Foreign Office) 42 years in prison, the longest sentence ever given
to that date for less than murder. He was deeply conservative, but
he surprised me in confiding that he found the Labour Lord
Chancellor, Lord Gardiner (Parker's superior for most of his
LCJship), too radical for words. Hubert Parker must have been
singularly exasperated to have said that to me.

When I developed what was long in being diagnosed as agoraphobia, I told him about it (but hardly anyone else, not even the
Headmaster). Perhaps he had some measure of it himself, for he
made a careful statement, which will be mentioned later.

The traumatic year of 1962 for Charles (and by reflection for me,
who was depressed by his injuries, both obvious and suppressed)
ended more brightly with a splendid television performance by
him. It was at the Royal Institution, where, in white tie and tails,
he held the television and the Institution's audiences completely

rapt with a nobly delivered address, containing the minimum of notes, entitled 'The Two Cultures and the Sorcerer's Apprentice'. It was an incontestable *tour de force* seldom seen on television before or since.

The playwright Sir Ronald Millar, whose works included *Robert and Elizabeth* and who later became the principal script writer for Prime Ministers Heath, Margaret Thatcher and Major, dramatized a third work of Charles's (after *The New Men* and *The Affair*) — *The Masters*. It was very successfully put on at the Savoy Theatre (the other two had been at the Strand) with Sir John Clements once again in the leading part, this time as Jago.

But, climaticaily and otherwise, the year ended ferociously. The 'ice age' returned for three months and, until March 1963, roads were impacted with ice and virtually impassable: water tanks froze repeatedly. Part of my duties involved being in charge of the Works Department, its 12 members too slender a quantity for the maintenance of the 100 staff houses, 12 boarding houses, sanatorium and multiple school buildings. Because the clerk of works' wife, hard enough done by through the load on her long-suffering, loyal husband (he was to die in harness), could not endure a telephone, all calls about burst pipes and other out-of-office-hour calamities had to be put through to me at home. I was up all night for a number of weeks directing Works Department emergencies. The success of the appeal had resulted in many major structural developments being carried out. Consequently, this meant heavier work for the department, which remained the same size but at least had the cooperation of the smooth, diplomatic professionalism of Keith Kellett, the school architect, leaving much skilful work to his credit.

The glacial conditions, however, finally overcame my reluctance to have an assistant bursar. The first to be appointed, a naval commander, not my choice, did not fit and left. I made certain that I had my way over the selection of his successor, Lieutenant-Colonel Eric Ingram, who had applied before and now got the job the second time round. He fitted, was comfortable to work with and stayed. He had the additional advantage of being an architect: his lasting memorial is the School Centre built on the sole remaining central (hence the name) site, regrettably restricted by financial stringency. Sir Denys Lasdun had shown interest in having the assignment for his old school but, having seen his work, I am glad that another concrete mass was avoided.

It is sad that the future will be confronted for seemingly as long as concrete lasts by postwar monstrosities, whose architects have been knighted for their 'inspirations', starting with Basil Spence and including Lord Rogers. What is more, these landscape blots (the Tricorn shopping centre cum car park in the heart of Portsmouth must rank as the most hideous of them, with much competition for the title) often have to be pulled down because of their technical defects, quite apart from their aesthetic offence. How can children be brought up to be reasonably normal in these ghastly high-rise urban cubes? My suspicion of postwar beknighted and benighted architects runs deep, not without reason, so many will agree, because there is nothing unfortunately original in this reflection or in the nostalgia that exists for the style of a Lutyens or Baker. Why isn't their most worthy heir, Quinlan Terry, knighted?

It was the grimmest physical end of a year and beginning of a new one that I was to experience. But, climate notwithstanding, the staff put on *An Italian Straw Hat*, with Anne as usual in staff plays taking a leading part.

Bert Howard died in 1963. For some years he and Charles had not been close. Charles did not approve of his peccadilloes, which could and did have serious consequences. Ager, headmaster throughout most of Howard's career, wrote to Charles: 'I was very sorry to hear of Howard's death. Though I have not seen much of him for some years I feel that both the school and individual boys owe him an immense debt for what he did for them so generously and capably.' Charles replied: 'I'm very sad about Howard. I wish I had been of more use to him. Somehow his life ought to have taken a different course.' Howard was one of the most stubborn of men. His influence on Charles was, with G. H. Hardy's and C. R. C. Allberry's, the strongest Charles knew among his men friends.

In 1964 I took Charles to the Cricket Writers' Club dinner in the most impressive Fishmongers' Hall. Whenever they came it was the custom to invite the Australian cricket team as guests. Elaborate

ABOVE. Author on change of career, 1952. *(Photo: Ramsay and Muspratt)*

ABOVE. Humphrey Evans, author's wife and daughter with author at Garden House Hotel, Cambridge, 1953. *(Photo: Humphrey Evans)* BELOW LEFT. Sir Will Spens, Chairman of Rugby Governing Body. *(Photo: Rugby Governing Body)* BELOW RIGHT. Author, captain of MCC v. Rugby, flanked by RES Wyatt and RE Bird, 1955. *(Photo: Leicester Evening Mail)*

were the menu cards (that year the menu was clear turtle soup —
knowing turtles as I did, I could not help feeling sorry about this
— scallops chablis, roast duckling with pineapple, lemon posset
and Scotch woodcock) and fascinating to the Australians was the
ceremonial 'loving cup' drinking, which the Fishmongers have as
their special ritual. I sat between Charles and Arthur Langford,
while my brother Eric sat opposite, next but one to Peter Burge,
the formidable Australian batsman who was an accountant. Burge
and Charles got on famously: this helped to make Charles's
evening because the speeches of 10th Viscount Cobham, R. B.
Simpson, the Australian captain, and E. W. Swanton were not, at
least on this occasion, noteworthy. Charles knew the first and last
named. Charles Cobham, formerly Hon C. J. Lyttelton, lived close
to, and was friendly with, Francis and Jessica Brett Young (I was
asked to handle their affairs when Francis died, but had to
decline). Charles had already done so himself, writing to Jessica: 'I
will find you a sensible chap (i.e. my brother).' Jessica talked of
Francis nonstop, Charles describing it as 'it seemed to me
bordering on a mania'. I was glad to escape that involvement. It
was not that I was shirking a duty, for I had never met the Brett
Youngs.

Cobham, not a prepossessing man like his distinctly handsome
father (both father and son were uniquely presidents of MCC),
had been Governor-General of New Zealand. I came to know him
at the International Cricket Conference and was sometimes on my
own in never thinking him very personable. With an unrefined,
heavy appearance, his features could not easily be associated with
the aristocratic profile of his father. I could not help observing the
contrast when, facing him across the narrow table in the MCC
committee room at Lord's, I would see him sitting directly, and
not fortuitously for him, under the portrait of the 9th Viscount.
The squareness of Charles Cobham's face seemed to be his alone
in the family: his sister was the mother of the present Duke of
Westminster — no heaviness of bone structure there. He was
certainly a robust raconteur, which apparently made him a hit in
New Zealand.

I wrote extensively for histories edited by Jim Swanton.
Avuncular in figure and style, he was an imaginative and crystal-

clear writer, far better in that capacity than as a television commentator. His biography of Gubby Allen, is excellent although Allen chaffingly told me, too full of Swanton, whose *Follow On* has a piece on the Snow brothers. When, in talking about his biography, I asked Sir George Allen why his knighthood had been so long delayed, he said that he had an enemy blocking it for years. He would divulge neither who nor where.

Charles wrote on 29 April 1964: 'I am sending three guineas for the dinner, with many thanks for an enjoyable evening. You seem to have been more affected than I should have expected.' This was his reflection on our relative states at breakfast (not on the return journey from the dinner to Cromwell Road when he had at times been scarcely coherent). Never did he have a hangover. He went on to write:

> If Pamela and I should die or be killed together, then someone has to look after young Philip. We should very much like you to do this. . . . The question of money does not of course arise. Apart from the trust, he is the main legatee of my estate, which is considerable. I should expect you to use the income from this estate to keep him and yourselves in reasonable comfort.

He had made me joint copyright holder of *Corridors of Power*. He wrote in a letter of 8 April 1964: 'As the trustees [there were two of us, the other being Edmund Williams-Ashman, his accountant] I am writing formally to assign to you the copyright.'

That year, Sir Edward Roberts (sic) Lewis, founder and chairman of Decca, not very voluble but generous on a large scale, joined the Rugby School Governing Body for a decade. He had turned down giving the first recording contract to the Beatles, not an unnatural act considering general first reactions to their sounds and appearance (it is easy to forget the shock of their initial impact except on the very young), but commercially costly. His nose, not a Jewish one, was for money, acquiring it and dispensing it. He was philanthropical, I know, towards his school.

When my delightful old friend, Sir Pelham Warner, died in his ninetieth year, I met — but only briefly — at his memorial service (which I went to with Gerald Steel, who died in the same year) Raymond Robertson-Glasgow. It was shortly before he died from an overdose of pills after a life of giddy euphoria and severe melancholia in and out of institutions as a manic-depressive. The extreme complexity of his character, like to some extent Charles Allberry's was tragically never to give himself as much pleasure as his brilliantly witty writing, often viewed from his own illustrious first-class playing experience, brought to others. His character sketches could not have been improved upon for their deftness, their discernment and their attractive presentation of personalities. The farewell gesture to Plum Warner was for me sad. But he was 90 and he had had an enviable life. It is difficult to absorb that he was half-Spanish and the eighteenth child of his father, an attorney general of Trinidad, who married twice, the second time to Maria Cadiz.

The first half of the 1960s was almost over. It had certainly been the prelude to that aptly named 'swinging decade' for me, if not always as one would have wished it to be, but then that is life's progress. I was on the sidelines in some of its closer traumas but I was glad to be near to Charles rather than on the other side of the world in his chronic trials. For him, things might improve: for me, they would be devoid of dullness.

3

A Glimpse of America and a Baron in the Family

The year 1964 was a distinctive one for me and for Charles in different ways. Another world now called me. Two bursars — one, Frank Walesby, the soul of amiability from coeducational Bedales, the other, David Sherwood, from the girls' school, Badminton — had been in the Easter holidays to look separately at schools in America for comparisons or contrasts with English ones in case we could learn anything, not least in the area of appeals, where America had almost been pioneers. Schools there in nearly all cases had their finances substantially supplemented by them.

The Bursars' Association had arranged for this tour by Sherwood as the secretary, a committee member and myself as chairman (and from a boys' school) to go and report. They gave a little financial support and we each obtained the necessary extra from other sources. Rugby helped me, as did materially the American government, which gave generous Foreign Leaders' Specialist awards containing dollars and éclat simultaneously. America had been kind to me since saving our existences in the wartime Pacific.

I could not go at Easter, as Walesby and Sherwood had done, but gave up my entire August–September vacation (so that I had no holiday *per se*) for what was in fact a most strenuous assignment. So as not to overlap each other, we had arranged for different schools to be visited: I also took in universities and Canada, particularly schools there that were members of the Public Schools' Bursars' Association. As the administrative and educational details were published as *Report on the Visit of Three*

84

A Glimpse of America and a Baron in the Family

Bursars to the United States of America in 1964 by the Public Schools' Bursars' Association and reprinted years later by Lord Craigmyle's professional fund-raising organization, I will simply mention here one or two personal observations.

Through my abomination of flying, I planned to go out on the *Queen Elizabeth* (83,637 tons) and to return on the *Queen Mary* (81,000 tons), finding the latter much the more congenial of the two. To the astonishment of my American government sponsors, I also planned all internal travel by rail or bus. As a result, at the end of the seven weeks' nonstop movement, I was still able to claim a degree of freshness. Also, because I never left the surface, it is unarguable that in that short time I saw more of their country than many had in the space of years.

Of all that I saw, I liked the Deep South the best and was utterly charmed by Savannah, Georgia, so underestimated in comparison with Charleston. A Mississippi paddle-steamer trip from Memphis, Tennessee and Hilton Head Island, South Carolina, still with its alligators and Fiji-like jungle (before the arrival of Evonne Goolagong's tennis-court complex), were pure nostalgia. In another existence and at a different time I would like to have been a benevolent cotton plantation owner living in a Palladian mansion with white Corinthian columns and ornamental lace ironwork approached through an avenue of oaks festooned with Spanish moss.

Buffalo and the Canadian Niagara Falls duly impressed: not so Quebec and Ontario provinces. New England's Choate, Hotchkiss, St Paul's, and the Phillips Academies of Andover and Exeter put England's schools in the shade with the quality of their equipment and many of their buildings. Yale and Harvard seemed prosaic after Cambridge and Oxford but Virginia University at Charlottesville had poetic qualities. Indian reservation trading posts had undeniable fascination when one shut one's eyes to mounds of tyres and derelict vehicles.

A most delectable sight to contrast with my daily immersion in sometimes overpowering academic confines was offered at the Peabody Hotel, Memphis. Its dozen ducks, resident overnight on the flat roof of the 12-storeyed hotel, would descend daily in the lift with a liveried, white-gloved Negro footman of immense dignity. Having rolled out a red carpet for them, to the rousing sounds of Sousa's *King Cotton March* he would lead the waddling single file to the marble fountain in the middle of the foyer. There, they would disport themselves all day until early evening when the carpet would again be unfolded for their procession in single file behind the footman to the lift up to the flat roof, a charming daily ritual.

I should have arranged my itinerary to have been by train over the Middle West to San Francisco instead of the visits to Quebec, Montreal, Toronto and Ottawa but as their chairman I had a duty to see our association members there. In New York, Pat Dean, the long-standing member of the Rugby Governing Body and then Permanent Representative at the United Nations General Assembly, arranged for me to observe proceedings in the Security Council Chamber. He also gave me a party at which I met Lord Widgery, the future Lord Chief Justice, as well as two Rugbeians, Lord Spens (the last European Chief Justice of India and brother of Will) and Sir George Coldstream, former permanent secretary to the Lord Chancellor. I could not refrain, although I hadn't played for nearly 15 years, from entering the *Queen Mary* table tennis championship. Although I was about 30 years older than most of the contestants (long-armed Americans going to English public — private in the American and correct sense — schools for a finishing year) and had to struggle, I was finally presented with a clock inscribed 'WINNER OF RMS *QUEEN MARY* CHAMPIONSHIP'.

It was not long before some bursars (or business officials or comptrollers, as they are more likely to be known in America and Canada) came across the Atlantic to see Rugby and me.

Corridors of Power had now come out. Its appearance was ironically before a happening that might have changed Charles's approach to its theme. When Harold Wilson won the general election in 1964, some of the papers tipped Charles as a possible minister, more likely, one paper thought, as Permanent Representative of the United Kingdom at the United Nations General Assembly.

All the same, I was very surprised when he telephoned me — in strictest confidence, only Anne to be told — that Wilson had offered him the post of parliamentary secretary to the Ministry of

Technology, a new ministry set up with Frank Cousins, MP, at its head. Since Cousins was in the Commons, Wilson wanted Charles to accept a peerage so that he could be the spokesman in the House of Lords. Charles would himself never have contemplated a safe seat in the Commons. I had once asked him years earlier (in 1951 when we were waiting for a bus on Oxford Street — I recall the exact place and year vividly for some reason) if he shouldn't go into politics. He said, instantly and firmly, 'No. Never under any circumstances.' Charles told me that Wilson had asked him to 10 Downing Street but to use the garden gate off Horse Guards Parade so that the media would not photograph him. It is remarkable that, even now, the media do not seem to watch that back gate, especially since visitors to No. 10 who are required to be incognito are probably often more significant than the ones who use the front door. This cannot be revealing a state secret, for the gambit must have been so often used by newsworthy callers.

Anne was rehearsing for one of the many staff plays in which she appeared, enjoying taking the female lead and doing it without nerves. I went to the wings of the stage, called her and whispered the news. Nothing could be known until the papers revealed it. Prior publicity could be death. I did not talk about it in Rugby and the fact that Lord Snow was my brother remained largely unknown for the rest of my time there. Had it occurred earlier and then been known while I was in America that I was the brother of Lord Snow rather than simply of Sir Charles Snow, there indeed would have been much reflected glory for me. He was well known as an author and pundit there. To have added to this that he was a statesman and a baron (the latter more than the former, such is its fascination over the Atlantic) would have increased interest in me: he became better known in America than in England.

The barony brought one or two pleasant posers. But first of all he had to ask my help: 'While I am a minister I don't want to know about my investments.' He was obliged to have a coat of arms. Pam took this largely into her hands, gaining much enjoyment in the process. The motto '*Aut Inveniam Viam aut Faciam*' was explained in a letter to Anne from Pam of 27 October 1964 as 'I will either find out a way or make one — a motto I chose for myself when I was 18 and hung on to with adolescent romanticism. It is fun to see it come true'. The crossed pen (arts) and telescope (science) embodying the two cultures, the snow crystals and the Siamese cats were all her ideas. It was not Charles's field of interest and he was rapidly becoming involved in the work in the ministry at Millbank. On 5 December 1964 Pam wrote to me that 'I must say C thrives on politics. He is out far earlier and back far later, but always comes in looking chuffed as hell.'

But it was not long before the novelty wore thin. Not the Lords, which he found absolutely ideal as his club and retreat into select company, but the ministry where he found that he had no power for channelling his ideas and that the job had some menial aspects almost approaching the taking of minutes or, at least, detailed notes of proceedings. I had often enough chided Charles with having escaped throughout his life the formidable chore of having to take minutes in any organization to which he belonged, whereas it was the fulcrum around which my own life since returning to England revolved.

Charles's work was inhibiting his wish to get on with writing, but he had to put up with the load for a year, the minimum Wilson required and seemed indeed the bare one in return for a peerage. It was in fact to be a year longer than the single one for which Charles had hoped. When he made his maiden speech on 18 November, Pam, Anne, Stefanie and I were as impressed as the more hardened peers by his use of absolutely no notes and by the impression he gave of having been there all his life. Many were the congratulatory messages passed to him as he sat down. He had previously asked the advice of Lord Astor about the custom governing speeches. Ironically enough, in view of the Eccles attack (referred to later), Bill Astor was confident that a high level of courtesy was demanded — unlike in the Commons. Charles had a fortnight previously been inducted into the House before the Lord Chancellor in a more than faintly comic procession behind Garter King of Arms, who was collaborating with me in a family history necessary for the heralds' records, and flanked by Lords Boothby and Bowden. Charles wore the hired ermine and tricorn hat with the aplomb that marked his always utterly unselfconscious wearing of any apparel. A predominant impression of the occasion was Boothby's remarkable gravel voice crunching over all the conversation, including that of Pam, Anne and myself at lunch in a private room.

New profiles among the Rugby School governors now included, since the additions of Corner and Dewey, the Dean of Westminster, Very Reverend E. S. Abbott, an unobtrusive person in the place of the bassoon-voiced Alan Don, Sir Edmund Compton, Comptroller and Auditor General who was to become the first ombudsman (more properly, Parliamentary Commissioner for Administration) and chairman of the Governing Body very briefly on Lord Parker's retirement, and Sir Alan Wilson, chairman of Glaxo, the last named bringing some scientific and industrial experience — they represented quite a mixture. But the Governing Body had the facility to absorb all types, some inevitably remaining mute and others, if vocal, then only in a controlled way. It was to me remarkable that people at the top of their professions would spare the time, even at least a whole afternoon, three times a year — and more if they were on the War Memorial trusts, appeal, finance, and Founder's London Estate committees. Compton had come up through the Treasury, which tended to fasten him to detail to the exclusion of broader issues.

Meanwhile, Lord Parker was steering the Governing Body in an almost indiscernible, certainly serene manner that was assuring as we neared an important piece of Rugby history.

4
Maharajahs, Innings and Outings

I n 1965 my close friend of nearly 30 years, since my first meeting in the sombre interior of Wing Zoing Wah's store at Nausori in Fiji, died. Dr Humphrey Silvester Evans was 75. He had been a splendid, rather elusive eccentric.

I would not have relied much on his medical skill: he himself had deeper interests than his profession. His motivating love, running alongside his unfailing eye for beauty of people and places (in that order), had been the administration of the locations furthest removed from telephone, radio and headquarters. He had enjoyed benevolent, aristocratic autocracy as much as he had been governed by the magnetism of fine-looking females in all his travels. While he was joint District Commissioner/District Medical Officer, Lau — for one of the longest spans of any official in a district (preceding Ratu Sir Lala Sukuna, whom I in turn succeeded after a lengthy span by him: there were only three substantive commissioners of the Lau archipelago within the Fiji Group in about 15 years) — his beautiful English wife, Phyllis, left him through his undoubted neglect of her but not before her genes and his handsomeness had inevitably produced two attractive daughters in Lomaloma.

As described in the first of these two volumes, when he and I first met in 1938 in Wing Zoing Wah's store at Nausori, he had a Lomaloma mistress, Seru, and there were other attractive daughters. When he married a second time, now to Hélène from Switzerland, he took her to the Rotuma group of islands, far more isolated than Lau, where she could not endure his preferences and committed suicide. He reverted to the faithful Seru and a Lauan household when he retired to Suva Point.

His breadth of interest, his Pacific scholarship and his cultural ambience had been treasured rarities for me in Fiji. Humphrey had indubitably, by a wide margin, been the best-read resident in the colony. He had been a prolific correspondent in a fastidious, elegant script. One of his manifold studies had been of Oriental calligraphy: he had become very attached to it on his peregrinations in Indo-China and the East Indies. The tragedy is that he never left any tangible works on the Pacific, though I tried hard to persuade him to put his knowledge and original thinking on to paper. There were multiple disconnected memoranda, but it was as though he could not face up to a sustained effort. Perhaps retarded by the meticulousness of his script, he never ventured into work of lasting academic merit. He would not undertake it if it was not the acme of perfection and comprehensiveness. One knows only too well of cases of pen not being applied to paper through such inhibitions. But he suffered from them more deeply than many, yet he was not fundamentally a man of inhibitions.

Without denigrating his noble looks, his nose was undeniably hawk-like but there was nothing else that was predatory except his insatiable appetite for recording beauty. Instead of talons, thin tapering fingers. He was a member of the Royal College of Surgeons and could no doubt if required or, more to the point, if he wanted, have taken on surgery of the most delicate precision. Those fingers would be applied to the camera at which he was almost a professional and, given single-mindedness, a near genius. Supreme aesthete as he was, there was also unarguably something of the poseur in him and also of the voyeur (in the nicest, most unconcealed sense). Humphrey was a philanderer in thought rather than in ultimate deed to its copulatory conclusion. For him (as for the Greeks), beauty was his ideal but virtually exclusively as belonging to females.

Not a complete isolationist (he was an indefatigable traveller but at the same time anti-gregarious), when in Suva he would accept annual invitations to the Governor's Royal Birthday tea party in the grounds of Government House. With his camera tucked inconspicuously about his faultlessly attired person (all in white or cream, the only one in the colony to wear the Trinity College, Cambridge tie), he would capture the most elegant women for his collection. He would take the inseparable camera too to the Fiji Arts Club amateur productions of ballet but would eschew almost all other social functions (to which he would not in any case be invited).

Other sure-fire captures would be distinguished entomologists, archaeologists, botanists, linguists and anthropologists visiting Fiji, for whom he would be almost their only unofficial contact. Even pre-advertised visitors on liners passing through Suva for a single day would be captured by him and, if they were eminent, he never missed an opportunity to arrange a *yaqona* reception ceremony for them in a nearby village. I remember being invited to accompany him to one he organized for Robert A. Millikan, the American Nobel prize winning atomic physicist. All these people would later become his correspondents: regular ones included Sir Julian Huxley and Dorothy Tutin (although she never visited Fiji. Nor did she ever meet Humphrey). They enriched his life and he was comfortable in their physical and epistolary company, as they were in his, a rare exotic bird to be encountered in the tropics.

Not many local residents understood him. He could be rigidly aloof, austere and abstemious. He kept a lean figure all his life, which could not have been a more utterly individual one. It was natural that his burial should have been conducted in Suva by Rotumans: he had left part of his heart in their group as well as in the Lau archipelago. I was sorry that he just missed seeing the publication of my *Bibliography of Fiji, Tonga and Rotuma*, for which he was inspirationally enthusiastic over the years and made a generous bequest to me for it in his will.

I had been his closest friend for the last 27 years of his life. When we had been together in Suva, Anne, Stefanie and I would be warmly welcomed by camera and by a cheery, sometimes self-mocking, greeting on regular weekend visits to his house on the beach at the Point. He was a never-failing source of unorthodox, entertaining and diverting instruction about the islands and their variety of people. Humphrey had a gift for imparting really fresh air from a healthy extra-island perspective, and his global assessments stretched across sometimes claustrophobic coral reefs to boundless horizons. I was only glad to know that his last few weeks had been brightened by having James Pope-Hennessy's *Verandah*, which I had sent to him in the belief that it was just his cup of tea, read to him by Lindsay Verrier, who spoilt this by telling me that he had never liked Evans. Verrier, a medical colleague, was also odd but in a generally unappealing way.

Humphrey Evans had been a fine eccentric and, for all that, had been one of the first striking personalities I had got to know closely. In the last decade and a half of his life I had seen him only intermittently in England but there had been unceasing correspondence. Having retired, he would send endless letters in his thin, individualistic script to which I, working very hard at the time, could send only one letter for every half-dozen received. His were paradoxically esoteric and eclectic, not expansive on people but on places and policies. He had eschewed comment on persons, recognizing that each should live the life that he or she had chosen — a reflection of his own stance in the world. I was impressed by the extent to which he could be enamoured by several women simultaneously, though, as in the case of Dorothy Tutin, always from a distance, mostly at the end of a camera, and yet remain associated with Seru, his Lomaloman housekeeper for many years and mother of two children being brought up in Lau. His utterly individual style in Fiji had enriched my life.

It was in 1965 that a Fijian, Inoke Lesuma, whom I had known in Fiji and who was training in England to be a district officer, brought to the house a Solomon Islander and a New Hebridean. The former was to become the first of his race to be knighted, as Sir Fred Osifelo, after distinguished administrative service, finishing as Speaker of the Legislative Assembly in the Solomon Islands where he had started as an office cleaner. The latter climbed higher and fell steeply. After becoming the first indigenous district officer in the British part of the condominium of the New Hebrides, on independence when the name of the country was changed to Vanuatu, George Kalkoa was elected its first president.

He himself did a name change — to Ati George Sokomanu — and was featured on Vanuatu's stamps. In the general unrest in the Pacific Islands in the late 1980s, he became dissatisfied with the Prime Minister, Father Walter Lini — was this another example of a meddlesome priest in politics? — and attempted to suspend the constitution, only to be arrested at the end of 1988 by Lini. The President was put on trial for plotting to incite the police and military to mutiny against the Prime Minister. Kalkoa was sentenced to a term of imprisonment in 1989 but had the verdict quashed on appeal. The Anglo-French condominium of the New Hebrides, as it was officially known before independence, used to be called unofficially the 'pandemonium'. The leopard did not seem to have changed its spots. A prime minister accusing his superior of mutiny was a classic example of nonsense.

In the year of the visit of the three very different Pacific Islanders — ranging from the bronze of Inoke, who perhaps was content to remain a district officer in Fiji, through the deeper bronze of Kalkoa to the real black skin of Osifelo — all sharing a bright, sharp outlook on their new world then not far from independence from the West, there was a rather uncommon occasion.

I joined a moderately rare number of people in an unusual manner, involving profiles that weren't quite what they purported to be. The occurrence gained front-page publicity in most of the national press to which the story had been sold. The Headmaster's secretary at Rugby School had been rung from the luxurious Leofric Hotel, Coventry, by solicitors acting for the Maharajah of Kapurthala with the request that, as the Maharajah was on a rare visit to England, he might visit the Headmaster and Rugby School with a view to putting his very young son's name down as a candidate. Edna Graham, the hyper-efficient secretary (mine, Enid Simpson, was equally so), replied that the Headmaster would be in London but that in any case the Bursar often, in his capacity as registrar, saw prospective parents and she would make the necessary arrangements with him.

Two or three days later at the appointed time a large black limousine drew up outside the Bursary and my secretary brought in the Maharajah, a tall, handsome, magenta-turbaned Sikh. He was accompanied by his fair, beautiful wife, a Parsee, and an anonymous looking young Englishman, his secretary, whom I thought dumb and whom I would not have engaged unless I were desperate. I nearly welcomed the Maharajah in Hindi, but, as he was to do most of the talking, all in near perfect English with the faint unmistakable tinge of an Indian accent, I was glad that I did not. He asked me about the history of the school and its curriculum, the elegant Maharanee in a dazzling orange sari with a plenitude of gold braid adding the inevitable requests for information that mothers make. I then showed them, as was my custom with prospective parents, the more ancient parts of the school and examples of newer building; parents' interests usually lay in the combination. Two very pale dark-haired young women with the small red-painted spot of faith on their foreheads and in saris draped over their foreheads in the manner now much seen in this country, who had been waiting in my outer office, were following quietly behind. They had not been introduced.

The visit lasted the usual three-quarters of an hour before they got into the limousine after the Maharajah's secretary had been given the prospectus containing entry forms for the three-year-old son left in India. It was advisable if they were interested, I said, to fill in and return the form without too much delay for, although prospective entry would be for 1975, we already had a large queue of candidates for that year. Completion of the entry was often done soon after birth, both by those who had connections with the school and by those who did not have any, like themselves, I added. I had stated, to add perhaps to their comfort, that there was a son of the Maharajah of Morvi already in the school with other Indians and co-Asians from Singapore and China. A good preparatory school for from age five to thirteen would be advisable, I concluded, but in my position I could not specifically recommend one.

Next morning the national press had on their front pages 'Successful Hoax at Rugby School'. It then emerged that the Rugby College of Engineering Technology, with which Rugby School had no dealings, was having a rag week and that the visit to the school had been engineered (they were all potential engineers) to raise money for it by selling the story (with photographs taken at their college, which apparently hoodwinked the press photographers also), to the principal and local newspapers. They described the Maharajah as of 'Capoorthala'. Had I seen anything beforehand in writing (I of course never did: it had cleverly been left to the telephone), I would have raised my eyebrows at that: Kapurthala was well known to me as the name of a state and of course the Punjabi Sikh was, if a serious interpretation were to be put on it, an impostor of the true Maharajah of Kapurthala. My initial reaction was of umbrage, not only for the waste of time but for being made to feel foolish, in particular by papers that did not publish the pictures which clearly showed the Maharajah as a genuine Sikh (named Harmohan Singh Bhatia) — the real holder of that office would be one — and the Maharanee (named Parni Kassan) as a genuine Parsee of the high caste to which that race belongs. The press did not make it evident that they were not masquerading Europeans. In retrospect, I wish that I had used a few phrases of Hindi, although it would have been a form of showing off, if only to see what effect it would have had on our meeting. They could never have expected that, and it might have disturbed their poise. Hamilton, on his return, was as surprised as I was. Telephoned by the press, he commented: 'There but for the Grace of God went I. Philip Snow is no fool, you know. My congratulations to the students. I was not there but I am taking it all in the spirit that was intended. There will be no repercussions. I was a student once myself.'

It was of course the only way to treat it. It had been successful in what it had set out to be. Never did I think that I would be the victim of a hoax. I later judged it to be a totally plausible one, as did the half-dozen bursary staff who were alone in seeing the visitors. Of course the Indian jokers had not thought that we dealt in genuine maharajahs which took, for those of us with inside knowledge, most of the edge off the performance. I had interviewed the Maharajah of Morvi earlier about his son as an entrant for the school: he was not a Sikh and was on his own a straightforward Indian aristocrat.

The final laugh could be said to be mine. The following week there was the college's first award of diplomas and of all people who had been invited to present them it was Charles. When I met him at the station he was highly amused, declaring that, as a hoaxee, I was one up on him. But the students perpetrating the impersonation — both the Sikh and the Parsee would be near their middle twenties but looked a little older — were full of trepidation when by then the astonishing coincidence of the college's guest of honour being Lord Snow, their victim's brother (when it had been intended that the victim should be the Headmaster of Rugby), was known to them. The organizer had said previously when there were no repercussions: 'That's a relief. Mr Snow's brother, Lord Snow, is presenting our awards next week. We hope he sees the funny side too.' I was reported as saying 'I did not know that there was a college rag. In the short time we had contact we of course had to accept them in good faith.'

At the assembly to which I had been previously invited by the chairman of the college's governors, Charles started off his speech by saying 'I am not a sixth former from Rugby School in disguise here to attempt to even the family score. The chairman has known me for 20 years and can vouch for my identity.'

Afterwards the principal of the college asked me if I would receive the two Indian graduates (by now) and allow myself to have the reciprocal honour of being shown round the college by them. The tour was dull (scientific institutions almost bore me: my engineer grandfather would not have approved of my apathy, though he would have enjoyed the particular circumstances) but the company was bemusing. For some time afterwards my leg was pulled by friends and acquaintances who felt a little let down by the real fact that the hoaxers were genuine Indians of high caste — if not quite the highest as they maintained successfully for three-quarters of an hour with straight faces.

Round about this time, both Charles and Walter Hamilton themselves suffered slight dents in their own *amours propres*.

Under the influence of Pam as a periodically chronic sufferer (she would be put totally out of action, having no recourse but with her powerful opiates to take to a dark room for hours), Charles had agreed to be President of the British Migraine Association. Princess Margaret as a sufferer was the active Patron. At an annual dinner of the association, Charles indulged heavily. He was later to be advised by Anthony Storr (descendant of Paul Storr, the distinguished eighteenth-century goldsmith), psychologist and close friend of Charles's, to cut down his drinking when he was reported to be near to making a public exhibition of himself. Pam was horrified to overhear Charles, who was sitting next to Princess

Margaret, saying paternally, 'My dear girl, it is a matter of...'
Pam did add, when telling me this, that Princess Margaret's
composure did not appear to be perturbed, which is contrary to
what has been described as her reaction (and no doubt royalty's in
general) to over-familiarity. Charles was only dented by Pam later
deciding that it was time to take him severely to task.

As for Walter Hamilton, he had arranged for me, as Chairman
of the Bursars' Association, to be the only bursar present at a
weekend conference of the leading dozen headmasters on the paramount question of the future of public schools, which Major
General 2nd Viscount Bridgeman, chairman of the governors of
Shrewsbury School, had convened on the invitation of the more
liberal than most headmaster of that school. The conference was
held in Windsor Great Park at an impressive house, which must
have been, or could be, a grace-and-favour apartment of some
size. All was based on informal talk except for a session that Lord
Bridgeman decided to preside over with the dozen headmasters
and myself seated around him in the drawing room.

The faces of the headmasters as the imperious Bridgeman
addressed them were a sight. He both told them what they should
be doing and what they had not done, and asked them what they
proposed to do. They were given the status of sixth formers but no
higher. Walter's face grew more and more thunderous — he was a
patient man — and the rest fidgeted in their comfortable gilt
chairs. I kept a straight face with the utmost difficulty. At the
coffee break Walter propelled himself across to me with his watch-
chain-dominated waistcoat protruding proprietorially: 'What right
has he to tell us our business? Damned impertinence!' The headmasters decided among themselves that their self-appointed mentor was not worth repudiating and the conference ended abruptly
with no contributions forthcoming but with Lord Bridgeman
continuing to look ebullient.

On the way back, Walter's state of high dudgeon was rigid
enough but changed in the train first to being 'vexed' (the word
that he would use in confiding any loss of imperturbability) and to
mild ruefulness. Then the anodyne of his customary tranquillity
took over as he mastered *The Times* crossword within the hour he
always allowed himself, observing wryly at the end of it that a

single governor had for once triumphed — or thought he had — at the expense of a hegemony of headmasters. Ironically, two years later, on leaving Rugby, Walter replaced Bridgeman as chairman of the Shrewsbury Governing Body.

Extraordinary notoriety from 1989 makes a note from this signatory mildly interesting:

IV:III:MCMLXV

Dear Mr Snow,

I wonder if you would like to speak in a 'Balloon' Debate on Sunday week. The theory of this is that five prominent people are sailing over the ocean in a balloon when it develops a leak, so that four have to be thrown out to let the fifth survive. We invite one speaker to represent each personality in the balloon and sing his praises as the most worthwhile passenger. Would you like to represent *Lord Snow*? It would only involve a speech of about eight minutes and will, I am sure, be very interesting. I hope you do accept.

Yours sincerely,

A. S. Rushdie (Hon. Sec.,
Rugby School Debating Society)

I sent a note across to Ahmed Salman Rushdie's boarding house asking him to come over the road to the Bursary and see me. I had to tell him that I could not be present as I would be at a Governing Body meeting in London. I cannot remember much about him except his, of course, Indian features (he was in fact a Muslim born in India) and extraordinary hooded eyes, not dissimilar in their hypnotic effect from a snake's and resembling closely those of an Indian lawyer who had often appeared in Fiji's courts before me. Rushdie was sorry that I could not be present and I did not see him again. He was never at ease, he has said subsequently, at Rugby.

In the Easter holiday of 1965 I represented the Governing Body at the funeral of Sir William Dugdale, who had died aged 93 in the Warwickshire half-castle/half-hall, on the site where his family had lived since the Norman Conquest. He had retired in 1963, when very deaf but mentally alert, after having been a governor of Rugby for 41 years. As a young man, after a collapse at one of the mines he owned, he had gone into the depths to achieve memorable rescues. He had also done the world tour, including Fiji, where he had been very impressed by Ratu Pope Cakobau: he was delighted when I took to the castle/hall, to see sepia coloured photographs of the visit, Ratu Pope's kinsman, Ratu Edward Cakobau, by whom he was just as impressed. He and Edward would have been intrigued by his grandson marrying a daughter of Ratu Sir Kamisese Mara, President of Fiji.

The only member of the Governing Body who could get to the funeral was Lord Willoughby de Broke, but in his capacity as Lord Lieutenant of Warwickshire. With those slanting eyes, the twentieth baron looked like a noble bloodhound. In the village we had had to park in a squelchy field. On leaving, we helped each other by pushing our cars which had sunk in the mud. Lord Willoughby de Broke, who led an outdoor life on estates, was evidently quite used to, indeed totally unperturbed by, such conditions as mud flying over his brilliantly polished shoes and Lord Lieutenant's uniform — the cleaning would no doubt be a valet's job. I was less happy wallowing about: country life in England was an unfamiliar and currently unwelcome setting.

From the Gritti Palace Hotel, Venezia, Charles wrote on 31 August 1965 that 'This is the best hotel that I've ever stayed in.' He had no better eye or feel than Pam for creature comforts, but their experience of so many hotels gave weight to that testimonial.

I had told Charles and Pam that Charles had the curious notoriety of having his name enunciated from the stage of a royal command performance — by Peter Cook, possibly widely known then but obscure now. Cook's reference from the stage was somewhat irreverent as well as being irrelevant: the audience's silence seemed to confirm this. Pam wrote on 18 November 1965 that 'We were very amused by the Royal Variety Command Performance. Peter Cook has a sort of obsession about Charles — he actually said in public that he was the thing he most hated.' Cook was heavily connected with the perpetually sued and perpetually paying-out *Private Eye*.

I was always very refreshed by the visits I had to make to

London for meetings of the Governing Body, and of the finance
and appeal committees, War Memorial trustees and bursars'
committee. Often I would have dinner afterwards with Charles
and Pam, sometimes staying overnight. Otherwise I would find my
own relaxation, as at Lord's, and catch the midnight train back,
known with the sardonic wit of the common room in the times
when all trains except that one bore names as 'the Fornicator'. It
may have been the effect of the claustrophobia of the school's
restricted society (friends were made as much in the town itself)
after the wide open Pacific spaces, but I always returned with a
clearer head for work and an extra spring in my step.

Almost exactly a year to the day after Pam had written that
Charles thrived on politics ('He is out far earlier and back far
later; but always comes in looking as chuffed as hell'), Pam wrote:

> I must say that the Preface [to my *Best Stories of the South
> Seas*, submitted to her in draft] is most beautifully adapted
> to its purpose. I wanted to read the stories at once. ... The
> Beachcomber piece is excellent and most touching. I can see
> the allure of this kind of life, even though it would never
> have allured me (too much dirt, too many insects, too much
> *dalo*). But it gives me a sort of longing, when one finds the
> Cromwell Road so solid with traffic that it is impossible to
> cross. ... I shall be pretty glad now when he [Charles]
> packs in his Government job [Ministry of Technology]. It is
> becoming more and more demanding, with more and more
> piled on his plate. We hardly see each other during the
> week-days and he always comes in fagged out. Of course,
> he is extremely good at the work, so gets used, in my view,
> as the willing horse a good deal of the time. I'm not too
> popular when I say this. His own brand of stoicism will
> never permit him to complain while a job is on but
> afterwards he will come up with the truth!

Later, there were two different but interesting comments from
Pam. On 27 May 1966, she wrote to me to say 'Yes, we shall be at
Eton for the 4th, but spending most of the day at Cliveden.' Young
Philip's being at Eton brought them into contact with the 3rd

Viscount and Viscountess Astor, with whom they became friendly, continuing so with Bronwen, who was Astor's third wife, after the death of Bill Astor not long following Cliveden's associations with Profumo. They told me that they never came across him. Then, on 2 July 1966, Pam sent a postcard saying 'how pretty Stephanie was looking'. Our daughter's auburn hair (there was a strain of it on my father's side: her uncle Eric had the same colouring) and brown eyes (like Anne's and unlike the blue in all the Snows) combined to make her outstanding to our obvious pleasure.

Incidentally, Pam and Charles always spelt Stefanie with a 'ph' rather than an 'f'. Stefanie had chosen the latter from when of independent mind at St Andrew's University.

We experimented for our annual train journey to Nice in August by travelling via Biarritz, San Sebastián and Zaragoza (the last named quite off the beaten track), where Stefanie's bronze-auburn hair was patently an unusual sight, heads turning among the pedestrians, vehicle drivers and café patrons. Then, from Barcelona, we broke our journey at Marseilles. The Marseillais have long included gangsters. Once Anne and Stefanie had retired to the hotel, I wandered about the old quays and was near a café on the Quai du Port off the Quai des Belges, where King Alexander of Yugoslavia had been assassinated in 1934, when an ambulance rushed up and promptly took away someone on a stretcher. A blood-stained coat lay on the pavement. As best I could, I understood from the excited voices that a fusillade of shots had been fired from a passing car at someone sitting at a table. It was believed that he had been killed. I was there before the police. Four of their vans rushed up and they started looking for something. I was told that the search was for bullets. Finding one in the gutter, I handed it to them. The next afternoon's paper (it had failed to get into the morning's edition as the shooting was at about 1.00 a.m.) confirmed that a leader in a vendetta had been bumped off. It was the nearest I had been to a murder. Marseilles had certainly lived up to its reputation for roughness.

On our return from holiday there were two functions of a different kind for me to attend. On the recommendation of Walter Hamilton, who was a governor of it, Gresham's School, Holt, asked me to help them with a rearrangement of their financial setup as their bursar was retiring and it was thought that an opportunity existed for change, perhaps on Rugby's lines. After a few days' visit there when the Bursar, a Rugbeian, was magnanimous enough not to mind my task and to put me up at his house, I lodged my report and was asked to be present at the interviews for selecting the new bursar. The choice fell on R. J. Purdy, whom I had known at Cambridge and who often used to get me out playing for Jesus versus Christ's. He had subsequently had a distinguished colonial career as a senior resident in the provinces of Nigeria and was to stay at Gresham's for some years.

In addition to making a presentation to me, the governing body of Gresham's, the Fishmongers' Company, asked me to their livery dinner. Seated next to the chairman, I thoroughly enjoyed the veritable banquet in such an inspiring setting as their hall over-looking the Thames. All went out of their way to be welcoming, from the Prime Warden, 11th Duke of Devonshire, downwards throughout the company. I had been to banquets in their hall a few times before. But always with the Australian cricket team and no Fishmongers: that alone seemed strange. Otherwise, there was no change in the ritual of the 'loving cup' handed all around the hall, no doubt unhygienically despite the wiping of the large silver cup with a napkin, with bows from the person on one side handing it to you, oneself also bowing and then, having drunk, bowing to the person on the other side, who received it with a bow. A ritual that never failed to be a high spot among the visiting Australians, but one that kindled something of a distasteful memory of the Anglo-Catholic communion services of my youth. I expected genuflection at any moment.

Grander surroundings still were Marlborough House, where Queen Mary lived in solitary magnificence (except for a vast entourage) after George V's death. These were for a reception by Anthony (later Lord) Greenwood, an elegant Secretary of State for the Colonies who did not stay long in the job, in honour of dele-gates to the Fiji Constitutional Conference preparing for the independence that was to follow five years later and now considered in some quarters not to have been thought out with the foresight that events of 23 years later required. At this affair, where Ratu George Cakobau was amused to remind me of the

'Maharajah's' hoax, which had even found its way into the Australian newspapers, I re-met many old friends, some after 13 years. What struck me was that in almost all cases their faces were markedly fatter: it made me ponder on the effect of the beer imbibing that Fiji's climate demands. I met again here Sir Alan Burns, former proconsul in British Honduras and the Gold Coast who had been to Fiji as the chairman of a commission of enquiry into land and population problems — had the commission not come up with some contentious findings for Fijians, he might perhaps have made a good governor for Fiji — and the current Governor, Sir Derek Jakeway, small but active-looking, fortunate to have reached gubernatorial status before the empire almost wholly dwindled, with Fiji close to bringing down the curtain on the imperial scene.

During 1966 Christopher Legge came to stay with us for a while. I had last seen him on my American tour *in situ* as custodian of the Fiji collection of the monolithic Field Museum of Natural History in Chicago. He had been a particularly close friend ever since my first view of him in 1938 coming down the Rewa River enshrined on a top-heavy deck chair astride a shallow put-put. He was top heavy in himself. Broad shouldered and with thin legs, he always seemed likely to topple over. I had of course seen him do this once, breaking his knee, in Levuka in 1947. He had a remarkable memory of years past but did not seem to concentrate on what was happening at the current moment. The former was endearing; the latter could be off-putting unless one knew that it was illusory.

Further American bursars also came, returning my visits to them of a couple of years earlier. My life was busy enough, even though I had finished a tenure of three years (a year longer than normal — there had only been three instances of three years' election, including mine) as Chairman of the Bursars' Association. The guest of honour at my last dinner in that company had been Lord Upjohn, Lord of Appeal, a convivial co-diner.

It was at about this time, and bearing in mind Lord Astor's advice to him about a high level of courtesy governing the House of Lords, that Charles was severely jolted. He was bitterly attacked by Viscount Eccles for sending, as a Labour supporter, his son to Eton instead of to a comprehensive school. Charles phrased his reply badly, saying afterwards that he was for once surprised as he had never previously been less than wholly at ease in thinking while on his feet. He had stated in the Lords that young Philip's half brother was at a public school and that I was the Bursar of another (the only time of course that I have been mentioned in the Lords). He intended to suggest that it was a mistake to educate children differently from their brothers, relatives and friends (I of course had been to a grammar school like himself, his relations and many of his own friends). The matter gave rise to much controversy in the press: letters showed that there was more grasp of the educational issue than of the Leavis or Lindemann affairs. Charles's friend, George, 2nd Earl Jellicoe, wrote to him: 'But I wish you to know how much I — and I am sure many of my colleagues — regret the remarks which David Eccles let slip at the end of his speech.' It was an indefensible position for Charles and the only time that he was wrong-footed in public speeches.

Eccles was a foe. Nor was T. S. Eliot a friend. Charles was asked by a Canadian correspondent about Eliot and replied: 'I only knew T. S. Eliot very slightly. I don't think I should be justified in giving any impression on the strength of a few meetings on social occasions. It is true that I disliked a number of his views.' No doubt those opinions included anti-Semitism, which Eliot scarcely concealed.

Of another contemporary, Charles told *Life*: 'I don't think I ought to review Zuckerman's book. I have always been on cool terms and I would not like to review a book for you in which there was even a suspicion of personal feeling. And I could not resist making some sharp comments since he is the world's greatest master at making the commonplace incomprehensible.'

Charles's life was intensely preoccupied: it was his last year as a government minister and he was anxious to escape the round of debates in the House of Lords, presiding at official lunches and treading the corridors of power in Millbank, new but leading nowhere. On 10 February 1966, Charles asked in a publicly reproduced letter for release by Harold Wilson ('I want to write some more books'): the press published the Prime Minister's letter of 5 April reluctantly allowing him to leave the government 'in order to resume writing'.

Christ's had delayed, through the machinations of some of those in power there, making him an honorary fellow. They only just preceded Churchill College's election of him as an Extraordinary Fellow. Charles's interests had moved to Churchill where he was finding posts for his friends. He was also attempting to secure honours for C. S. Forester, Enid Starkie, J. B. Priestley and J. H. Plumb: to the latter he made a rare comment on age: 'It is wonderful ... to have no commitments of any kind.' He thought that there was much to be said for retirement at 60. And to Lady Aberconway he made one of his sweeping generalizations, namely that 'Russians are nearly as bad on their feet as Americans. I sometimes think the bigger the country the worse the public speaker.'

Earlier, Charles derived special pleasure from unveiling a Greater London Council blue plaque at 13 Hanover Terrace, London, NW, where H. G. Wells had lived for the last ten years of his life. This was on the centenary of Wells's birth. I wonder who will unveil a similar plaque in 2005 on Charles's terminal residence at 85 Eaton Terrace, London.

At the time of Profumo's resignation from government, names of those who had been guests of Bill, 3rd Viscount, and Bronwen, Viscountess Astor, at Cliveden were bandied about. Charles and Pam had received hospitality there quite often and Charles felt impelled to write to the editor of *Time Magazine* about their story of the Ward affair: 'I should like to put on record some facts about Lord Astor which were relevant to the suggestion that he "was never really intellectually attuned to his sophisticated circle ..." I know that he has given generous and selfless help, financial and otherwise, to a good many writers and artists who were in need.' Bill, son of Nancy Astor, was uncle of the proprietor of *The Times* and brother of the editor of the *Observer*. This quotation by Charles is included as it has been maintained that he never chose to come out publicly in the matter.

At the risk of name dropping, I cannot resist mentioning that an unexpected meeting for me was with Field Marshal Viscount Montgomery. He wished to pay a visit to Rugby to meet some of the boys but he wanted nothing organized. Walter Hamilton introduced me to him in his study: we exchanged but a few words.

He was obviously a laconic man in all circumstances. His face, with his inordinately long canoe-like nose, was every bit as pertinent as I had seen depicted. Tête-à-tête, I perhaps fixed him with my look, searching for a quick judgement of his character. But his rapid-moving eyes seemed to be looking round for the next face. Perhaps he was always hunting for something he seldom possessed — except self-confidence, jauntiness and a lack of nerves amounting to an ability to achieve insensitivity, which helped his indifference to the outcome of decisions once made. By that, I mean his setting the battle and then going off for a sleep not to be interrupted — like Marshal Joffre in the First World War. Joffre's imperturbability, mammoth meals and good nights' sleep nevertheless, with General Gallièni's poker-faced grimness, miraculously saved Paris at the last ditch in the Battle of the Marne: Gallièni, after being Governor-General of Madagascar, was the city's military governor. But Montgomery's concern to win with the lowest number of casualties was to his eternal credit, like that of Field Marshal 1st Viscount Plumer of Messines, commander of the 2nd Army, British Expeditionary Force 1915 to 1918, who contrasted with the otherwise scandalously carefree attitude of many generals in the First World War about losses in attacks from the trenches. But then Plumer, for all his intense religiosity and belief that 'God meant Right for the Allies', had shown the same caring attitude prompting him to pronounce against General Sir John Monash being passed over as governor-general of Australia because he was Jewish. This brilliant Jew, commander of the Australian Army Corps in France, had been earlier accepted as the most efficient leader on the European front in the First World War.

Charles was always deeply interested in opinions about generals. He would tell me that whenever he came across pundits on this subject a consensus of view was that the highest class in our country's generals in the last war was limited to Field Marshals Viscount Slim, Earl Alexander, Viscount Montgomery and Viscount Alanbrooke. Wavell and Auchinleck did not have the luck so essential for success: otherwise they would have made up the half-dozen. In their case, as in that of Admiral of the Fleet Viscount Cunningham, it was apparently damaging almost beyond repair that all three were tongue-tied in Churchill's presence. It was another gap in Churchill's judgement that he demanded articulateness above all else. Had it been the First World War, Churchill would somehow have eliminated Haig for this reason, whereas Lloyd George had not succeeded in doing so, even when motivated by other reasons.

Montgomery has so often been contrasted with Alexander that there is nothing for me, having met both briefly (one extremely so) to comment on, except an absolute preference, if I had been given the choice, for serving under Alexander.

Shortly after meeting Montgomery I came to know one of Montgomery's and Alexander's assistants, Lieutenant General Sir Oliver Leese, ultimately Commander-in-Chief, Allied Forces South East Asia 1944–1945.

Fiji had been the first country, with Ceylon (as it then was) and the USA, to be elected an associate member of the International Cricket Conference, of which the full members were England, Australia, the West Indies, New Zealand, India and Pakistan. South Africa had been expelled and the conference had just changed from being 'Imperial' to 'International'. Leese, as President of the MCC, was automatically chairman of the ICC and could not have been more charming to the newest accretions over whose admission there had been much controversy. Gubby (later Sir George) Allen, England's delegate, had been vociferously opposed: he was still gruff in his gravel-voiced manner and remained so for a few more years until he was magnanimous enough to admit publicly that it had been one of the two mistakes in his life (he did not reveal the other but no man could be so convincingly obdurate or self-sure) to have resisted the admission of associate countries to the International Cricket Conference. There were in all (with the three latest representatives, Gamini Goonesena for Ceylon, John I. Marder for the USA and myself for Fiji) 17, a small enough number for Leese to accommodate at a barbecue outside his Chelsea flat in St Luke's Street. The major countries had two delegates to each associate country's one.

At the first meeting of the International Cricket Conference I was in no way intimidated, speaking for half an hour. So far as I recall, I strongly pressed for major countries to have teams visit minor ones for the purpose of stimulating them and assessing each other's strengths. It was the germ of the idea for the associates eventually to play each other in a competition so that they could formulate some estimate of relative status in one-day matches. That took 13 years to accomplish in three ICC trophy competitions — or nearly accomplish: one-day cricket cannot be the real test, nor can English pitches and weather, but I like to think that I set what is now quite a big ball rolling. As I spoke, I remember Allen looking, when not inscrutable, unencouraging, but Charles Cobham and the Maharajah of Baroda every now and again gave endorsing nods. Goonesena and Marder spoke only to say that they agreed entirely with my view. I was pleased to have been given such a receptive hearing. From that time in 1966, the major test playing countries have always listened politely to associates' opinions, which are stated guardedly in the presence of wider contacts with top international administrators.

It is revealing to compare the group photograph of the International Cricket Conference of 1966, my first, with that for the present. The growth not only in size but in the knowledge of the associates, largely through what they have picked up from the major countries, has been striking, one of the most fundamental developments in cricket at, or next to, the top. Over the next quarter of a century I was to meet many interesting representatives of different countries.

At the first official dinner in 1966 Sir Arthur Sims, a self-made millionaire from trade in sheep, wool, timber and land, and then a philanthropist, was New Zealand's main delegate and had been since their election in 1926. He had played for New Zealand and held the eighth wicket partnership record of 433 with Victor Trumper for an Australian XI (he moved there) against Canterbury. He established an unsurpassable record of 40 annual imperial and international conferences, putting my 30 consecutive years, the next longest, in the shade. He made a most gracious, warm speech of welcome to us three newcomers from another class of cricket. Charles Cobham was New Zealand's number two: as its governor-general, he had been much given to public speaking in a country that could not have too much of it.

The Maharajah of Baroda, whose friends were light-heartedly encouraged to call him 'Prince' or 'Jackie', was India's number one. Congenial, quite without pomposity, he had an infectious sense of humour. When I told him of the impersonation of the Maharajah of Kapurthala at Rugby, he said that he was a friend of the genuine one to whom he would recount the story and who would be entertained. Baroda told me of Kapurthala's never-to-be-forgotten, inextricable gaffe in proposing a toast to Lord and Lady Willingdon when it should have been to their successors nearly two decades later as Viceroy and Vicereine of India — Lord and Lady Mountbatten. Sadly, Baroda, a first-class cricketer whom I had met earlier when he was manager of an Indian team, died at an early age in 1988.

Walter Robins was Australia's number two through his friend-ship with Bradman. I would like to have observed personally the leadership of this dynamic Middlesex and England captain on the field. Vitality and vigilance were qualities I strove for myself as a captain and seldom saw in others — but noteworthy in Jardine, A. B. Sellars, Benaud, Bradman, F. R. Brown, W. A. Hadlee and, at a lower level, A. W. T Langford (MCC) and Gil Tebbitt (Northants and Rugby Town). From early on I made every possible special study of captaincy, which formed my greatest enjoyment in cricket. It always seemed to me that on the field, it was necessary to express imperturbability, punctuated with expressions of pleasure and encouragement of course (not overdone, perhaps a handshake — never a hug) when there was some ordinary or extraordinary feat, never raising one's voice, always taking up (before the absurd era of helmet protection of course) the potentially most dangerous position of silly mid-off, having the fielders instantly ready to comply with any signal for a move not seen by the batsman, never showing displeasure however much it might be going through the mind, unrelenting vigilance, conveying the sense of being on one's toes at all times. Any lapses from this were tantamount to losing control of an individual or even a team. With hindsight I recognize that I did tend to shirk from taking bowlers off if I thought that they were not tired enough. I hated disturbing them when they were on and not being expensive and not manifestly fatigued but keeping batsmen relatively quiet.

Australia could not then afford to send over two delegates all that distance very often: Bradman himself disliked flying and was not overfond of the sea. Robins, like all the others, could not have made me feel more comfortable. Gubby Allen, also a captain of Middlesex and England, was in later years the acme of friendliness: I was pleased to have gained the approval of so formidable an authority. He once confided in me that he had just warned a writer that he would 'take him to the cleaners' if he published that he was a son of Sir Pelham Warner. This was at a time when there was a publicized recrudescence of that belief.

From humble cricket administration in Fiji in 1939, I have since been absorbed by the game on the international level, which has richly increased my acquaintance and friendship with its leaders. Their tenure of office was, however, often (with the ubiquitous exception of Gubby Allen, it seemed) only for three years. The year 1965 saw my début on it and 1994 my retirement from the International Cricket Council, when all the others from the start had departed from the administration or from life itself. I never tired of it. When it expanded sixfold in my quarter-century (and more), incorporating countries or regions as disparate as Malaysia, Kenya, Argentina, Denmark, Gibraltar, Holland, West Africa, Singapore, Hong Kong, Bermuda, Bangladesh, Canada and Zimbabwe, my absorption increased correspondingly.

It has made so much about the inside of the game and its antics — successes as well as failures — comprehensible, not least the delicate interplay but the international intrigues reflecting more often than not the vacillations in world politics generally. I sometimes feel that I would have liked a career in the diplomatic service if it could have led to ministerial or ambassadorial status and if that was not an absurdly pretentious ambition to have entertained. With hindsight, and from what I can remember of what I said at conference annual meetings (as refreshed by the printed minutes), I am glad to have lacked timidity and to have shown that a smaller country might have something modestly to contribute.

As a result of my experience, E. W. Swanton asked me to write for the vast encyclopaedic *The World of Cricket* about smaller countries and islands playing the game round the globe. I already had quite a dossier of knowledge but a good deal of research was involved before publication in 1966. Since then, there has been a second edition in 1980 and a third, with expanded pieces by me on the countries and ICC associates' history, in *Barclays' World of Cricket*, edited by George Plumptre, son of 21st Lord Fitzwalter, under Jim Swanton's remarkably able, synoptic and balanced eye.

TO THE MEMORY OF CRICKETERS
OF ALL LANDS WHO GAVE THEIR
LIVES IN THE CAUSE OF FREEDOM
1914–1918 ✦ 1939–1945
SECURE FROM CHANGE IN
THEIR HIGH-HEARTED WAYS

ABOVE. Ratu Sir Lala Sukuna, Field Marshal Earl Alexander of Tunis, President of MCC, and author, on the presentation of the painting of Albert Park, Suva, for the Imperial War Memorial Gallery at Lord's, 1956. *(Photo: Sport and General)* BELOW. Charles, Pamela and author outside the Bursary, Rugby, 1962. *(Photo: Look magazine, USA)*

ABOVE. First meeting of the International Cricket Conference, in succession to the Imperial Cricket Conference, at Lord's, 1966. *(Photo: Sport and General)* BELOW. Lord Parker of Waddington presents author to the Queen on Rugby's 400th anniversary, 1967. *(Photo: Rodney H Huntingford)*

5

The Queen's Golden Touch

Lord and Lady Snow
at home
The Eve of Twelfth Night
(Thursday, January 5th)

Leicestershire Supper
RSVP
199 Cromwell Road   *Dress: What You Will*
London SW5   *8.30 p.m.*

This party to open 1967 took some organizing. Eric had to bring two huge cheeses, a whole Red Leicester and a whole blue-veined Stilton plus Leicestershire pork pies by train from Leicester to Rugby where I was able to help him. Charles had told Eric: 'The food is exactly what we want. We shall add chicken ourselves locally for the rather curious reason that we happen to have a couple of Orthodox Jewish guests.' We then boarded the train for London but it was held up for nearly two hours at Rugby station. We were able to warn Charles by telephone. He met us in a hired Daimler at Euston and we reached Cromwell Road just before the guests. Eric, an expert on Leicestershire customs, cut the Stilton in wedges. To several enquiries, he firmly declared that it is never scooped and port is never put in it. It only used to be when the cheese had been cut incorrectly and had wrongly been allowed to dry out and crumble. The ornamental silver cheese scoop was a Victorian introduction, completely unhistoric.

As a record of the sort of people whom I was to meet a few

times and get to know, this was an attendance list of names of those with more than a domestic fame. At the further risk of name-dropping, I mention the following whom I can think of as being able to be observed close at hand.

These included Joyce Grenfell, untheatrically pleasant, whom I did not somehow associate with having a husband, who was also present; Norman Podhoretz, widely acclaimed as the leading literary critic in New York; Arthur Crook, editor of the *Times Literary Supplement*; Tony Benn, whom Charles had helped in the curious campaign subscribed to by friends to suspend his viscountcy (Stansgate) for life and whose brown eyes burned as incandescently and wildly as those of my giant, light-transfixed Fijian moths; Larry Adler, the world's outstanding harmonica player who describes himself officially as a 'mouth-organist' — a man of quick-fire Jewish riposte and half-Yiddish, half-American expression; and Boothby to whom I have already referred.

Also, there were Alan Maclean, the genial, gentle leader of Macmillans in the absences of Harold and Maurice, who was to help so much over my *Stranger and Brother* because of his long friendship with Charles and Pam; the 7th Earl and Countess of Longford, the former dishevelled and donnish-looking with soft spots for lost souls, and the latter quietly distinguished, in appearance a non-matching couple; Lady Antonia Fraser (now Pinter) whose looks, fortunately for her, followed those of her mother, Elizabeth Longford; Sir Kingsley Amis, resembling and being an 'old soak', much given to immersion in drink on those occasions but never known to acknowledge that it was Charles who was first to give *Lucky Jim* the boost that really launched him (although in my humble view it was the only book worth recognizing in all his output); Harry Hoff (William Cooper, a protégé of Charles's); and Susan Hill, a protégé of Pam's.

Kingsley Martin, editor of the *New Statesman*, with eyes as surrounded with black skin as Larry Adler's or a panda's, was more distinctive looking than most of the literary figures there and was never short of company at the party. The friendly US cultural attaché, Philip Kaiser, was fascinated by English scenes like this; while Sidney (later Sir) Nolan, the Australian artist, whose first patrons in England were Charles and Pam and whose dramatic, memorable, if not always comfortable paintings other than depicting Ned Kelly decorated their house, was rather ill at ease.

Also present were William Gerhardie, of another age and background, with reclusive charm; Enid Starkie, whose name did not spread far beyond her deep European knowledge; the sisters Margaret Drabble and A. S. Byatt, daughters of a judge, loyal friends of Charles and Pam's and regular attenders at their parties; Kenneth Rose, the *Sunday Telegraph* columnist for a great number of years, biographer of George V and Curzon, and hardly rivalled since Chips Channon in the sharpness of his surveys of the social scene and his instinct for the bizarre; Lord Shackleton, who had crept ahead of Peter Scott in recognition of personal achievement while sharing paternal fame; and Alun Gwynne-Jones, a journalist with a distinguished war record who had become Lord Chalfont, Minister of State, Foreign and Commonwealth Office. On his behalf Charles had strenuously refuted irresponsible reports in the press that Chalfont had asked Garter King of Arms if he could take the title Lord Plantagenet.

Sir Ronald Millar, the indefatigable and skilled adapter to the stage of Charles's novels, was of course there, as was Sir Stephen Spender, suspiciously rouge-cheeked, statuesque and belonging to an earlier age. Also present were John and Madeleine Bingham (7th Lord and Lady Clanmorris), by their own right part of literary circles; Sir John Clements, who came without his invalid wife, Kay Hammond, and looked as though he were still on stage (as, in connection with Charles's plays, he nearly always was); Harold Macmillan's assistant, John Wyndham (1st Lord Egremont), and his wife, who were close friends of Charles and Pam's; and Patrick Blackett, Charles's scientist friend dating back to the 1930s, whose craggy profile has already been commented upon. Charles's aristocratic friends were represented at the party by the 10th Earl and Countess of Bessborough, Mary Duchess of Roxburghe and Viscount Hinchingbrooke (heir to the disclaimed tenth earldom of Sandwich).

Other literary, artistic and entertainment figures included Michael Ayrton, Anthony Curtis of the *Financial Times*, Anthony Storr, David Cornwell (John Le Carré), the light ginger-haired Bamber Gascoigne, L. P. Hartley, Marius Goring and Alec Clunes.

Sir John Betjeman, accompanied, of course, by Lady Elizabeth Cavendish, was his freely unstuffy, hilarious self. Field Marshal Lord Montgomery, with whom Charles was friendly, was expected at this particular party but did not turn up. These names (I met most of them on other occasions) have been dropped to indicate who Charles and Pam's friends were, constituting their party circle and giving me glimpses of their variety of profiles. Their conversation was esoteric and inbred.

As usual, what is interesting in such lists is the omissions. No writers of the stature of Anthony Powell, Graham Greene or Anthony Burgess were there, although Charles did have contact with them, particularly with the gentlemanly Powell and the forthright John Wilson (Burgess) but only distantly with Greene. In the 1930s and 1940s writers like Wells, Galsworthy, Walpole, Bennett, Conrad and Shaw would all have been together in what could almost have been described as a trade-union atmosphere. There were no professional politicians and no French figures, although Pam coveted the Légion d'honneur and merited some recognition for her intense study of Proust.

Christ's people such as Plumb, Downs and Putt never came to such parties. At this particular one there were no Russians, though Yevtushenko did on occasions visit them at their next house. There would always be a sprinkling of Americans and after the move from Cromwell Road to Eaton Terrace these included the still dazzling figure of Douglas Fairbanks. The list is lengthy because Charles and Pam gave virtually no dinner parties — and no lunches whatever: it illustrates fairly a cross section of classes of the inner Snow circle of London, imparting some idea of their self-imposed limits on sociability. There were 60 at this particular party, the absence of the Prime Minister, Harold Wilson and his wife being the only cause of the hosts' regret. On 13 January 1967 Pam wrote:

> We are so glad you enjoyed the party and grateful for all the help you gave us. I must say it was a riot: I have scads of letters almost hysterical about the originality, gaiety and the glories of Pork Pie. ... I suppose most people are so conditioned to horrible risottos reeking with garlic, or

Robert Carrier recipes, that the recall to the food of their youth (pork pie and chips in more cases than you might suppose) was a ravishing experience.

Charles was himself chauvinistic about Leicestershire in one respect only — its cheeses and pork pies. For years the only food specially ordered by Charles and Pam was pork pie from Leicester and when this coincided with a brace of pheasants from Lord Nelson, head of English Electric, this made Christmas tolerable for them.

The year 1967 was a quieter one for Charles but by no means for me. He was now accessible at almost any time and revelled in his new freedom — at least such freedom as he permitted himself. He was his own taskmaster. There was the unfailing, daily application of pen to paper, writing a quota whether he felt like it or not. In this fundamental discipline he was unremitting. He could, of course, never have been as prolific — much of it on top of a working life — without that gift of rugged application. It was the most fundamental advice that he would pass on to any writer.

When Charles was in America I told him that the *Sunday Telegraph* had reported that he would like to be Master of Churchill. There then appeared a cable to the editor: 'Churchill College story total fabrication. I am not suitable for this position and further would not accept any official position anywhere. My views as to possible successor to Cockcroft already in possession of Vice-Master. Must ask complete retraction. Snow.' On his return to London, he wrote to me on 20 October 1967 that 'I expect you have seen that I sent a cable from New York. I was certainly grateful to you for taking such prompt action. It would have been a great mistake to leave it for another week.' He told me that as the mastership was a Crown appointment, rebuttal was of the utmost importance. When Cockcroft died in 1967, Charles was pleased both with the obituary he had written for *The Times* and its reception.

For me the year was a relatively gigantic one. It started quietly enough with a visit from a friend of then nearly 25 years' standing, Reginald Caten. His rolling eye, like that of Groucho Marx, was mentioned in the first of these two volumes — it was one of the first sights I noticed when freshly arrived in Suva. But his humour was droll and kind, not inverted and acerbic like Groucho's. The fact that his eye rolled gave an impression of languor but this concealed an energy and imaginative drive for culture that made him invaluable in Fiji, where he was not specially attuned to that country's way of passing the time. His father had gone from England as bandmaster of the Fiji Defence Force. Reg himself was as Anglophile as anyone long exiled from England could be. He wanted, on retirement from the deputy registrarship of the Fiji Supreme Court, to be a guide in Westminster Abbey or St Paul's — more than anything else in the world. He would have been superb.

Early in the year (on 3 February 1967) I had written to Pam: 'Anne and I lunch this Monday at Marlborough House with the King and Queen of Tonga — he's not the charmer Salote was but a comparative South Seas intellectual. *Best Stories of the South Seas* comes out on March 9.' Herbert Bowden, MP for Leicester and later Lord Aylestone (a title Charles had contemplated with more territorial claim but was passed over for Lord Snow of Leicester), subsequently a neighbour of mine in West Sussex, as Secretary of State for the Commonwealth, was host. Two there whom I did not take to were Judith Hart (later Baroness), toothsome and wearing, and John Silkin (whose brother, Sam, later Lord Silkin, I had played cricket with at Cambridge). But quite different was the Queen's private secretary and King George VI's from 1937, Lieutenant Colonel Sir Michael (later Lord) Adeane — delightfully indiscreet. I suppose that if you live in a perpetual conclave of confidentiality and if you have to talk at all — which you can't help doing at a function like this — your contribution is bound to be a cascade of small, harmless indiscretions. There were 16 of us; no speeches and marvellous food and wine from the Government Hospitality Fund.

It was through Herbert Bowden, as our MP, that Anne and I had been able while on leave in 1946 to witness what was to us staggering. Churchill's wartime name in Fiji's distance from Britain was close to being sacred. When Bowden obtained tickets for us to attend a Commons debate, we indeed saw Churchill. Our horror was utter on seeing him rise to speak from the opposition, into which the electorate had, to antipodean people, mystifyingly put him, and be greeted with howls in the house of 'Sit down,

Churchill!' Yes, his name was called out against parliamentary protocol. It was the visual and audible toppling of, to us, a near idol. Our astonishment was complete.

It was not until the postwar years unrolled that Churchill's defeat became explicable. And of course, even when weighed against the strength of his character thwarting the appeasement gang of Londonderry, Chamberlain, Simon, Halifax and Hoare, he had made some terribly naïve blunders, echoing his record, like Gallipoli, in the First World War Cabinet. Nevertheless, he did seem to be the only figure of a dimension capable of drawing the country round him in the Second World War.

This year, Sir Alec Douglas-Home, later Lord Home, succeeded Leese as President of the MCC and Chairman of the International Cricket Conference. I was able to talk with him quite a bit in his second capacity. It surprised me that his hair was inclined to be reddish and his eyebrows positively ginger, but one's impression was dominated by the combination of half-rimmed or half-moon shaped spectacles and his lack of chin. That his jaw had recovered from tuberculosis was remarkable. It provoked sympathy but it sadly diminished the all important impression that television so ruthlessly demands and to which Macmillan rose so curiously from his unpromising younger phases of looks. Alec Home had, as Lord Dunglass, been a first-class cricketer and was an able chairman of the conference. I realize that, having met him at the conference, I have in fact met all prime ministers after Churchill except Callaghan and Heath, who aroused no interest whatever in Charles and me.

During this conference, the delegate from India, the Maharajah of Baroda, gave a party of imperial style at Veeraswamy's Restaurant in London, which he owned. The colour of the saris of the non-cricketing guests' ladies was kaleidoscopic; the food was delicious. I took Stefanie to it and we both thought it radiated the Orient quite exotically.

In 1964, passing a Philadelphia bookshop, I had noticed a book, *Best South Sea Stories*. As this was the title of a collection Faber & Faber had invited me to edit and, although my selection was different, we held up publication under the title *Best Stories of the South Seas* until 1967. A paperback edition followed five years later: it was in the railway station bookshops and I had the esoteric satisfaction of sitting in a carriage opposite a stranger reading it. It included two chapters and an introduction by me, but as it was commissioned there was virtually no pecuniary satisfaction, for me at least.

Preparations for something quite exceptional at Rugby School had started in 1966 — and it was not a reception for a bogus maharajah. Rugby was coming up to its four-hundredth anniversary year since its foundation. Quatercentenary was an awkward word, too often confused by the *non-cognoscenti* as quarter-centenary, a very different thing. Walter Hamilton wanted me to undertake most of the organization of it. On top of it, Lord Parker had succeeded in obtaining the consent of the Queen and Prince Philip to attend part of the celebrations. Although the only person in the school who had had experience of quasi-royal (gubernatorial or viceregal) arrangements (Hamilton had received the Queen twice at Westminster School, and there had been the visit of the Queen Mother to us), I knew full well that this was to be altogether more elaborate.

I was considered the obvious person for the task of organizing both the Royal visit and the separately timed celebrations proper. Walter told me that he was determined to move from Rugby before either the quatercentenary or the Royal visit occurred. Since I had set up committees to help me with both parts of the organization, he could not have been more delighted when he was offered the mastership of Magdalene College, Cambridge. His successor was Jim Woodhouse, a master from Westminster aged, incredibly, 33. He was just as kindly as Walter and had an innate dignity. At that age his job was not going to be easy but he carried it off.

Coming half way through the preparations for the Royal visit, which was to be in May and the quatercentenary proper which would occupy about a week two months later, he readily accepted without change what had been planned and was now being rehearsed. Philip Moore (later Sir Philip and on retirement Lord Moore after being private secretary to the Queen from 1977 to 1986) had been appointed assistant private secretary to the Queen in 1966. The Royal visit was to last three and a half hours and it is some measure of the work that goes into such events that he came to see me eight times in all before May. Each time we went over the route, checking the time of each leg of the programme. I had drawn up a dry-weather timetable and a wet-weather alternative. The Queen had asked to see as many of the boys' activities as possible.

Came the day in mid-May, black and full of threat of rain. I arranged for such of the Governing Body as would be coming to have lunch beforehand. Lord Willoughby de Broke was in the not overimposing uniform of Lord Lieutenant of Warwickshire. His peaked cap belonged more to the Salvation Army. Surely it should have been a plumed cockade, like that of a field marshal or a governor? But then I have a thing about plumes of feathers on male headgear: indeed, I believe that before the First World War lords lieutenant did have them. Languidly, at 1.45 p.m. he told me that he was driving himself down to the station, five minutes away, to greet the Queen. I replied that I would line up the Chairman, Lord Parker, the Headmaster and his wife, other governors and their wives, followed by the officers of the Governing Body designated for presentation at the welcome, with the Second Master and his wife, myself and Anne and the President of the Old Rugbeian Society (a former headmaster).

At 2.00 p.m. exactly the royal limousine, preceded by the Chief Constable of Warwickshire, with whom I had had many preliminary discussions over security, drew up at the red carpet. Lord Willoughby, who had been following in the car behind, opened the royal vehicle's door and out stepped the Queen with Prince Philip behind her to be welcomed by Lord Parker, now completely drenched. In common with most of the Governing Body, he had no umbrella. The rain was coming down in torrents and I noticed that the Second Master's MA hood had filled with rain. I checked mine and was surprised that there was no water in it at all — mildly puzzling. Philip Moore had joined the descending party with an umbrella, which the Queen insisted on carrying for herself. I had a very large spare one but it was not called for. Prince Philip was in a modest raincoat and trilby hat. All the bared heads of the male presentees glistened with water: no one could wear a hat except the half-dozen wives.

The Queen extended to all her gloved hand and an individual

smile as Lord Parker took over the presentations. Prince Philip, immediately behind, overheard the names. When he had shaken my hand and gone past me, he suddenly darted back to ask with a grin: 'So you are the chap who fixes the fees like those I get from Gordonstoun? Do you manage to balance the books?' I held back the riposte that Gordonstoun's fees were higher than those of any school except Millfield but in any case he had gone on to the end of the line. Now the architect was summoned by the Chairman (Lord Parker had no rehearsals for his part which virtually ended here) to meet the Queen and present her with the gold key for opening the commemorative gates.

It was my suggestion that the Queen should have something specific to do for marking the occasion and that a miserable rustic gate leading into The Close, which was universally noted for its location of the supposed start of rugby football, should be replaced by a pair of high ornamental wrought-iron gates. Based on the roughest of sketches of mine, with a curved ironwork overhang bearing the school arms and motto (*Orando Laborando* − by prayer and work − I did not set much store by the former) and set between two pillars, they had been handsomely executed by the architect, Keith Kellett. Soon one could not recall anything as inferior as that pastoral sheep's gate ever having been in such a prominent position.

Philip Moore had been coached by the architect and me in opening the double gateway time and again: the main point for him to get over to the Queen was that the key had to be turned anticlockwise. The Queen duly inserted the key and turned it anti-clockwise without being reminded. Of course, it happened. The gate refused to open. She tried three times. Being gold, the metal now twisted. Something had providentially prompted the imperturbable architect to carry an ordinary steel key in his pocket. With extreme difficulty, while the assembled school, masters, parents and public were locked inside awaiting the royal entrance, the architect extricated the bent key and offered the substitute.

This was making the Queen's day: apparently, as one heard later, she (and Prince Philip) enjoy nothing more than a break in the well-practised routine. She was smiling broadly. Prince Philip was saying to her erroneously and equally gleefully: 'I knew that you would muck it up.' To a great cheer, she opened the recalcitrant gate and acknowledged the crowd. She surprised me by walking to the side of the red carpet, dodging puddles, to the narrow entrance of the oldest part of the extant buildings, insisting on holding her own small umbrella and not using my extra large one, which courtesy required I should not unfurl for anyone else.

In our rehearsals, Moore and I had overlooked that in the event of rain there would be a pronounced crush behind her of the official party, the Marchioness of Abergavenny, lady-in-waiting, the Crown equerry, the Queen's police officer (Commander Albert Perkins), the Lord Lieutenant, Lord Parker, governors and officers' wives, all anxious both to be out of the rain and also not to miss any of the proceedings. There was a solid jam behind the Queen and Jim Woodhouse, who was to keep with her, just as I was to keep with Prince Philip for the whole programme. Once we were through that bottleneck it was my duty to present the three oldest surviving serving members of the non-teaching staff (also far senior in service to any teaching staff). But I was behind the many who should not have gone in ahead.

I felt myself pushing a raincoated figure in the semi-darkness of the passage. It was Prince Philip's back. I asked to be excused to be able to go in front so that the leading order, necessarily in single file, was Woodhouse, directing the way through the labyrinthine and, in the prevailing gloom of the day rather dingy, corridors with the Queen behind, then me, followed by Prince Philip. Somehow I managed to squeeze past to the old building, which had once housed the only three classes held simultaneously in it and where now were lined up Harry Gay, accountant, Jim Boneham, head porter, and Arthur Reece, shop manager, each with more than 50 years behind them since they had started in the humblest posts in the school at the age of 13. Their families and other non-teaching staff were the audience. These three were satisfactorily presented and we were able to visit other buildings. No more bottlenecks existed.

I had sent out to the four corners of the school word, as the Queen had first approached in her Rolls-Royce, that the wet-weather programme was the one that was operating. It was all fairly obvious, but it had been left to the very last moment lest the rain should stop, for we were desperately anxious to be outdoors and the Queen wanted to be seen by as many people as possible. Even so, the message did not reach some parts and boys, now dispersed, were still running fervently round tracks, high- and long-jumping, playing tennis and cricket in the torrents as we drove round the grounds.

I was intrigued to notice at one point, when the Queen had completed an around-the-room load of presentations and I had informed Jim Woodhouse that we were running five minutes late, that the Queen tapped her foot lightly on finding that Prince Philip, this time escorted by a master, was only half way round the room. I had to go over and hurry him up. He had an obvious penchant for trying to trip up officials. Showing him the Speech Room and explaining that it was used for film screenings, he said huskily and rather sharply that he did not see how it could possibly have that purpose. I told him that a screen was lowered from the roof over the stage and that there were, if he would kindly look, apertures in the rear for film projectors. He did not comment further. I think that he would have liked to have caught me out as his guide somewhere along the line: it would have relieved the tedium for him, although I must say that he looked nothing but keen throughout.

The unexpected, however diligent the rehearsal, must plainly occur in three and a half hours. It had happened with the gold key. It was to happen with the gold fountain pen I had purchased for the Queen to use for signing the visitors' book seated in full public view. The rain had at last stopped but somehow so had the ink flow. It simply would not work — to the simple pleasure of the Queen and Prince Philip. I had taken the precaution of buying two: the second performed its function. The Queen must have reflected that all that is gold does not glister.

When they had departed, we were all left with a strong sense of anticlimax. I had enjoyed the first-hand contact for so long a period but it seemed to have vanished in a third of the time, reminding me of Einstein's truism of relativity that talking to a pretty woman for an hour seems like a minute, while sitting on a hot stove for a minute seems like an hour.

Although the weather was so bad the colour pictures were

surprisingly good. I was asked to take them to Buckingham Palace for the Queen to see. Moore took them from me to her in the room next to his and returned to say that she liked them very much but did not want to add any to her collection, which I had supposed must be immense. (I later learned first-hand that she, unlike Prince Philip, collected nothing.) I had a delayed shock in seeing one taken at the open-air swimming bath alongside which she met some of the teaching staff. I had stood back in the fairly confined space and there is a picture showing my heels and the bottom of my gown virtually overhanging the bath to which I had my back. The slightest further movement backward and I would have been floundering as a non-swimmer in the shallow end of the bath, no doubt to the high enjoyment of the royal couple. That *would* have made their day.

All this over, there were now the final preparations for the July arrangements for some 3000 former members of the school, for the current pupils and their parents and for the staff. These involved some rehearsing and imposed a very heavy burden on top of my bursarial and other work. I had chosen to take everything on, but should have asked for a temporary administrative assistant.

Anyway, all had been gone through in advance many times on paper. It only remained for two zeppelin-sized marquees to be put up on The Close, one for the assembly (and later for meals) and the other for the ball. I had seen Sydney Lipton, whose orchestra I had often heard over the wireless at the Grosvenor House Hotel before the war, and liked him: he was engaged to make a personal appearance. He was, I think, Jewish, like so many of the prewar dance band leaders, and certainly from London's East End poverty. In his last years he acquired further fame, reflected this time when he went to live with Celia, his daughter and singer in his orchestra, who became the wealthiest English person in America when she married the inventor of milk cartons and was the regular hostess for royalty.

Beforehand, I had the advantage of being a guest of Ian Merry, the Bursar, at the Clifton College Centenary Ball. Ian, a former police commissioner in Ceylon, had succeeded me as Chairman of the Bursars' Association: I never saw his rubicund face less than anything soberly living up to his name in my many contacts. The

Governor of Fiji just before my time, Sir Arthur Richards (Lord Milverton), a Cliftonian, was broodingly interested in my Colonial Service past. At the ball I was fascinated by a West Indian steel band and resolved to add one at Rugby, where they played on The Close out of earshot of Sydney Lipton's orchestra but within conga-line contact. I also arranged for floodlighting of the school's best buildings, as well as of the carpeted path across The Close from the Queen's gateway and of The Island with its majestic trees. It was a great relief that catering was in the professional hands of David Physick, the Rugbeian head of Searcys. He had been an ADC to Richards in his governorship of Nigeria just as I was ADC to his successor as Governor of Fiji, Sir Harry Luke. The whole night scene was memorable.

But before then there was the morning assembly of about 3000. This time the weather was golden: hot enough to require the flaps of the marquees to be raised. I was asked to lead the Governing Body and Headmaster to our chairs and sit with them all in a row on the rail-less dais in front of the sea of faces. There was no more organizing to be done. If it had not been thought of by now, it was too late. So I relaxed on the end chair of the platform with governors ranged alongside. Lord Parker and Jim Woodhouse made felicitous speeches. When the end came, we all stood for the school song, with the school band playing just next to and below me. Suddenly, I felt myself wildly swaying (as Mountbatten did, and was seen by millions on television to do, while holding up the huge Sword of State at the opening of Parliament three years later). I thought for a moment that I was going to fall the two or three feet off the edge of the platform on to the front row of wives of governors, Governing Body officers and their wives, including Anne. I was sure that I must be seen to be swaying like a slow-gear metronome and that I would have to sit back on my chair. This was all too conspicuous and somehow I stayed — unsteadily, very close to collapse — while the seemingly endless verses in Latin of *Floreat Rugbeia* went on. My relief was enormous when the platform party, I now at the tail end of it, trooped off in reverse order and the audience dispersed. I now felt absolutely all right and enjoyed the lunch immediately following, as well as all the rest of the strenuous activities, including the ball of which I was in charge.

For six months I had a clerk to deal with tickets for the ball, which were £6.30 for a double. In 1937, when I had run the May Ball at Christ's, they were 37s. 6d. for a double. So, in 30 years the increase was modest. But this was to be an altogether larger affair. Sydney Lipton had no singer. Otherwise, I might have exposed myself to self-rebuke for breaking my own rule of no dancing with the singer; I had been irresistibly vulnerable to female 'vocalists' on more than one occasion, for which I can't easily account.

Afterwards, literally hundreds of congratulatory letters came addressed to me from grateful former members of the school and parents, and Anne, Stefanie and I were able to go off to Nice for utter relaxation.

But once, after dinner there, strolling down the grandly wide boulevard of the Quai des Etats-Unis towards the Promenade des Anglais, I felt again that disturbing swaying. Only once, but I had never had it before the experience on the platform, which I had put down to being a reaction to the very hard work and to the realization that the task was virtually over.

When we returned to Rugby from Nice I found a letter from the Lord Chancellor appointing me a justice of the peace for Warwickshire. I had been sounded out about it earlier in the year. This had not been the first time. Years before — not long after my appointment to Rugby where it was known that I had been a magistrate in Fiji for 14 years — I had been twice approached, the first time by a senior master who himself was a JP (one of only two in the school). He was a kindly person but I could not sum him up until I had introduced him to Charles, who later accorded him the unique and totally apt description of 'a vivacious bore'. I was told that the JPs would like me to join them if I were a Freemason. I declined and was rather appalled by my naïvety in not having thought before that this was how benches of magistrates were composed in this country. That was then. This has not been the case for the last quarter century or so. I had thought that you could be appointed if you belonged to the Conservative Party or perhaps the Liberals. Of course, now the pendulum has swung the other way, with trade unions and the Labour Party nominating at a furious pace, time of work lost having the carrot of being reimbursed officially.

A second attempt was made, this time by the chairman of the

bench who equally openly said that I would be welcomed if I were to become a Mason. I found the suggestion derisory. In any case, I had been long enough on the bench in Fiji on far more serious matters, including preliminary hearings for murders and man-slaughter sent on by me to the Chief Justice for sentencing. I was not attracted by my name appearing in the weekly local press as one of a panel of three, the other two Masons, judging the most petty crimes and vehicle offences.

In 1967 I was, however, approached by Sir Jack Scamp. This was different. He was a man I liked enormously. The epitome of friendliness, without any semblance of side, he was delightful to play tennis against, singularly difficult to get the ball past. John Gunther, Minister of Labour, had spotted this man, the son of a railway porter, as exactly the person he wanted as his trouble-shooter for strikes, of which there were a lot. Jack Scamp had been in industry all his life: he was sweet reasonableness and fairness itself. A tall, dignified, sleek, immaculately-dressed man, he asked me to keep him company on the bench which, he said, was changing in character.

He and one or two robust former Labour mayors (they had been put on the bench in their mayoral year of office — it was then the automatic practice — and had found the work so absorbing that they had both been encouraged, almost without precedent, to accept it on a continuing basis) wanted someone independent like me. I had the utmost respect for Alderman W. A. Robotham and Alderman W. A. Manning (both known as Bill, both William Arthur and both former Labour mayors) who symbolized com-mon sense, old fashioned courtesy and fundamental justice. No local Conservative could match them for polite, gentle firmness. So I said that I would be willing to have my name put forward if my chairman, Lord Parker, agreed.

The Lord Chief Justice unhesitatingly gave me the encourage-ment I needed: he considered I had just the right background and that it would bring credit to the school for its bursar to be a justice. I said that I would make up the loss of working school time by taking in Saturday afternoons in addition to the Saturday mornings I had worked in all my jobs. He did not think I should do that, but in fact I found it unavoidable to do so for keeping up to date. Incidentally, for the elucidation of American readers, where the office does not contain much *élan* and is of course far less historical, justices of the peace in England, who date back to the fourteenth century as officers of the Crown, do not conduct marriage ceremonies and are purely judicial officers. I had carried out marriage ceremonies in Fiji as a district commissioner: in that country justices of the peace were largely honorific, with no judicial powers other than to sign a few legal documents and witness signatures.

Charles approved and on 13 September 1967 wrote to me saying that 'It's splendid your becoming a JP. You must tell us about your experiences.' I think that Pam in particular, who was always on the lookout for bizarre and sensational material for her novels, was hoping for something less than pedestrian — or at least vehicular, which composed about 90 per cent of the cases. I cannot recall being able to tell them anything of moment, compared with my Fiji experiences on the bench.

At the swearing-in at Warwick Assizes before the county court judge, in reading the oath at an assembly of a few hundred friends or relatives of the 15 new justices for the county (Anne did not think it required her to attend; nor did I) I felt for the first time uncomfortable standing in front of a crowd, albeit a small one in the gallery and lower floor. It was nearly akin to the sensation I had felt on the quatercentenary dais, but this time I was able to grip a lectern. All the same I was disturbed, particularly as the discomfiture persisted when seated on the bench (knowing that once there I was there for three hours at a time — a kind of claustrophobia).

The feeling came on sharply one day afterwards when I was on my walk from the house to the bursary which was a few yards ahead across a road. I struggled, or rather dashed raggedly, across regardless of traffic, told my secretary that I did not feel well, and was driven the few yards back home. I feared that it was the beginning of some sort of attack but a doctor who was called did not think so. After many walks along empty roads (I now distrusted myself where people were about, believing that I might collapse and hence disgrace myself), I seemed to be only marginally improved.

A Time of Renewal

There were many consultations with my doctor who prescribed
Parstelin, a drug known to be dangerous if taken with meat
extracts, broad beans or cheese — a bizarre blacklist. I have since
heard that Chianti wine has to be avoided but that was not known
at the time, which was experimental for the drug. It did not
restore my confidence and on holidays in France and expeditions
into Italy Anne had to be my food taster to detect if any cheese,
now known to be lethal even in a sandwich, was present. My life
was for the first time becoming circumscribed. I had been the least
valetudinarian of people. A whole personal dimension was being
lamentably lost.

Librium replaced Parstelin with no effect, but Valium proved to
be just what I needed. I told my chairman that I had been off
colour since the quatercentenary, but hoped that it would wear off
with the reduction of the load. Lord Parker's velvet brown eyes
settled on mine — normally he was too shy to exchange much by
way of eye contact — before he said in a careful judicial manner:
'I am awfully sorry to say this, but I think that it could be with
you a long time. A mental ailment can be much more of a
nuisance than a physical one, which yours isn't.' This made me
wonder whether he had, or was under, some similar strain, as he
was known to keep himself much to himself. Eventually, a name
was put on it —agoraphobia. Not as one might think from the
Latin *ager*, field, but from the Greek *agora*, market place.

Agoraphobia is often erroneously described as a dislike of open
spaces. In fact I am at ease in fields and often on soft surfaces such
as beaches where I can sit down, if necessary, surreptitiously. What
is hardest of all to cope with is a wide stretch of hard material,
such as tarmac or slabs. And harder than that is being among
crowds. Precincts are for me anathema. I can handle assemblies or
parties, from which I do not have to drive of course, if I have in
advance a small sherry of the sweetest possible kind — for the
most rapid form of anaesthesia — with a Valium tablet. Not only
can I handle then the assemblies and enjoy them (without drinking
at all when once arrived at the function, which is ironical and a
waste of free liquor), but with that combination (and a driver) I
have been able to do things that were otherwise ruled out of my
life — with one or two exceptions, for example, meeting the

Queen again before a considerable formal assembly. The proximity of a chair is otherwise essential, together with the need to know that I can use it inconspicuously or under some valid pretext. If life began for me at 40, as in some ways it did afresh, it nearly ended for me, at least as I liked it, at just over 50.

I mention this ailment and how it affected me not out of self-pity, hypochondria or morbidity (although it is demeaning) but in case a candid, unashamed reference to it is of the slightest assistance to anyone attacked by a still largely unknown and certainly largely incomprehensible (to victim and bystander alike) nuisance. It can vary, however, so much in the form that it takes with individuals. I have now had to live 30 years with it but I am not complaining in the absence of physical troubles except the addition of arthritis, a pretty limiting partner with agoraphobia, since approaching 80. But I won't deny for a minute that I have regrets for the circumscribed effect that it has had on my activities for which I am blessed, however, with the drive in spirit and stamina that one can hope to continue to enjoy.

At the swearing in of the justices, Alderman (later Sir) Charles Smith-Ryland was present as High Sheriff. From the following year onwards I was to see something of him because he succeeded Lord Willoughby de Broke as Lord Lieutenant of Warwickshire. A commanding, handsome figure, he was a sensible and helpful contributor at the Governing Body meetings where he took his place ex officio. He helped me additionally in my capacity in charge of the agricultural estate of 350 acres belonging to the school and adjacent to it. I was very surprised that a man of such stature, recently knighted, should die in 1989 of a heart attack at merely 52: there seemed to be to me no one stronger-looking whom I had known.

Charles at this time produced what I sometimes think is his neatest work, *Variety of Men*. I only wish he had written more biographical — and of course autobiographical — material. He could have been persuaded to the former. Indeed, I always put the pressure on, with some success, as in *The Realists* and *The Physicists* and in a promise for a second series of *Variety of Men*. But he was obdurately against an autobiography: there was never a chance in that direction. Just as one could never steer him into a monologue. He could endure one but not out of choice. Conversation was for him inexorably a matter of interchange of words. Dialogue was his forte. He followed *Variety of Men* with a much less pleasing book, *The Sleep of Reason*. I did not enjoy it. He claimed that the account of the death of our father was the 'best single piece of writing I have done'. Because that is markedly good it is generally assumed that he was present, but, as already explained, he was in America at the time and obtained the facts via Eric and me.

In a 1968 BBC talk produced by Kay Fuller (also producer of my *Calling the Islands* broadcasts in the 1950s), Charles again proudly proclaimed that one grandfather had been 'an artisan, a skilled workman, the other a gamekeeper on Lord Burghley's estate, which brought a trace of vicarious grandeur'. He was never slow to refer to this dichotomous ancestry, the Industrial Revolution contrasting with the rural scene. For 'gamekeeper' strict accuracy requires that this should have been 'house painter'. By 'Lord Burghley', he really meant the Marquess of Exeter, the owner of Burghley House, Stamford. Lord Burghley is the title of the heir. In the same programme, one participant, Maurice Cranston, a philosopher, said 'he [C. P. Snow] gives me the impression sometimes of being perhaps a retired Colonial Governor ... somebody who had once been responsible in a rather paternal way for some Colony or some society of people.'

At this time, and indeed almost continuously every year, sometimes twice a year, Charles was in North America, both the USA and Canada, accumulating honorary degrees. The process, begun in 1960, was to continue to 1979. Their fascination for him cannot be understood if it is not accepted that he hoped to set a record in the number collected and variety of places in which he had been given them, 30 in all and one posthumously. His Russian one was unique, indeed contrived. English universities were pointedly parsimonious: he made no attempt to court them but, for that matter, neither had he solicited American institutions, whose variety, Catholic and Jewish, not least, gave him such surprise and pleasure.

Pam, while concerned greatly with the pros and cons of moving from Cromwell Road to Eaton Terrace, expressed herself strongly on mutually repulsive ground by saying in a letter to me of 6 August 1968 that 'We had a p.c. from Stephanie who rightly takes a poor view of bull fighting. Disgusting display.' Pam and he eventually moved to 85 Eaton Terrace, a house with a fine drawing room and long windows looking out west and east but vertically uncomfortable in contrast to the one-level flat at 199 Cromwell Road, which had become intolerably busy, whereas Eaton Terrace has a quiet, dignified, leisurely Georgian ambience.

At the dinner in Fishmongers' Hall for the 1968 Australian cricket team, Charles and I sat opposite in this grandiose setting a glum, almost sullen looking I. M. Chappell, who was on his first tour. To try and bring him out I said that I had seen his grandfather, Victor York Richardson, play. I always understood, perhaps wrongly, that Richardson was one of the more gentlemanly Australians to have toured England. But I. M. Chappell could scarcely have been ruder. He spoke to no one. Subsequent sights of him on television confirmed my opinion. Latest reports are that he has mellowed, as do many men of substance. Certainly he had been a most undislodgeable batsman. In any list of those put in to bat for their lives, if that were necessary, one might perhaps have to consider him. As it was, we wrote him off that festive evening.

What delighted Charles was to have a long talk at the dinner with Herbert Sutcliffe, the Yorkshire and England professional who had given a speech in a most polished voice and still looked like Tyrone Power. He, Charles, Brian Close (Yorkshire and England) and I sat afterwards in a corner talking for an hour. Close's accent could not have been broader. Charles asked Sutcliffe how he had lost his accent. The answer was that he (Sutcliffe) thought that it had disappeared gradually as his tours abroad and mixing with amateurs increased. Herbert could have been the 7th Lord Hawke himself. One waited in vain for the slightest lapse. After all, he had, as an orphan, left school at 13 to learn how to fasten boot uppers to soles. On retirement from his playing life as a professional, he became a businessman, living in a mansion run by servants. The rubbing off of dialect in Sutcliffe's (and Compton's) case was applicable to Astill of Leicestershire and England, who had a similar social development — so much so that he was scarcely taken for a professional in the last half of his career, though professional he was (and the first ever to captain a county for a season).

When Stefanie turned 21 this year, Charles gave a grand party in the Lords. Charles had written a year earlier, on 6 June 1967: 'I am duly booking the Cholmondeley Room for the party on June 11th 1968. I should like to stand Stephanie this party as my birthday present. Is that all right?'

The Cholmondeley Room was made available by courtesy of the Lord Great Chamberlain, the 5th Marquess of Cholmondeley (whose office has to be differentiated from that of the Lord Chamberlain, a royal courtier). It has a terrace overlooking the Thames. Charles and Stefanie were photographed on this, the imposing lanterns of the Houses of Parliament forming an artistic background. The occasion glistened, as did some of Charles's guests. Lords Chalfont and Shackleton were wearing decorations for a dinner on to which they were going. It was a mixture of Charles's friends and Stefanie's, including some relatives. Stefanie followed his speech with the auspicious opening: 'Never in my wildest dreams did I think that I would make a speech in the House of Lords.' It was a charming performance. Afterwards the family went to the Dorchester Hotel where I gave a dinner.

Stefanie, thanking Charles on 12 June, wrote: 'I shall always remember last night for Lord Chalfont and his medals to the little drake on the parapet which was one of the most charming gate-crashers I have ever met.'

Soon there was to be a curious letter from Charles from 85 Eaton Terrace, marked 'confidential' and dated 6 January 1969:

I have had to conceal from Anne [Seagrim] that the move here [to Eaton Terrace] is a *fait accompli* — though now I have broken it to her that it will probably happen during the Spring. Obviously it is a blow to her since she feels we shall be more cut off. I shall try to find an office — when we are thrown out of EE [English Electric] House — where I can do a little nominal work: that would solve the major difficulties. The point of this letter is, if I should be *incommunicado* up till March and she gets in touch with you I am still to be regarded as in the flat [Cromwell Road]. With good luck this won't arise but you ought to be warned. She has been more than good to me, and I want to spare her what little I can manage to spare her from.

On 25 February 1969, I wrote to Charles on a different tack:

Miss Haddy [his English Electric Company secretary] has also given me the latest American press cuttings — the great majority of them, which is about as much as one can expect, are excellent. They lead one to wonder what will follow *Last Things*. I believe you said you were going to write something entirely without restriction or connection with anything else, as an utterly free agent. Your American public would seem to like a combination of three things in one — pure autobiography to cover the past, comments and advice on the present, predictions and advice for the future. I don't know of anyone who has put this design in one volume. The first part would be fascinating by way of true running comparison with the fiction of *Strangers and Brothers* and could include extensions of *Variety of Men* that we could all do with more of: the second and third parts the world ought to have from you. I think you said that when the series was finished you would set out to enjoy to the utmost the next one. Perhaps something on the above lines is what you have in mind. I am sure it would give wide pleasure.

During the 1960s Charles came to know a Northern Irishman, Donald Harold Wauchope Dickson. This was to have significance, for Donald Dickson was subsequently to devote his retirement to writing a biography of Charles after the essential six months' perusal of all the papers in the archives of Texas University where he became the first C. P. Snow Fellow. Dickson was regarded by Charles as one of his 'new men', like himself a scientist by training but equally interested in the arts. As Principal of the North Antrim Further Education Area, he invited Charles to open the area's new headquarters at Ballymoney in County Antrim.

On retirement from the post in 1985, Donald Dickson wrote

perceptive essays on Charles and there germinated in his mind
Science and C. P. Snow: First Things and Some Others and *C. P.
Snow and Pamela Hansford Johnson: A Literary Partnership*. He
expected the biography to take about a decade. It is now nearing
completion. A comprehensive work can be anticipated, having, as
he does, first-hand knowledge of both Charles and Pam, as well as
complete familiarity with their works and the immense archive at
Austin, Texas, occupying 50 yards of shelf space. He has been
given by me exhaustive assistance in his task.

Charles was taking on something new. He wrote to me on 15
July 1969 that 'When the Post Office Corporation is set up in
October I am to be chairman of a kind of forward thinking group.
This will provide me with an office and various amenities and
might be mildly interesting. It will also give me a good excuse to
move to the cross-benches, as you can see.' The 1st Viscount Hall
was in overall charge and history will not endow the idea with
much record of achievement. It suited Charles from the physical
side until he moved to the cramped basement conditions of 36
Craven Street, Benjamin Franklin's home and part of the
American pilgrimage in London.

His move of offices first from English Electric and then to these
two addresses did not fortunately result in any loss of his archives.
For all his stoicism and rationale, Charles was superstitious,
privately admitting it only to Anne Seagrim (who told me) and in
a letter to his long-standing friend, Alan Maclean of Macmillans. I
personally never saw any evidence of it (this was the 'stranger' side
of the 'brother') and only reluctantly acknowledge having any
form of it myself, so well concealed that no one would know of it
(like the agoraphobia). It partly accounted for his distaste for
telegrams, which he expected more to convey bad than good news.
He had no great liking for the telephone either.

But I did not conceal the agoraphobia for long from Charles, to
whom I wrote on 21 July 1969:

> I have been pretty much off colour for the last few weeks
> but after a complete check over by a consultant it appears
> that I am physically absolutely all right but mentally suffer-
> ing from complete exhaustion due to a recurrence of the

pressures of extra work which I had two years ago and still shows more sign of growing.

Charles replied on 22 July, 'So sorry that you are not well. If I were you I should be very careful about the kind of drugs they give you. One is usually better at looking after oneself.' Immediately I replied, on 24 July, 'It's the penalty of living twenty-four hours, seven days a week, geographically on the job and not being able to move freely outside the gate.' Quickly, on 4 August, he wrote to me at the Shanklin Hotel, Isle of Wight:

> Your affliction is obviously very tiresome. Librium is a very mild drug and nothing to be concerned about. I thought they were medicating you much more heavily. On the other hand, if you are still feeling agoraphobic I fancy you ought to consider consulting a psychiatrist. I have almost no faith in psychiatrists for important things but they tend to be used for these more or less mechanical ailments. They are not uncommon in people doing official jobs.

To a young American correspondent he made a judgement I found surprising:

> I congratulate you on your originality. No one has ever thought of comparing me with Kipling before and I doubt if anyone will ever do so again. I only wish I was half as good a writer. I dislike a great many of his attitudes but I have no doubt that he was a writer of real genius — one of the very few in the English language of the last two generations.

In our dining room at Horton House, Anne and I had a dinner for ten in honour of Ratu Sir Kamisese Mara, who was breaking his journey on his way down from Holyroodhouse where he had been knighted that day. He was Chief Minister on the verge of being called Prime Minister as Fiji's independence materialized. He and Jack Scamp, a fellow guest, got on famously. Kamisese told me later that Jack was just the sort of man he wanted for sorting out a number of problems in Fiji. Kamisese stayed up with me over cigars and a bottle of whisky until 4.00 a.m. Naturally introverted, he literally poured himself out to me as I poured out the whisky. We discussed, among so many subjects, what form the Fiji government might take in its independence. I asked if it would be a republic (and said I hoped not), if it would be a kingdom like Tonga, or a dominion like New Zealand. He ruled out the first, poised over the second idea and did not dismiss it, but thought that the most likely outcome would be a self-governing dominion. That is what it did become, although, as in the case of New Zealand, 'self-governing' and 'dominion' seemed to be contradictory, self-cancelling terms.

We had, we thought, two domestic problems. The day of the visit was Friday and Kamisese was a Catholic, but I checked and found that we could have a fish course so beloved by Fijians. The second was how his 6 foot 7 inch length could be coped with on our beds, or any beds from anywhere in the school for that matter. He disposed of this by disclosing that he invariably slept coiled up.

Next day I took him to see Warwickshire versus the West Indies at Edgbaston, where my old friend from Sir Julien Cahn's visit to Fiji in 1939, Cyril Goodway (he died in 1991) was a very attentive and charming chairman. What we lost in cricket — rain prevented any — was gained in more discussion. Kamisese was pleased to meet the West Indians, in some cases re-meeting them. He had captained a Suva team (not even the representative Fiji team) that had played the West Indies (including Sobers, Ramadhin and Valentine) when they had passed through on their way to New Zealand in 1956. Suva had batted first, scoring only 91: the West Indies were 30 for 0. Kamisese had been one of the opening bowlers. He told me: 'With a blinding flash of insight I took myself off.' The next bowler went right through the West Indians who were dismissed for 63, an astonishing result.

I was delighted when an old Indian friend from my Naduruloulou days, Gajadhar Singh, let me know that he was in England. He had been the court clerk who had helped me with my Hindi while I taught his son Latin and whose family had constantly ganged up against me at ludo. It had given them vicarious pleasure to have invited the only European ever to visit their house and then to have beaten him. He was now 70 and had had four serious heart attacks but made his way to Rugby to stay with us. He was in his usual form, interested in everything, not least in matters European. He had never been to England before and we had a vigorous interchange of views. I had not seen him since he had been the sub-accountant on Taveuni 21 years earlier. A stimulating friend, he lived in New Zealand for a few more years after his visit to Rugby. His son, Harry, writing from New Zealand to tell me of his death, said that I was 'the best European he had known'. It was one of the highest compliments that I have received. We were always Mr to each other. I would occasionally address him, by way of extra respect, without the 'Mr' but as Gajadhar (pronounced Guj-ah-dha, with emphasis on the middle syllable) Singhji, like K. S. Ranjitsinghji and K. S. Duleepsinghji (whose names were properly Kumar Shri — meaning Prince — Ranjit Singh and Dulip Singh). The suffix 'ji' means worshipful.

There had been some changes in the Governing Body with which I had to work so closely. They brought a crosscurrent of knowledge and experience. The eminently wise and intelligent Sir Robert Birley, who had been so liberal a headmaster of Eton that he was known there as Red Robert for some minor reform he initiated, had joined with Brian (later Sir) Young (son of the Governor who surrendered Hong Kong to the Japanese) who went, like fforde, from headmastering to television administration.

In 1953 Birley, in an address to the British Association for the Advancement of Science entitled 'Greek or Chemistry or Both', had anticipated the theme of 'the two cultures', for which Charles was later to be the prime expositor and user of that title. 'I believe that we must face the existence of this dichotomy in our culture', Birley had said. Charles was to develop this famously but Birley's address may have been forgotten. Charles and he were simpatico, not least over resistance to apartheid. Birley was a formidable opponent of the South African government on the spot and Charles was about to have joined him in a gesture of solidarity when other arrangements got in the way.

Sir Derek Hilton, a solicitor, joined the Governing Body in 1967 as the Lord Chancellor's representative, succeeding Bibby and contributing soundness and considerateness, which elevated him to the deputy chairmanship in quick time. Birley and Hilton both strengthened the standing of the school to which they gave much of their time. The former was the Oxford University representative: both had been boys at the school.

To my great regret, Lord Parker decided to retire as Chairman of the Governing Body. He had been courtesy, consideration and competence itself: I could not have had a more comfortable person under whom to work for the past seven years. He was succeeded by Sir Edmund Compton, who was a governor only for eight years. Diminutive, with blue eyes that darted about, he represented quite a change.

I had been present, before a meeting of the Rugby School War Memorial trustees (of which I was secretary as well as a trustee), when two other trustees, Parker and Compton, were the only other people in the room. This was in 1967 when Compton had just become Parliamentary Commissioner for Administration, the first holder of the post universally known as ombudsman. Lord Parker had said to Compton: 'I can't congratulate you as I believe that your functions will overlap those of the courts which naturally worries me.' I do not know whether Lord Parker's fears came to be justified. At times it seemed that they might, but the post of ombudsman has scarcely featured prominently. Edmund Compton served as Chairman only briefly until 1971, when he resigned to take up the appointment as chairman of the Local Government Boundaries Commission for seven years. Some of the decisions taken on that commission's recommendations have subsequently been reversed, notably the elimination of Rutland and artificial, unhistoric creations like Avon. There are no claims that the commission showed wisdom and imagination in the face of the strongest local, and a good deal of national, opposition.

My *Bibliography of Fiji, Tonga and Rotuma* now came out — after terrific struggles with proofs and the impediment of distance between myself and Canberra, where the Australian National University Press took a lot on themselves without any reference to me. Their errors still lie awaiting correction in the second volume that has been prepared unremittingly by me since 1969 — or rather 1966, when the entries necessarily closed for printing so highly detailed and intricate a volume. Started in 1937, it contained over 10,000 entries ranging from the obvious such as

history, languages, anthropology, entomology to more esoteric
entries for herpetology, vulcanology, ichthyology and malacology.

The *Bibliography* received excellent worldwide reviews, estab-
lishing me in other scholars' eyes as one of them. The most
remarkable accolade was that of Père Patrick Georges Farell
O'Reilly who had published masterly bibliographies in his native
French language of the New Hebrides, New Caledonia, Tahiti and
French Oceania. The world's expert on regional bibliographies
was most lavish in his praise of my work. To have the leading
authority's seal of utter approval was the principal reward of my
30 years' work on it with many vicissitudes (in the early stages
including being burnt, lost in the flooding of the Rewa River and
insect depredations). I was always regretful that I never met
O'Reilly, missing him narrowly in La Musée de l'Homme. In the
war he had heroically helped the Resistance, escaping by a
hairbreadth the penalty for doing so. Immensely modest, Père
O'Reilly was one of the world's many unrecognized top persons in
an important top field, although the whole of both a French
Polynesian and New Caledonian stamp imaginatively bear a
portrait of him issued after his death, inscribed '1900–1980'.

Scholars using my *Bibliography* round the globe have written to
say how warmly appreciative they are for the short cuts that it
provided in their research. That, together with the adulatory
review in the anonymous and circumspect *Times Literary
Supplement*, made it worth while. I had made nothing out of it
financially. Indeed, the reverse. It cost me thousands of pounds,
since its start 20 years earlier, in travelling to libraries in the world,
correspondence, transcription, airmailing 10,000 entries and
proofs for them across the world (only Anne's mammoth typing
was free). There were no royalties anyway. It went out of print at
the Australian National University Press and Miami University
Press, which published simultaneous editions, before they closed
down. Neither university had anything left over after covering
their publication expenses for so intricate a printing job as a
bibliography containing numerous languages. But the work gave
me a niche in the academic world. Clamour grows for the second
volume, despite abbreviated versions having been printed for *Fiji*
by G. E. Gorman and J. J. Mills (1994), who acknowledged mine

to be the most comprehensive work by far, and directed by me for Tonga to Martin Daly, both in the World Bibliographical Series.

Separate visitors to us were father and son of real standing in our affections. Ratu Sir Edward Cakobau, whose wit, urbanity, courtliness and generosity of spirit were legendary, stayed with us in the month of Kamisese Mara's visit before becoming the first Deputy Prime Minister on independence. When I met him at the station, an elderly woman ahead of us put down her case for a rest at the end of Rugby's seemingly endless platform (one of the longest in the country). Without a word to her, the bronzed Edward, under a large velvet trilby, picked it up and carried it down the subway to the road outside where he deposited it at the taxi rank. She could not make out who he was or what he was doing so imperiously. No one looked less like a porter. At first I think she was concerned that he was making off with it. She was disconcerted that anyone, apart from his having a different coloured skin, could be so gratuitously helpful. Ted did not pause to be thanked. He was all things to all people. A prince among princes (as the son of King George II of Tonga, he was virtually one) and an ordinary man among ordinary men and women.

He told us that his son, Ratu Epeli Nailatikau, by his wife Adi Vasemaca, was at Oxford with his cousin Tupouto'a, the Crown Prince of Tonga. So we invited him to stay with us in Rugby. We had not met him before. He had many of his father's mannerisms, not least signing himself in our visitors' book as 'Soldier, Fiji Military Forces'. He was then a lieutenant and was to become the first Fijian to reach the rank of brigadier. It will be described later why Ratu Epeli went on to become Fiji's first ambassador in England.

An unexpected visitor to Horton House, Rugby in 1970 was Sir John Betjeman. He had come with a BBC television producer, not to see our house, though it was to his liking, but to judge whether Rugby or Keble College, Oxford, would be the better setting for a programme on the architect, William Butterfield, shared by each institution. There were only the four of us to lunch: it was in the middle of the holidays with virtually everyone away. Betjeman was in magnificent form, chuckling hugely and entertaining his small audience with his hilarious account of what his disapproving future father-in-law, Field Marshal Sir Philip (later Lord) Chetwode, Commander-in-Chief, Indian Army, said to the impoverished journalist Betjeman, whose countenance was governed by tusk-like protruding teeth and whose name Chetwode could only remember or think suitable, since he believed him to be Dutch, to render as Bargeman:

> Now that I have given consent to the marriage to my daughter, Bargeman, how are you to address me? It can't be Sir Philip. That is too familiar. It can't be Commander-in-Chief. If you were in the army that would be correct. But as you are not in the army, it can of course only be, and should be, Field Marshal. You will call me that.

Betjeman was a difficult man to drive about. If he saw anything architecturally intriguing to him, he would say to me, 'Look at that. It is a most unusual feature. We must examine it.' I had to point out that we were in a one-way street with a constant flow of traffic and no waiting. All that I could do was to drive around the block and approach the feature again as slowly as I could. This did not assuage his thirst. We had to go round the block four times. Even then he felt deprived. In the event, Keble was chosen in preference to Rugby. He would like to have done both. As it was, he was a most stimulating unorthodox companion for a day that passed all too quickly.

6

Some Profiles in Half a Decade

The year 1970 was memorable in a few respects. For Fiji it meant independence, which the Fijians did not want but were compelled by the United Nations to accept (although, as regards Pacific territories, the UN has not forced France similarly in French Oceania, Chile in Easter Island or the USA in American Samoa). Deep down, Fijians felt that there might be trouble with the Indian majority of population (which was then the case: that majority exists no longer) and were conscious that the British administration had held the balance judiciously. But, of course, Fijians realized that they would have extra power, at least in name. At that stage there were about 320,000 Fijians compared with 350,000 Indians, 4000 each of Europeans and Chinese, and 10,000 part-Europeans. The eight Rotuma islands, population 8000, remained a dependency of Fiji. Queen Elizabeth was still Queen of Fiji. The new flag of the Dominion (which colonial status had glided into) in place of the Union Flag contained the historic coat of arms and a small Union Flag in the corner, more like the flag that government vessels such as the *Adi Maopa* flew, except that it was light and not dark blue. It was rather a token change.

Just before independence became a reality, the leading Fijians and the Indian leader of the opposition came to England. Charles said that he would like to meet those names of whom he had heard so much. If there were more than three guests for a House of Lords' meal, a peer has to have another to support him. Lord Clifford of Chudleigh, a millionaire hereditary baron, was invited by Charles to join him, Ratu Sir Kamisese Mara, Ratu Sir Edward

<small>ABOVE.</small> Stefanie, author and wife listen to a speech by Charles in the Cholmondeley Room at the House of Lords on Stefanie's 21st birthday, 1968. *(Photo: Desmond O'Neill)* <small>BELOW.</small> Ratu Sir Penaia Ganilau, Adi Lady Laisa, author and wife at Rugby, 1970. *(Photo: Rugby Advertiser)*

ABOVE. Ratu Sir George Cakobau, Adi Lady Lealea, author and wife at Angmering, 1980. *(Photo: author)* BELOW. Sir Colin Cowdrey introducing author and wife to John Major at 10 Downing Street, 1991. *(Photo: the Prime Minister's Office)*

Cakobau, Ratu Sir George Cakobau, Siddiq M. Koya (leader of the opposition) and myself for lunch.

Kamisese told Charles and Lord Clifford that he and the others would like to 'have the opportunity to case the joint, as it were', explaining that Fiji was about to have for the first time two houses, one a senate, the other of representatives. The lunch was most cordial and the party from Fiji appreciative of the scarlet carpets, gilt ornamental ironwork and the trappings of the House of Lords that so greatly impress visitors.

With his complete command of the English language idiom, Kamisese's mannerisms sometimes appeared as much European as Pacific Islander. He seemed inclined to be introverted when so many from the South Sea Islands were the opposite. Uniquely among Fijians, he has published an autobiography. Charles observed shrewdly the close affinity between Kamisese and Edward. My favourite sentence of any speech by Edward was 'I wear my kilt like a *sulu* principally because my ancestors ate shipwrecked Scottish sailors, thereby making me half Scottish by absorption.' How often did I hear this sure-fire rib-tickler?

The contrast between Edward and George intrigued Charles. Although cousins, Edward being descended illegitimately from an elder son of King Cakobau and George legitimately from the youngest son, there was no resemblance facially or in character. Edward's Polynesian light bronze from his father, King George II of Tonga, who reigned from 1893 to 1918, stood out in relief from George's darker bronze, which was unalloyed Fijian and Melanesian. George was not exactly ill at ease but seemed so by the side of Edward and even Kamisese.

Koya seemed just typically Indian to Charles: nine years later he was to defeat Mara in the first elections, but astoundingly had neither predicted such a result (when Indians outnumbered Fijians) nor lined up a government. In the paradoxical impasse of Koya failing to get a team of ministers together, the Governor-General, Ratu George, called on Ratu Mara to be Prime Minister again, thus saving Mara's political future although there seemed to be little empathy between George and Kamisese (and no family inter-marriage which there was between the descendants of the other paramount leaders, Edward, Kamisese and Penaia). Kamisese wrote

A *Time of Renewal*

to Charles from Marlborough House, London on 30 April 1970:

I am writing to thank you very much indeed for the very pleasant lunch party you arranged for my colleagues and myself at the House of Lords today. We all enjoyed meeting you and hearing from you of the warm feelings expressed in your House towards Fiji. It was a real occasion for us to lunch in the House of Lords provided it does not give us too expensive ideas for our own Upper House.

With warm regards and sincere thanks from myself and all my colleagues,

Yours sincerely,
K. K. T. Mara

Charles himself wrote to me on 5 May to say 'Here is a copy of Mara's letter. I thought the lunch went off extremely well.'

Edward's first job, in addition to being Deputy Prime Minister, was Minister of Labour and Immigration. Stefanie, with a Fiji birth qualification, applied for dual nationality. Edward regretted having to say that Fiji's new laws could give no option: so she has kept her United Kingdom qualification through her parents.

Charles had now met all the leading Fijian chiefs except for the late Ratu Sir Lala Sukuna, the greatest of all, and Ratu Sir Penaia Ganilau, who was to have the most worldwide publicity of any of them. I was to see Penaia twice in quick succession shortly after. Though he had been appointed manager of the Fiji rugby team's tour of England, which would straddle the independence celebrations, he was also in charge of those celebrations in Fiji, something of a geographical anomaly. Peni had come the 22 miles from Leicester to Rugby by taxi, returning the same way, while the team was touring. He then returned to Fiji for Independence Day, 96 years after the cession of Fiji to Britain, and then came again to Rugby, this time with his second wife Adi Lady Laisa, as expansive as Penaia, who had brought for Anne and me a *tapa* sachet reserved for VIPs and containing arrangement details about the celebrations, an honour and kind thought much appreciated. They had again come by taxi from Leicester, returning there for dinner in the same manner.

Some Profiles in Half a Decade

Peni was as broad in his gestures as in his build. Tongan-sized and, as he grew older, Tongan-looking, he was physically the largest of Fiji's pre-eminent leaders (Sukuna, Edward, George and Mara), all with chief-like body structures. Like a gentle bear, he was a tactile, extroverted, gregarious person. Laisa died relatively early and when he remarried, this time to Adi Lady Davila, the widow of Ravuama Vunivalu, she too died. His fourth wife, Adi Lady Bale, Jonati Mavoa's widow, survives him. His second visit was a few days after the Fijian rugby players came to The Close at Rugby to see where the game had started. I gave the party of 30 lunch based on as close to Fijian items of food as possible after they had seen the wall plaque, saying: 'This stone commemorates the exploit of William Webb Ellis who with a fine disregard for the rules of football as played in his time first took the ball in his arms and ran with it, thus originating the distinctive feature of the rugby game AD 1823.'

It was Ellis's sole claim to notoriety: he went into the church and is buried on the bluff at Menton overlooking the Franco–Italian border. Rugby is a game about which I have never been enthusiastic, for I do not look with favour on any sort of physical grappling between men. In particular, I never thought it suitable for Fijians, in whom it can bring out latent aggression against whomever they are 'playing'. At the lunch I gave a speech in Fijian from a seated position and before the meal, in the manner of the country. I found it easier than a corresponding speech in English. The manager was part-European, with no command of the language of his 30 team members: he replied in English standing up. It was all a little bizarre in its setting but at least the Fijians were not bored by yet another welcoming speech in English, which is the fate of many touring parties.

Later, the party adjourned to our house for beer, the 30 or so squatting on the floor in Fijian fashion and a hefty forward, to my apprehension, on top of our large television. Whether the one testing his weight was Sitiveni (Stephen) Ligamamada (Light Hand) from Drekeniwai, Cakaudrove, at the bottom end of Natewa Bay, as recorded with all the others' names in our visitors' book, I do not know. After the return of the team to Fiji, he changed his name to Sitiveni Rabuka. It was he who, as a lieutenant-colonel 17 years later, deposed his brigadier, Ratu Epeli Nailatikau, in an act of mutiny, which will be alluded to when we reach that year as it had notably the largest impact known in Fiji events.

With independence impending, I was invited to a reception at Marlborough House, with Lord Shepherd, Minister of State for Foreign and Commonwealth Affairs, presiding for the delegates attending the final talks on the constitution for Fiji. Then, with independence all worked out, it was confirmed that Fiji was to become a dominion, the first of that status since New Zealand in 1907; to me, this was a contradiction in terms. How can one be independent and yet be dominated? There was to be a celebration at Marlborough House. Anne wrote to Pam on 1 October 1970:

> Charles spoke to Philip on the telephone about arrangements for Saturday, October 10th [at Marlborough House]. Whether Philip can make it with us is uncertain. From before the time of your visit to Rugby he has not walked anywhere where people are nor gone to any stand-up gathering: he has driven every day the few yards to the office and back. To keep as fit as possible in these difficult circumstances we have driven each evening to a country lane and walked along that for nearly an hour. But this has been no test of course for him as there has been no one about. He is all right sitting in his office and in fact sitting anywhere else (though not probably in a theatre or that kind of place) and meeting people sitting down and doing anything in the house. It is a great problem his getting from A to B, even a few yards, with people about, or standing talking to them for more than a minute or so, due no doubt to our having lived so long over the shop, as it were, where we can't escape for 24 hours of each day. ... It really is irksome. He is desperately trying to aim for Marlborough House.

Pam replied, on 2 October 1970: 'I do hope Philip can make it. I am dreadfully sorry to hear that he isn't yet making much progress and that life is such a strain to him. It is much that he can get to his office.'

As it was, with Anne's psychological support in the purely psychological dilemma, we were all at the function attended by ex-Fiji governors, officers and clerks alike; I greatly enjoyed it once the champagne had circulated. Charles was entertainingly diverted by a former governor in my time in Fiji, Sir Alexander Grantham, cornering me to ask in his strident voice the name of the governor who had succeeded him. I was taken aback as much by his not remembering his name as by his harsh judgement of him and looked over my shoulder in the fervent hope that his widow, a friend of mine with whom I had just been talking, was out of range. The host was the High Commissioner, Josua Rabukawaqa, an ex-teacher, lay preacher and one of the earliest Fijian district officers. A commoner from Bau, he had played cricket for me in Rewa more than a quarter of a century before.

Invitations came to me thick and fast. One was to a lunch of a dozen people at Marlborough House in Josua's honour given by Anthony Royle, MP (later Lord Fanshawe, elegant and suave), Permanent Under-Secretary for Foreign and Commonwealth Affairs. Jo gave a cultured, apposite reply to the toast to Fiji written for him by his adroit counsellor, Kenneth Bain, a New Zealander and former Fiji administrative officer, whose part-Tongᵤ, son at Rugby reminded one of a Tom Brown, running away from the school on his first day towards the railway station only to be brought back and end up years later at the very apex as head boy of impressive presence. In exact yet easy English, Jo's speech had been delivered with great dignity in his morning dress and pin-striped *sulu*. With his public face as his striking asset one could not imagine a more prepossessing looking diplomat. He was ultimately knighted.

The year 1970 also brought Tonga's independence, although it had been effectively autonomous for a century since King George I's time. Again at Marlborough House (I seemed to be continuously there in my leisure moments during that year) there was a function to celebrate, which continued at the temporary house at Kilburn of the prepossessing, noble first Tongan High Commissioner, Va'ea, now Prime Minister of Tonga. He soon moved to more commodious quarters where Anne and I were invited to meet again King Taufa'hau Tupou IV of Tonga and Queen Mata'aho when the King's uncle, Ted Cakobau, was also present.

A Time of Renewal

In the summer of 1970, this crowded year, there had been a cricket function of note. Leicestershire (or rather my brother Eric as curator, honorary secretary and archivist) arranged for contemporaries of George Geary, the England all-rounder, to be present when a painting of him (given by Eric) and also of his late colleague, Ewart Astill, were unveiled for the pavilion in Leicester. Charles and Pam were there with Anne and myself. I derived special warmth from being part of George's day. A group photograph of all those who had played with Geary was taken but I missed it. I had known him since the end of the 1930s (he gave me a little coaching and was captain when I took the field as twelfth man versus Somerset in 1938) and obtained for him his final post as coach at Rugby School. He was in splendid form. A stand on the ground was subsequently named after him but none has been given Astill's name, a typical historical failure to commemorate a local player of England calibre. Equally unimaginative was the county club's belatedness in making Geary the first professional to be a vice-president. It took a disproportionate measure of pressure by Eric and me (from no official position) to achieve that for him, and by me for Eric himself. As I tried to tell in my obituary of George in *The Times* of 9 March 1981, he was a man and a half:

Mr George Geary, the Leicestershire cricketer and a leading all-rounder for England, has died. He was 87. Eldest of 16 children of a bootmaker, he was born in Barwell, 15 miles from Leicester, to which he would cycle daily, roll the ground and bowl all day, returning by cycle to roll the Barwell ground before dark. He played first for Leicestershire in 1912. Ewart Astill, a name forever associated with his, and he were two of the four survivors (the other two A. L. Hosie and F. E. Woolley) from the pre-First World War era in the country still playing in 1938 when Geary retired. His talent for detecting ability with his sharp brown eyes and his flair for coaching were unsurpassed. He was at Charterhouse 1939–58 (P. B. H. May, currently President of MCC and Chairman of ICC, was one of his products) and at age 67 went to Rugby where he stayed until he was 76.

Always bowling in a cap, his best performance in an

innings was 10 for 18 in 1929 against Glamorgan (16 for 96 in the match), the most remarkable figures before Verity's 10 for 10.

As he aged, his batting improved: he scored three centuries out of his career total of seven in his last season. Geary was one of the best slips in the world. ... In the final Ashes-winning Test in sweltering heat at Melbourne in 1929 Geary created a record for endurance in Test cricket in Australia with 81 overs in an innings.

He was made an Honorary Life Member of MCC. All his distinguished performances and dedication apart, the most lasting impressions for the humble Barwell villager were tiger hunting, eating off gold plate and residing in suites in Maharajahs' palaces.

It was pleasurable to meet on this occasion again Eddie Dawson (he had come to my house in Rugby about a dozen years previously, as mentioned earlier), another of my schoolboy heroes. To be a hero one did not have to be of international class, although this Cambridge and Leicestershire captain who played for England was that, but primarily fine looking and gentle mannered. Aubrey Sharp unveiled the portraits. He was often at the ground. Breezily provocative, effervescent and original, he was pure entertainment for the connoisseur of personalities and techniques.

I had forgiven the fact that when he was on the Leicestershire committee before my going out to Fiji he had obtained a place in a match in the county side for his son, whose record did not approach mine, when it must have been a question of him or me for the opportunity. General Sir John Sharp, a contemporary of mine at Cambridge and considered by his father a rival to me for a place in the Leicestershire team, died at 60 when Commander-in-Chief of the Allied Forces in Europe. His had been a recessive, retiring character for one of his calling and rank. There was a story — which I never believed — that he had been fatally poisoned by Russians when near the frontier in Scandinavia.

John (I knew him as Jack) had been a frail colleague in the county 2nd XI side when I was captain. He had, however, been to a public school. With the aid of his father Aubrey (who had been a charismatic character and most distinguished and able player with a nervous staccato cough heard all over the ground when he was batting: in a later era he would have been considered almost good enough for England), Jack always had the social edge over me. I would never have thought him set to be a professional soldier and, even less likely, to have the qualities for an MC. But from there he went from strength to strength. Except once. He was the famous ADC to Montgomery on a visit to Russia. While Montgomery would contrive not to swallow the drinks in front of him at the dinner, this was more than an ADC was allowed to get away with. At the end of the visit he was prostrate under the table out of the Field Marshal's sight. Montgomery left for his aeroplane, asking about Sharp and being told that he was in the lavatory. Sharp was smuggled aboard and locked in an aircraft lavatory while Montgomery slept. Miraculously, Montgomery never did know what had happened to Sharp, who was able to get off the plane at the right time. Had he not been protected by the ascetic Montgomery he might never have made his generalship.

I met him again when he had attained that rank and I was still bemused by the fact that he had reached it: he never seemed to me a military figure. But I was palpably wrong. If it had not been for his relatively early death, it is considered that he would have inevitably become a field marshal. Aubrey Sharp, a solicitor who enjoyed speaking and always had a ready wit, had unveiled the portraits not without a playful dig from Geary, in his comfortably self-assured speech, at Sharp's legendary parsimony. Other former captains, besides Dawson and Aubrey Sharp, arranged by Eric to be present, were 2nd Lord Hazelrigg (whose father had once bowled lobs for MCC when I was batting against him — they were infernally troublesome to deal with) and Michael Packe, the latter, like Jack Sharp, a contemporary of mine at Cambridge but a better batsman than I was, with Sharp behind us both. Packe's father, like Hazelrigg's and Sharp's, had been on the Leicestershire committee but Michael and Arthur Hazelrigg achieved their places in the county team on merit, although Charles had thought that, had I stayed in England in 1939, I, not Packe, should have captained Leicestershire, which had a most dismal last season before the war under him.

Some Profiles in Half a Decade

A quite different memorable feature of 1970 was the completion of Charles's monumental sequence of 11 novels, *Strangers and Brothers*. Congratulating Charles, I wrote on 26 October 1970 to ask 'Am I right in thinking that you first mentioned the concept to me in your room at Christ's about 1936?' The next day he replied that 'I probably mentioned its concept to you in 1935 rather than 1936.' *Last Things* had made a reasonably satisfactory concluding book after the other ten in the sequence, though I personally felt that it came low in the total order. For recommendation to anyone wanting to embark on reading C. P. Snow's fiction, my private preference by way of an introduction for them would be: (1) *The Light and the Dark*, (2) *The Masters*, (3) *The Affair*, (4) *The New Men*, (5) *Homecomings*, (6) *Last Things*, (7) *George Passant*, (8) *Time of Hope*, (9) *The Conscience of the Rich*, (10) *Corridors of Power* and, a long way behind, (11) *The Sleep of Reason*. But I would have recommended above all, except the first four and *The Search* (outside the *Strangers and Brothers* sequence), the non-fiction minor masterpieces *Variety of Men* and *The Realists*.

In July, Charles's 'The Case of Leavis and the Serious Case' was published in the *Times Literary Supplement*, squashing forever those Leavisites who couldn't escape the demolition of Leavisites. It had been a deliberately long-delayed reply, answering with dignity the questions that Leavis had raised with such venom.

Mr and Mrs Philip Snow

Mr Harold Macmillan requests the pleasure of your company at an evening party on Tuesday, December 8th 1970, at The Ritz in honour of C. P. Snow and to celebrate the completion of his 'Strangers and Brothers' sequence.

No one seemed less half-American than Macmillan. Pam had told me that he showed no interest in women at all. Misogynists I find faintly rebarbative but Macmillan was one of the most intriguing men I have met: no politician/statesman has transformed his public façade in later life as well as he did compared with his insipid appearance in youth and early middle age. His lifelong hypochondria ('the nervous strain of the speeches seems to get worse as one gets older', Alistair Horne reported) and the vomiting that preceded television appearances and superlative speeches was consummately concealed, like his being the great grandson of a poor Scottish crofter (except when it was convenient for him to refer to it). Ignoring the 'bounder' Boothby's affair from 1929 with Lady Dorothy to her death in 1966, he magnanimously put Lord Boothby of Buchan and Rattray Head at the top of his first list of life peers.

Macmillan at the Ritz party was elegant as usual and renewed his interest in my having been one of the principal characters (Martin Eliot) in the sequence. He told me that few things had given him more pleasure than seeing the whole series through his press after Faber & Faber had let it slip through their grasp. Charles's relief on the conclusion of a 35-year-old concept with a war in between hit him consciously at the function. He staggered away from it with Pam, Anne and me. I hailed a taxi, Charles promptly slipping off the back seat to sit bolt upright on the taxi floor back to front, while Anne sat opposite Pam and I managed to pull down the folding seat somehow with my feet tangled around Charles, all the way to Eaton Terrace where I propelled him up the stairs from behind. He had conversed over the entire distance, but it cannot be said with total coherence.

I wrote to Charles on 12 December 1970 that 'We all greatly appreciated the party, myself the last two and a half hours more or less completely. I was not sufficiently primed for the first half hour. Apparently Eric was rather the reverse. He did not seem too well after about the first hour and tells me that he retired about half way through.' Eric suffered from almost the same form of agoraphobia as myself, though not so severely or for as long. Charles was out of control after the party momentarily, for he was able to cast aside for the first time since 1935 any bounds of commitments. That state for a man of such conscience and responsibility was the sweetest of freedoms.

Nevertheless, it was characteristic of him that, relieved of the seemingly never-ending cycle of novels, he would take on what to many would seem an arduous task but one he relished and at which he excelled. He accepted an invitation to review a book each week for the *Financial Times*. That sounds light enough but he insisted on being sent six books each week. He would read every one and decide on the one to be reviewed without having made a note as he read it or on any of the others. It was a literary landmark of the last decade of his life. Always, between 1970 and 1980, I would find him with the weekly half-dozen tilted at impossible angles, heaped untidily around his chair and sprawled across the drawing room coffee table. He disdained to notice dust jackets: these would lie torn and flapping loose, diminishing the value of resale to half, instead of near full, price to a tame bookseller.

I submit that the hundreds of reviews should be held in the highest regard from two aspects, representing as they did some of his finest, sharp writing and also as a fascinating, timeless parade of his powers of selection of people and of what is interesting about them. They deserve to be published, with the agreement of course of the *Financial Times*, as a collection. I pass that opinion on gratuitously to some publisher, though why I should I can't imagine when a combination of taste and acumen is not in rich supply among leaders in the trade (such as have not lost their identities in mergers) in the current demeaning climate with profit-making, mercenary policies submerging quality.

Charles told me buoyantly that the investment he had made for young Philip was now valued at £50,000. Of his finances generally he declared: 'As with most writers my income fluctuates a certain amount but averages at something like £30,000. There is a 25 per cent chance that for the next three to four years it may be in the appreciably higher region.'

Since I had been puzzled as to the identity of Francis Getliffe in the *Strangers and Brothers* sequence he confirmed to me that the character was an amalgam modelled on two liberal scientists, Lord Blackett and Philip Bowden, but that the political views expressed by Getliffe were drawn entirely from Blackett.

A little while before, on 22 July 1970, he had written 'You have the distinction of receiving the only 100 per cent review I have ever seen in the *TLS*.' This was a reference to the *Times Literary Supplement*'s assessment of my *Bibliography of Fiji, Tonga and Rotuma*, published the year before. Harry Maude had been the guiding force for several years behind its being printed.

Related to Angus Maude (later Lord Maude of Stratford-upon-Avon), his appearance, fair, wan, frail, almost vapid, was wholly deceptive. With his intelligent wife, Honor, the world's expert on Oceanic string figures (how stately a governor's lady she would have made), he survived early privations in the Gilbert and Ellice Islands where he started as a cadet and ended as Resident Commissioner before retiring early from the Colonial Administrative Service. He became associate professor of Pacific history at the Australian National University, where he easily but without acknowledgement put the professor, J. W. Davidson, in the academic and administrative shade.

Not relishing academic infighting, however, Harry Maude retired as early as he could and was instantly in demand for writing prefaces to books. He wrote one for my *Bibliography* but all this impeded his unselfish progress on his own learned works. I have known him well since 1938 when we saw each other daily at the office of the Governor and High Commissioner for the Western Pacific. His is a friendship, as he advances into his ninth decade, I put high on my valued list. Seldom in my experience has an apologetic profile belied such gifts of imagination, tenacity, judgement and inner strength.

At the same time as he commented on my *Bibliography*, Charles recorded that 'Grandfather [whom I was too young to know] was a splendid example of an upright, intelligent, agnostic working man. He had some typical books — George Eliot, Renan's *Life of Jesus*, bound copies of *The Penny Magazine*. I imbibed them all.'

As 1970 turned into 1971 I wrote to Charles that 'I doubt whether it will have escaped your notice in the Honours List that Edward [Cakobau] has been given a K ... he was semi-disguised under the Fijian form of Etuate and his Tongan name Tugi. It is a reasonable move by Mara. ... It may also be a pointer to the next Governor-Generalship.' Ted came over for his investiture by the Queen. Charles and I arranged a party at Eaton Terrace for him but this had to be cancelled as Charles had to go to Russia.

When I confided with a friend, Billy Griffith, the MCC Secretary, about my agoraphobia, he confirmed his having it incipiently. He said that it was so ridiculous and irrational when he had had the lives of thousands in his hands at Arnhem without worry (he received a decoration for his command) and now he couldn't go the few yards from his house to his office without wanting to avoid anyone and everyone *en route*. He had to avoid the tarmac path behind the Warner stand and was forced to cut across from his house the curve in front of it over the turf between the grandstand and the pavilion. Meanwhile, I managed to cope with England — and, most importantly, London for meetings, increasingly accompanied by Anne on the train from Rugby.

A governor since 1939, Sir Patrick Dean, so much better known to me (from as long ago as 1952) than Edmund Compton, took over as Chairman. He was 63, blue-eyed, blond-haired, of an exceptionally strong frame, straightforward and modest. I was to have my closing years at Rugby working with him. Pat Dean had taken me in the course of my tour of America in 1964 to the United Nations General Assembly where he was Permanent Representative of the United Kingdom, and had arranged for me to sit in at a meeting of the Security Council listening to an Indonesia–Malaysia dispute, which had loomed large at the time but was small fry. While everything was being translated into French, high up in the building at the bar he introduced me to representatives from a number of countries, divulging that almost all business was conducted by lobbies at the bar. After that post Dean had become Ambassador to the USA and it was because on retirement from there he could now be in England for almost the first time uninterruptedly that he could become Chairman of the Governing Body.

Once, on a visit from his Washington posting, he turned up late and looking preternaturally flushed for a Governing Body meeting in mid-afternoon. After it, he explained to the Chairman, Lord Parker, that, with two other ambassadors (to France and Germany, if I remember correctly), he had been 'carpeted' by George Brown, the Foreign Secretary. He said that they had never been so insulted in their lives and that Brown had drunk too much at lunch before seeing them. Pat Dean also said that Brown had the reputation in all quarters of being the most impossible person to have held the high office (Eden had been difficult to deal with for the different reason of inheriting uncontrollable rages from his father: both tended to gnaw carpets) through his blatant rudeness.

I had never before seen Pat Dean ruffled. Nor did I see him in that state again — far from it. True to his diplomatic training, he was in control of affairs, whichever way they might turn. The beauty of his wife, Patricia, who had been on important secret liaison war work in London with Resistance movements, was eye-riveting. They were an imposing ambassadorial pair. He was ultimately to retire in 1984 from the Governing Body after what was almost certainly the record period of 45 years' membership. He and I talked the same language and I was very happy to have my closing years at Rugby working with him. I could not have been more fortunate.

A friend for some years, Bryan Valentine, the Kent and England player, retired from his post as manager of his school fees insurance firm. Effervescent and at the same time sagacious, he had dispensed delightful hospitality from the box at Lord's for test matches. My relationship with Colin Ingleby-Mackenzie, his successor and light-hearted, adventitious leader of Hampshire to the county championship, as amicable as with Valentine in settling parents' claims for loss of value for fees, was maintained to everyone's advantage.

I had also come to know better Freddie Brown, the Surrey, Northamptonshire and England all-rounder, for we were on the International Cricket Conference's committee of five from 1971 to 1975 (the other three were the Maharajah of Baroda and John Warr, both dry-witted, shrewd and sociable, and the sensible, modest Ben Barnett, Australia's prewar wicket keeper who had fought in New Guinea during the war) making the very first arrangements for a cricket World Cup one-day series, which was going to be quite a daring experiment.

I have never believed in one-day cricket. I would have been ashamed of the outcome if I could not have claimed to have stood out against it, as did Gubby Allen, on the grounds that anything bearing the description 'World Cup competition' could not possibly be based on less than matches of four days' duration. And this was without being able to envisage the excruciatingly vulgar impact of commercial sponsorship. The ludicrous pyjama game, surmounted by baseball caps and plastered from hideously helmeted head and totally countenance-covering visors (all this against monotonous bowling of no more than medium pace) down to astonishingly ugly footwear with beer and lager advertisements like racing car drivers, is garish, revolting and juvenile.

We had of course foreseen the elementary slog and scamper being the peak of any strategy, such as it is, with its statistics so meaningless as not to be worth looking at or recording for a moment. All lowering every conceivable standard in cricket. Having fulminated to that salutary extent when there is so much media space given to its glorification, I must in all fairness look at the reverse side of the coin or coins. For, if meaning less than little in criteria of teams' and players' relative abilities, the crude reality is that financially it brought in economic salvation when much of cricket was barely ticking over. It has become the lifeblood of associate member countries, which can now go in for widespread coaching, have some tours and pay without agonizing searches for participation in their periodic ICC trophy competitions.

The more I saw of Freddie Brown, whom I was to know further when he in turn came to be President of MCC and Chairman of the International Cricket Conference, the more he impressed me. As I have implied earlier, he would have been the sort of captain, like Jardine and, on a lower plane, Arthur Langford, I would never have tired playing under, although only experiencing once Brown's leadership personally on the field. Otherwise, I always preferred to be my own captain.

Brown had succeeded as Chairman Sir Cyril Hawker, a competent holder of the office, if not first class as a player, and an international banker, and before him Maurice Allom, the versatile Surrey and England fast bowler, a member of a top-class dance band between the wars and a writer of cricket tour books with a light touch, who in turn had succeeded Ronnie Aird. With Punch-like features, Aird had been a friendly and self-effacing Secretary of MCC before eventually becoming President. They had followed Arthur Gilligan, the good natured and unassuming captain of Sussex and England (I had played against him before the war when he was captain of Sussex 2nd XI). They were all friendly, as were Brown's immediate successors, Aidan Crawley, the former junior Labour minister and biographer of de Gaulle, and Lord Caccia.

A Time of Renewal

Lantern-jawed, sombre, without the temperament to stay as a player although of international calibre, Crawley wrote memoirs inclined to be wooden. But his life has had more than its share of domestic tragedies, with the death of his wife in an accident unconnected with that of his two sons killed together in an aircraft. Lord Caccia had been a former ambassador to America. All Caccia's diplomacy was called for when an unprecedented event occurred immediately before he opened the conference (which now had about a dozen additions to Fiji and the USA as associate members). Israel had been put up as an associate member country. I was among the one or two who spoke up for it as I had studied a history of the progress of the game in the country, not very promising but, by virtue of the number playing, worthy of support.

The Pakistan representative (and also a government minister), Abdul Hafeez Kardar, who had not been entirely separated from trouble in his associations after Oxford with Warwickshire, objected strongly, if predictably as a Muslim, to Israel's supporters. Rather than face a vote on Israel's admission, Kardar stalked out of the committee room not to return to the conference. Lord Caccia made a last-minute plea as Kardar reached the door. It was unavailing but it did not matter. We got along without Kardar, whose supercilious manner never earned him many friends. Pakistan's representatives in the 1980s were lieutenant-generals, who could not have been more Anglo-European in their approach and appearance, adding markedly to conference harmony.

I had been a fellow of the Royal Anthrolopological Institute for 20 years before a visit to London on Rugby work gave me an opportunity to attend an annual tea party in Bedford Square. Prince William of Gloucester was succeeding Princess Alice, Countess of Athlone, as patron and I was able to meet both. They seemed to be unusual members of the Royal family, Prince William enterprising and alert (his father, the Duke of Gloucester, was not known to have either quality) and Princess Alice unconventional and interested in everything esoteric. When Prince William was killed in an air accident, the Prince of Wales, who had read anthropology at Cambridge, succeeded him.

Before Charles visited Newfoundland University to collect an honorary degree, he was persuaded by me to raise a question in the

House of Lords: 'To ask HMG whether they are aware that the library at the Royal Anthropological Institute requires financial support to preserve it undispersed in this country and whether they will take steps to procure this support.' The best library of its kind in the world, it had been very helpful to me in my researches. It is still intact and in this country. This remains the only hand that I have had in this country's legislative assemblies.

Back in Rugby, our visitors, always welcomed by Anne as readily as by myself, included Raymond Burr, the Canadian actor with a fine gravelly voice overlaid with a salty timbre and bulbous eyes above sagging pouches. He had bought the Lau island of Naitauba in the Fiji archipelago, where the Hennings family had lived since purchase in 1899 from Walter and Herbert Chamberlain, brothers of Joseph Chamberlain of Birmingham, who had been taken with its commercial potential on their rather Philistine round-the-world trip.

Raymond, through me, became a friend of Charles's, who was invited to another island refuge of his, this time in the Azores, but Charles could not find the time to get there. Burr had come to Rugby to see my library of Pacific books, said by experts to be the best in private hands in this country (we were not sure whether Sir David Attenborough's was superior: Sir David has confirmed that he has fewer books). The library had been collected since 1937.

Raymond, whose existence was frenetic, flying from Fiji to Los Angeles and then to all parts of the world ceaselessly, told Anne that he could think of no happier way of spending a week (a long time in his hectic schedule) than browsing in my library. Seeing a pampas flowering with full plumes at the bottom of my garden, he ran down to check it. The back view of him — almost the broadest man I have ever known — was like that of an elephant lumbering, his knock-kneed legs waving outwards. He could not believe that Rugby could share the plant at all, even so spectacularly, with California and Mexico. I have noticed that actors and actresses try to avoid being photographed in spectacles. When his secretary and friend, Robert Beneveds, warned him that he was being photographed by Stefanie, saying sharply: 'You've got your glasses on, Ray,' he fairly whipped them off.

Raymond had divorced his first wife, lost his second in an air crash (the one that killed Leslie Howard) and his third through cancer, as well as his only son, and obviously needed to have to be endlessly on the go to keep morbidity away. He asked me to send him any Pacific books I came across in second-hand shops. I knew where I could come across some but, not having his resources, asked if he could send me a float for purchase and dispatch. It proved impossible to pin him down in any part of the globe at any one time and the arrangement never got under way. When he sold Naitauba, it was sadly occupied by a weird American religious sect. Also, in my view regrettably, the Japanese have moved into my beloved Lau by purchasing Mago from the Borron family, the beginning of a so far triumphant territorial progress into Fiji by the losers of the war.

Commendably, in Fiji attention was being paid to choosing a biographer of Ratu Sir Lala Sukuna while there were still alive a few people who had known him. Unfortunately, after the first spark of activity, when a committee set up to consider the work thought of approaching James Pope-Hennessy (his *Verandah*, the biography of his grandfather Sir John Pope-Hennessy, governor of no less than Labuan, West Africa, the Bahamas, the Windward Islands, Hong Kong and Mauritius, is masterly) but was stopped in its tracks by his murder in his London home, there was little further imagination shown.

One or two of us who had known Sukuna intimately were unable to be released from our posts for research and essential interviews in Fiji, principally with those Fijians whom we knew to have had much contact with him, but would not be at ease in any language other than their own. We regretfully could not allow our names to be put forward. (Jane Roth had proposed me to the committee. Kingsley — her late husband — would have been a natural first choice.) George Milner's non-availability was a notable loss. He was the outstanding exponent of the Fijian (and Samoan) language under the patronage of Ratu Sukuna. He would have combined scholarship and personal knowledge of a high order. The committee's choice was an Australian who had never met Sukuna, did not know the language and islands and neglected to consult those who had known the subject best. The result, with its grave shortcomings and peculiar twisting obliqueness, was neither the scintillating nor profound, correct and comprehensible study of a unique personality that it should have been. Filipe Bole, about to be mentioned, would have been an appropriate choice as biographer: he had done research for a degree on his subject — or Ian Thomson, who had known Ratu Sukuna particularly well during the final decade of his life.

A curious complication arose when Va'ea came as the first High Commissioner for Tonga in the United Kingdom. He had no other name but could not very well be addressed as just 'Mr Va'ea' or 'His Excellency Mr Va'ea' without initials or preceding names in the court circular on presenting his credentials or at other functions. So the King of Tonga created a barony specially for him with, as is that country's procedure, a territorial appellation. Baron Va'ea of Houma came to see us in Rugby on a few occasions with the stately Baroness Tuputupu, his first secretary, David Tupou, and his glamorous and entirely personable wife, Saane Tupou, who had been Miss Nuku'alofa (the capital of Tonga). Va'ea was a close relation of Ratu Edward's and had been asked by him to keep me in close touch with special Tongan occasions in this country.

Va'ea was a new friend. An old friend since the 1948 Fiji cricket tour of New Zealand was Walter Hadlee, who visited us. Subsequently, he became even more widely known as the father of Sir Richard Hadlee, New Zealand's most successful all-rounder. Walter had been captain of Canterbury against Fiji in 1948 and as captain elect of the New Zealand team to tour England the following year he had asked for my help in naming those whom I regarded as the most formidable of our opponents. All those whom I mentioned to him were selected. It was delightful to have him as our guest in Rugby and later in Angmering, and to read his excellent *The Innings of a Lifetime*. Walter brings common sense, imagination, dignity and articulateness to everything that he takes on. Apart from his own playing eminence, in international administration he was outstanding and remains a model for representatives of all countries on the International Cricket Council. New Zealand could fittingly make him their second cricket knight.

Peter Waine and Stefanie had become engaged. On 21 January 1973 Pam wrote that 'Charles and I are both immensely taken by

Peter. He is a dear, so easy and so extremely intelligent. Stephanie [*sic*. Pam and Charles never absorbed Stefanie's change of spelling] glows and so does he. It is lovely to watch them.'

And from Charles on 29 January 1973:

> I am very glad about the MCC. You deserve recognition in several different directions, and it is nice that one of them has come off. I am very sorry about Billy [Griffith]. As you say, it seems particularly absurd. After all, he has made a career out of being matey. Of course I won't reveal to him that I know in the very unlikely event that I see him but if he ever shows to you any indication that he wants someone in London to talk to you might remind him that I am a moderately sensible character.
>
> I am most favourably impressed by Peter.

Charles had known Billy Griffith from his Cambridge days as one of a handful of spectators at most times on Fenner's. Indeed, Billy told me that throughout play one whole, chilly May day absolutely the only spectators were Charles and G. H. Hardy (mentioned in my preceding book) huddled under a rug carried for such weather by the heavily bi-sweatered Hardy. Charles did not possess a rug. Nor would he have been so mundane as even to think of one, although he would remember to go in a sweater. Unable to spare more than a very occasional visit to Fenner's to sit in their company, I did not observe that spectacle. But even on the warmest of days (sitting all day oblivious to the discomfort of an armless, backless bench facing south and west), Hardy would be in a sweater turning a deeper hue than a copper-skinned American Indian, whom he resembled. He disdained sitting in the pavilion with its north and east vistas. Billy Griffith was an outstanding secretary of MCC, constantly calm and cheerful with a refreshing element of imaginativeness in his thinking and an abundance of charisma.

I had been elected a special honorary life member of MCC for services to international cricket, a long haul from the painful process of having played to qualify and then later to captain and manage MCC teams before retiring at the age of 50. I greatly esteemed finding myself on a list that naturally contained Bradman's name, something I could never have conceived as likely to occur.

Peter Waine, a specialist in personnel and executive management, later to be chairman of his own head-hunting company in London, was the type of hyper-alert person to whom Charles was specially attracted.

Stefanie's wedding dominated 1973. Peter's parents (his father a medical consultant) lived in Rugby. There was going to be a problem with the number of guests if, as Stefanie wanted, the marriage was to take place in the school's War Memorial chapel and the reception in our garden at Horton House. Although it was June, the weather was diabolical before the event. The marquee could scarcely be transported by the contractors out of the swamp of a field where it had been for a previous function: it arrived sodden 48 hours before the day. It had been too wet to mow the lawn.

Yet the day itself turned out to be absolutely golden. The marquee had dried, and the lawn both inside and outside it could be mown. The New Dawn and Albertine roses along the wall had recovered from being bedraggled. Everything was superbly set up. Only I with my agoraphobia was a difficulty. We had engaged as MC a colossal gypsy, Carl Dane, whose feats were notorious. He had once pulled a bus up a hill on a rope with his teeth. He was one of two used by Rank to beat the gong at the opening title of his films. In his company (he was watching the presents when we were to be away from the house) while all but Stefanie had gone to the chapel, I fortified myself with a few very sweet sherries and so much enjoyed the occasion, with Stefanie on my arm, that I forgot to take my place at the one vacant chair after giving her away. It was scorching hot and I was glad that I had ordered grey morning dress: this I knew to be infinitely cooler than the black, and to my mind more sombre, form. The Close made a splendid background for the numerous photographs, for which Rupert (later Sir Rupert, 13th Baronet) Shuckburgh, one of Peter's closest friends, as chief usher superintended the various permutations.

In the marquee Charles started the speeches on just the right note: 'My Lords', he said, 'Oh! I'm forgetting where I am. Forgive my lapse if I am not correct.' Stephen, Peter's brother and a barrister, made a splendid best man's speech to follow up Peter's task excellently performed. The quality of the three speeches was very high: it was a pity that they were not recorded. After them, Charles, who never liked champagne, took himself and Pam into the house where, with whisky at their sides, they watched a test match on television.

It has to be mentioned that the route out for guests lay between their chairs and the set. So everyone eventually had to troop past while Charles craned his neck to look round them at the progress of the match, murmuring farewells to those who spoke to him. We who knew him were amused, but we were not sure what others, seeing him for the first time and not knowing his idiosyncrasies, made of it. It must have seemed especially bizarre to the hyper correct High Commissioner for Fiji, Josua (later Sir) Rabukawaqa.

We had sent a courtesy invitation to Edward Cakobau in Fiji: he had known Stefanie all her life. We commented that we had no reply: Ted was punctilious in social courtesies. Two days later I heard that he had just died. His funeral was filmed in Fiji throughout its duration. Only one up to that date could have approached it — Ratu Sir Lala Sukuna's — in the volume of people and ethnic mixtures paying their respects. I had little thought when Ted had stayed with us two years earlier at Horton House that it would be the last time we would see him. Then he had come over for his investiture by the Queen as a knight.

Ratu George Cakobau, the younger of the two by four years and living with an entrancing wife, had been appointed Governor-General at the age of 60 in November 1972. This spelt the end for his cousin's chances of a post that he would have filled superbly. Inwardly, Ted felt this too, I think. A psychosomatic rapid decline then set in — it took little over a couple of months. I have always believed that if Edward had been made the first governor-general in 1970 for three years, letting George succeed him then, he might not have been afflicted. I fear that he may have died a disappointed, frustrated man.

It was striking to see how much respect Ted commanded in his family. Brigadier Ratu Epeli Nailatikau, now the Ambassador to Britain, in speaking of him always refers to him as 'Ratu'. Fijians outside his family called him 'Ratu Tui', Tongans 'Tugi'.

Apparently Ted died in exactly the same way as his half-sister, Queen Salote of Tonga — only two months off colour in each instance. Both went to New Zealand for cures of what was known to be cancer, only to return because it was inoperable. They are said to have looked astonishingly alike when terminal illness was taking over. I never knew a more impressively mannered person. His courtesy from one of highest rank extended effortlessly, as we saw from the incident on Rugby station, to the most lowly placed. It was such a loss: Ted could always be relied upon to elevate any occasion. He would never fail to capitalize on his ancestors' well-known supremacy in cannibalism. When studying the menu on the *Matua* he confessed to the table steward that he found little to his taste and asked him to bring instead the passenger list. He seemed ageless. Ted was the personification of goodwill and charisma. His death was one of those that left for me a chasm.

My skin may be smooth (and thin) but my profile has been metaphorically pockmarked with near disasters, if not actual ones. Now I nearly blotted my copybook by poisoning a trio of auditors. Throughout my working life, starting with the most eccentric of them all on my first day in Fiji, I was pleased to have specially good relations with these guardians of rectitude, for whose rather soulless, sadly essential occupation I had sympathy. During the annual audit of the Rugby accounts, it was my custom to take the auditors to lunch with two members of my accounts staff. At the Grand Hotel — within a month of closing before demolition to Rugby town's discredit — the first to select his course was one of my staff who chose steak tartare. We all followed suit except the lady member of my staff who ordered chicken. My mind was on other things until I saw a most inedible plateful put in front of me. I had not had the dish before and was surprised that it was cold and apparently raw meat. As host, I could not very well send it back. Somehow I forced it down. No one commented on the dish.

An hour later, I went home from the office feeling feverish and pretty ill without being so. Next morning I learnt that my male accountant had been similarly stricken: not so the female who had had the chicken. One auditor was laid flat with it. The two youngest were all right — until the rest of us had recovered, when they themselves went down with worse consequences. Salmonella (pronounced, after Dr Salmon, who identified the bacteria, with a silent 'l') poisoning is now much in the news. Well, three of the bursary shared it with three auditors. It was the least we could do. It would never have done to have poisoned our auditors of all people. And still the course is not officially banished.

We had met the snooker players, Rex Williams and Eddie Chariton (and Fred Davis, who was not with them on this occasion) on the Isle of Wight where they were giving exhibitions. Now they were doing the same at Rugby. What astonished me was that both who came round to Horton House after 11.00 p.m. stayed until 3.00 a.m. eating sandwiches and drinking brandy (the driver a mere modicum of it) with a return of 50 miles by road and another evening's test of such fine precision ahead of them the same day. But I think I was even more fascinated by the fact that they talked of the technique of snooker and billiards (Rex was currently world billiards champion and the Australian, Eddie, a former miner for 22 years and world championship finalist twice at snooker at this stage) the whole time, going back to the era of Walter Lindrum of Australia, Joe Davis, Clark McConachy of New Zealand, and Tom Newman, names from my youth and before theirs. It surprises me that it is apparently as interminable a subject as cricket.

To mark the centenary of the introduction of cricket to Fiji — it was the same year as the cession of the islands to Queen Victoria — I was invited by Ratu Penaia as Minister for Communications to design three stamps. Stamp designing was a work with which I little thought I would be associated. But I knew what I wanted to do with the opportunity. From photographs of Viliame Mataika, the sleeping policeman and a striking bowler in my 1948 team in New Zealand, Petero Kubu, the spectacular fielder and thrower from the boundary on that tour, Harry Apted, stylish batsman and Pat Raddock, neat wicketkeeper with me in New Zealand in 1948, I drew my impressions (disguising the faces) for the Crown Agents, which then used professional artists for delineation and colouring. The results were most attractive and the Crown Agents — and Stanley Gibbons's *Commonwealth Stamp Catalogue* — credit me with the design. The only trouble is that they are so scarce. I arranged for a few to be sent to friends when they were issued in 1974 but, not appreciating that there would be relatively few printed for a short period, failed to build up a stock for myself. But I look back with pleasure on achieving something in a subject — philately — that has a few fascinating facets for me.

I helped send off one pupil I could call a protégé to Fiji. Another earlier one on a scholarship from Rugby had been John Lourie, of Jewish stock (his uncle was the Israeli Ambassador in London), who later distinguished himself as professor of biology at Papua New Guinea University and is now a leading orthopaedic surgeon back in this country. Paul Alban Christopher Vincent Geraghty, Irish Catholic of a class background otherwise not too dissimilar from my own except that he was a day boy at Rugby, was awarded, like John Lourie, a travelling scholarship from Rugby to Fiji. There he taught for a year but he became so enamoured by the country that he went back — it seems permanently — after returning to England for a Cambridge degree.

Paul obtained a leading position in a new project for a Fijian dictionary entirely in the language and incorporating its dialects — a massive, pioneering undertaking eschewing English — and has remained there ever since, walking about Suva in a *sulu* barefooted or in sandals. After having been able to give attention to the language, dialects and customs unprecedentedly without the diversion of any other post, he must be the leading European exponent in the long history of European–Fijian contact. Only George Milner and Professor Al Schütz of the University of Hawaii can be linked with him — and the American anthropologist, Marshall Sahlins, with regard to the Fijians' tribal history. Paul's interest extends to custom throughout the country's disparate regions. Not seeing him, but hearing him on his weekly broadcasts in the language, one could not suspect that he was European. The same could be said in reverse of Fijian chiefs Ratu Sukuna, Ratu Mara, Ratu Edward, Ratu George and Ratu Penaia, who were all educated outside the country (though Ratu Penaia only briefly).

Another protégé did the reverse route, coming to see me after about 20 years. Harry Apted, part-European Catholic, was 23 when I had taken him as the youngest member of my cricket team touring New Zealand in 1948. He was the second most successful batsman after Bula and, despite a right arm bent at right angle that he was never able to straighten after a greenstick fracture in his childhood, was dazzlingly the best of an outstanding fielding team. It is always touching not to be forgotten by the young. His son, Alan, was to be captain of the second Fiji team to tour England, in 1982. Regrettably Harry, like Bula, was never seen playing in this country. Their standard, and I am sure Walter Hadlee would concur, ranked with that of the New Zealand teams.

Another visit from Fiji was a first and tragic last one. Superintendent of Police J. A. J. Walker came to see me as he was interested in helping me with the second volume of my *Bibliography of Fiji, Tonga and Rotuma*. About 40, reserved and intelligent, he would have made an excellent collaborator for continuing the work from 1969. But, shortly after his return, I received a real shock. Apparently, he had a Fijian mistress and had assaulted a Fijian man who had come to see her. Agitated no doubt by the position in which a police superintendent should find himself, he went to the police armoury and shot himself.

No one of course is without inconsistencies. Charles had few. But he was inconsistent when, having declared earlier that clubs had little interest for him, he resigned from the Savile, of which he had been a member for 30 years, saying that he 'liked clubs less and less', and from the Athenaeum, which had never held any attraction for him and to which he had only been twice in the last two years, he promptly allowed himself to be elected to the Garrick. This surprised me, particularly given that he belonged to the grandest of them all at the Lords.

It was a pity that Charles's first new work of deliberate choice after the end of the *roman fleuve* — a choice that need have no links with his literary past — should be *The Malcontents*, in my judgement the most alien of his works and untypical of his capabilities. It could have suited Pam's spectrum — I think that she was largely responsible for the theme — but not his. The time was right for more biographical vignettes, a follow-up to his charming *Variety of Men* (Rutherford, Einstein, H. G. Wells, Stalin, G. H. Hardy, Churchill, Robert Frost, Lloyd George, Hammarskjöld): after all he had met others almost as rich in character as the first team depicted in it.

There were two reflections by him at this time, one global, the other personal. To an American correspondent he commented that

'We live in an astonishingly silly age.' And to an old (but still young) American friend, Violet Ketels, he said 'I am pretty well and in my usual mixture of moderately high spirits tempered by stoical gloom.' In describing Charles, a New York women's journal, *Women's Wear Daily* commented that 'Snow has a way of peering at one through his glasses that inevitably suggests a sage and stout owl.'

When I commiserated with Charles about the Nobel prize for literature again being missed, he replied on 23 October 1973 that 'It would have been much worse if Greene had got it. The Leavis affair has to be extinguished.' Charles could not see anyone in this country having a superior claim to himself on the record of what he had written. Of the two distinctions he secretly (or at least made known to me and obviously to one or two others) coveted — he scorned the CH — he would have put the Nobel prize before the OM. At least this was before the former was utterly debased after his death by its being awarded to William Golding. Charles was certainly mystified by awards of each as they occurred. It was he, more than anyone, who had pushed Jack Priestley towards the OM — to receive few thanks from Priestley or his wife, Jacquetta Hawkes. He found it hard to understand Zuckerman's acquisition of it: he had less respect for him than for almost anyone in semi-public or public life.

Pam and Charles had been active. Pam in 1974 brought out *Important to Me: Personalia*, which I regard as her most attractive book. I wish she had indulged more in autobiography and biography. I have always regarded her powers as a critic as of the highest class in written reviews: her novels, except for *Catherine Carter*, have not managed to grip me because I sense that her strength, never properly given play, was in seeing people as they were rather than the invention of imaginary characters on which she concentrated.

Charles brought out also in 1974 *In Their Wisdom*, not quite, in my view, up to the standard of the first half of the *Strangers and Brothers* sequence — or even earlier, such as the underestimated *The Search*. Sir Ronald Millar adapted it quickly into *The Case in Question* at the Theatre Royal, Haymarket. The *Daily Telegraph* reported:

A Time of Renewal

When Millar first met C. P. Snow he asked if he might adapt *The Affair* for the theatre. With a dubious grunt, Snow invited Millar to tell him what the book was about. Millar replied, 'I believe the key to it is on page 329' and pointed to one speech. 'You've got it,' Snow replied.

The play ran for a year at the Strand Theatre. For the fourth time now there was a new Millar play for a Snow novel and for the third time with John Clements in the lead.

Charles, discovering that Belgravia, where he lived, was named after Belgrave in Leicester, a district rather like our ancestral Aylestone, could not resist so telling me. I tried to induce him to allow himself, now that he had a modicum of leisure, to take up a request by Fabio Barraclough of the Rugby art staff (whose grandfather, a humble Spanish villager, had been summoned to be resident artist at the Madrid royal court) to paint him. There was at that time no painting of him. There was not even one subsequently. The excellent picture reproduced on the cover of my *Stranger and Brother: A Portrait of C. P. Snow* is from a colour photograph taken in 1977 by Bern Schwartz of La Jolla, California, who died on the last day of 1978.

Fabio Barraclough painted two of me, one poor and the other said to be a real likeness; he insisted on going on painting me for no apparent reason. Edmund Geoffrey Fabio Barraclough, who signed his paintings Fabio y Valls, had as father a Yorkshireman, an official in the Madrid Chamber of Commerce, and as mother a Catalan. Fabio was highly entertaining, a most unorthodox and highly gifted member of the school staff who retired to Madrid. Diminutive, with a rapid, short-stepping walk and black beard (unusual in his time at Rugby), he was only the second person I had observed collapsing to writhe on a floor in hysterical amusement. The first occasion was when sitting behind an undergraduate in the pint-sized Cosmopolitan Cinema in Cambridge before the war. I was entertained to see him slide off his seat under the one in front of him in a paroxysm of uncontrollable laughter over some Marx Brother quip or antic. Sadly, Fabio's request never came off for Charles, the more's the pity, although there are numerous black and white cartoons and heavily photographed coverage from the 1950s, if not much before then.

Charles had surely time enough for sittings (the better one of me, large as it is and painted from a transparency, required only an hour of my time) despite this report from Pam of 28 March 1974: 'Charles is busy taking a crash course in French at the Berlioz School and becoming enviably fluent, though the sounds he makes aren't particularly Gallic.'

Charles made a unique visit for him in 1974 — to French universities at Lille, Paris (the Sorbonne and Collège de France), Rouen and Caen, giving lectures on himself and his books. He was always disappointed that his works never seemed to flourish in that country and that Pam's expert knowledge (she was with him) of Proust seemed to go unrecognized.

Jack Plumb wrote at this time: 'I was at Balmoral last week and in the Queen's sitting room saw *The Affair*. In the principal guest room is *Variety of Men*. Both of them had inside blue labels "The Queen's Book".' Plumb had been researching for his and Huw Wheldon's *Royal Heritage*.

When Pam was given a CBE (I said that it should have been a Dame of the Order) in the New Year's honours in 1975, she wrote on 2 January 1975: 'Thank you both for your sweet letter. Of course I am pleased — and I really didn't want anything more. When I am 80 I shall accept a pantomime title if they offer it. ... Your congratulations were more than welcome. Bless you all of you, Affectionately, Pam.'

She was almost wholly responsible for the selection of records attributed to Charles when he at last succumbed to an invitation from Roy Plomley of 15 May 1975: 'At the Garrick Club the other evening you were kind enough to intimate that the next time I invited you to take part in "Desert Island Discs" you would consent — so I'm hastening to extend the invitation. We really would be delighted to have you with us, and promise that the whole procedure is quite painless.'

This was his reply of 10 June 1975:

I am sending you this list of what I should like to ask for in Desert Island Discs. Since I am not musical, and propose to make that clear, some of the items may give you a little trouble. Hence this notice.

1) PROUST'S LITTLE PHRASE. This occurs in the sonata for violin and piano in D minor by Saint-Saens ...
2) THE ORCHARD SCENE from HENRY IV PART II. Is the production with Olivier as Shallow obtainable?
3) HEBRIDEAN BOAT SONG
4) THE 23RD PSALM. Read from the Authorized Version and from the New English Bible. Just read clearly so that we can hear the words.
5) 'IF LAWS WERE MADE FOR EVERY DEGREE ...' from BRITTEN'S BEGGAR'S OPERA.
6) KUTUZOV'S SONG on the fate of Russia from PROKOVIEV'S WAR AND PEACE.
7) THE FARMER AND THE COWMAN SHOULD BE FRIENDS from OKLAHOMA.
8) BEETHOVEN'S NINTH SYMPHONY — any selections you like.

Since Charles was not only not musical but completely tone deaf, this can go on record as being Pam's choice 100 per cent. None of them would have been mine, where Mozart's Piano Concerto Andante No. 21 in C Major would have been top of the list, followed by *La Vie en Rose*, Chaplin's *Limelight* theme, Massenet's *Méditation* based on Anatole France's *Thaïs*, Warren and Gordon's *The More I See You* sung by Chris Montez and arranged by Herb Alpert, and almost any piano-dominated recital, either classical or as modern as Alan Price's *Just for You* or, in between, like Scott Joplin. *Stephanie Gavotte* by Czibulka would have come high on my list: we derived our name for Stefanie from it. My father would have approved of some and been a little astonished by the rest being not totally lowbrow, not least that I had long after his death expressed a liking for the piano, which I would have given so much to have been able to play.

I believe that one is allowed to select for Desert Island Discs a book to take in addition to a Bible and all of Shakespeare. In my case, I could do without them. With my predisposition for facts, I

would opt for a set of *Encyclopaedia Britannica* (if a set would not
be cheating), preferably a 1920s edition with pictures of cities with
trams and without the effects of the Second World War.

Now, just an octogenarian, can I claim the privilege of having
reflected on and observed just two aspects of present-day adolescence for comparison with my own in the late 1920s and early
1930s? In doing so, my granddaughter, Philippa, will, I know,
regard me as far from being cool (I pull her leg in describing users
of that word as coolies, a term that has to be interpreted to young
generations as not carrying much standing in former times).

First, what I greatly lament as something they are missing is that
melodies and tunes have vanished to be replaced by an (apparently
hypnotic) cacophony of primitive sound and movement utterly
removed from the style of the 1920s and 1930s, stilted as it may
have been and caricatured not entirely justly by today's youth.
Surely no previous 'icon' of youth has been as grotesquely
androgynous and sick-looking as Michael Jackson, followed not
far behind by other groin-stroking 'guitarists' and gesticulators? It
seems that the current 'music' of adolescence and youth, although
it has always varied through the decades, has now really dissolved
under the term 'pops' into the sound of non-music for the first
time. It has reached perhaps a final end. Nihilism. Like ultra
modern 'art' and so-called architecture, with its extraordinary
appellation 'state of the art', whatever that may mean. This is not
to say that my granddaughter does not find pleasure in one-
fingering the Swedish film theme (*Elvira Madigan*) of Mozart's
Concerto No. 21 just mentioned and playing on her saxophone
Gershwin's *Summertime*.

In this pompous sermonizing, I reflect as to how those who were
octogenarians in the late 1920s and early 1930s felt about the
'music' of us adolescents and youths. I recall that my father, a
classical musician in his late fifties, used to be driven out of the
room by the then comparatively new appearance of the saxophone
heard on the equally new wireless. Yet, for me, its contribution to
that period represents real nostalgia with its sweeter sounds. I
suppose that octogenarians then can have only held in esteem, say,
Strauss, who still has his appeal, however, to this day in the lighter
area of music for the very young, except that it covered the

generations in a way that is missing in adolescent and youthful sounds of today.

A second point of sympathy I have for the young of today is, of course, their growing up against a background of violence, too graphically depicted on television, in films and extensively described in print, when they could otherwise be blessedly free from the brutality of the world wars, which were the traumas of this octogenarian's background. Perhaps, when perspective is drawn, we may be given just a modicum, no more, of credit for having done our best to see that those horrific times are less likely to recur and to have helped localize minor wars in a half century of relative peace, the longest in this country's history since the start of the Victorian era.

In 1975 Charles was 70 and I was 60. It was quite a year for Charles. In a phase of vacillating health, he penetrated Tanzania and accepted the presidency of the Society of Civil Service Authors.

A little before his birthday both Charles and Pam were unwell. He told me 'I with lumbago. I haven't had it for 20 years'. It was not diagnosed as such but simply assumed by Charles. With hindsight, I believe that it was a series of spasms associated with the cause of his death five years later. Pam seemed in far worse shape, collapsing, breathing stertorously, eating nothing, smoking nonstop and drinking whisky from 10.00 a.m., but it never showed unless you saw her actually replenishing her glass. At this time I began to be seriously concerned that she could not outlive Charles. They managed to accommodate overnight Yevgeny Yevtushenko in Charles's study — the only visitor ever to stay either at Eaton Terrace or Cromwell Road or even at Clare except Anne and me.

For his seventieth year a fuss was made of Charles by both Christ's College and Macmillans acting with Penguin Books and Curtis Brown, his literary agents. An anonymous benefactor (guessed to be an American) had established a C. P. Snow triennial lecture and the first to give it was Sir Peter Medawar, the distinguished-looking scientist of Middle Eastern and Jewish origin who had recovered from a major stroke. Charm matched his looks: I sat near him at the Christ's high table to which Anne and I were invited. The Master, Lord Todd, had never been close to

ABOVE. The International Cricket Council at Lord's, 1994. *(Photo: ICC)*

ABOVE. Ratu Epeli Nailatikau, author's wife, Ratu Sir Kamisese Mara, Adi Lady Lala Mara, author and Adi Koila Nailatikau at Angmering, 1992. *(Photo: Worthing and District Advertiser)* BELOW LEFT. The three generations: author's wife, Anne, their daughter, Stefanie, and granddaughter, Philippa, 1995. *(Photo: author)* BELOW RIGHT. The author's granddaughter, Philippa, aged 16, 1997. *(Photo: Richard Blower)*

Charles. I had met him once or twice before and found him short of charm just as Medawar radiated it.

Others present were Jack (later Sir John) Plumb, older at Newton's School than me by three years, a fellow of King's before and after the war spent at Bletchley, and a fellow of Christ's from 1946, soon to be Todd's successor; Lord Adrian; Sir Alan Cottrell, metallurgist and Master of Jesus College, Cambridge; and Sydney Grose — he in his nineties — who was Arthur Brown, the master-maker in *Strangers and Brothers* as well as in real life. Among others was Margo, the widow of Philip Bowden: they had both looked after Anne on her odyssey in 1940 in Melbourne and Bow-den had been Charles's collaborator in the unfortunate vitamin misdiscovery of the early 1930s.

Ungraciously, I thought, but it may have been against custom on an occasion like this, Todd made no speech. Charles made his own to the gratification of the fellows and their wives at the refectory tables in the body of the hall. The pudding at the feast was face-tiously shown on the menu as Lord Snow's Wig, the name an invention of some light-minded don. Much overrated, the base was unidentifiable and unmemorable, its main feature being strands of spun sugar on top.

The visit of Anne and me to Cambridge for the event was facili-tated by Walter Hamilton, now the Master of Magdalene, and Jane accommodating us. They looked absolutely right in the Lodge. They were worthy of this transition from Rugby. Unfortunately, Walter was too old to be vice-chancellor when he might have obtained a knighthood. Jane was described absolutely accurately in Walter's obituary notice in *The Times* (by James Hunt?)as being startlingly pretty. She never failed to make one look at her rather delicate bone structure. She had been a great capture for Walter in advanced bachelordom.

The reception for Charles given by Macmillans, Penguin Books and Curtis Brown at the Stationers' Hall marked both his seventieth birthday and the simultaneous publication of his *Trollope*, a sumptuously produced biography, which Charles characteristically thought would have been better without any of its fine illustrations. It was on this occasion that Philip Kaiser, the American Ambassador to Hungary, commented to me on the proximity of Harold Macmillan, standing in the middle of the ante-hall, to the pair sitting on a settee — Lady Dorothy Macmillan and Lord Boothby: 'Where else but in England would you find so civilized a *ménage à trois* publicly exhibited?'

Shortly after, while guests were moving into the main hall for canapés and champagne, I had a quarter of an hour alone with Macmillan, still in the centre of the ante-hall. He was in most relaxed form, going over Charles's publications by Macmillan, which he knew by heart: he liked all of them, although I expressed my reservations over *The Sleep of Reason* and *The Malcontents*. He seemed to have no other thoughts than his conversation with me and when the major-domo came in to tell him that all were assembled in the next room we went in, he to behind a table where Charles was already standing. I was surprised when Macmillan immediately launched into a smooth, effortless, elegant encomium of Charles. Surprised because he had given me no indication that when talking to me he had in his mind the requirement to make a quarter of an hour's speech without a note. Charles reported later to Charles Scribner of New York that Macmillan at the age of 81 had made an admirable speech. He himself followed it in similarly relaxed manner.

There was a cross section of distinctive guests to meet or re-meet at the Stationers' Hall — Mary, Duchess of Roxburghe, Sir Victor Pritchett, 3rd Lord Windlesham, Sir Osbert Lancaster, Ronald Millar, Dame Iris Murdoch, Olivia Manning, Rayner Heppenstall, V. S. Naipaul, Plumb, Medawar, the Priestleys, A. L. Rowse, Lord Robbins, Anthony Storr, Sacheverell Sitwell, Norman St John Stevas, Lord Trevelyan, Harold and Mary Wilson, Lord Willis, Lord Chalfont, Lady Selina Hastings, 4th Lord Aberdare, 2nd Earl of Gowrie, Lord Rees Mogg, Melvyn Bragg, Russell Harty, Michael Ayrton, Frank Cousins, Douglas Fairbanks Jr, Lady Diana Cooper, Margaret Drabble, Larry Adler, Maurice Edelman, Gavin Ewart, Lady Faber, Lord Goodman, Joyce Grenfell, Lord Hall, Michael Holroyd, Sir Alan Hodgkin, 5th Lord Harlech, Lord Jenkins, the Longfords, Sir Sidney Nolan, Lord Llewellyn-Davies, Antonia Fraser, Sir John Wheeler-Bennett, Yevtushenko, David Cornwell (John Le Carré), the Clanmorrises, as well as Boothby and Lady Dorothy Macmillan of course. Eric had come from

Leicester to join Stefanie, Peter, Anne and myself in this company. It was about as representative a list of Charles's inner and outer circle — a record useful for his biographers — as could be corralled to mark the occasion, the last, as it turned out, that could be celebrated for there was to be no eightieth anniversary. I had met some before and I would meet them repeatedly: others not again.

I could not think of anything to give Charles, never a collector of any material objects, except honorary degrees if they can be regarded as material, for this special birthday except a gold fountain pen, knowing full well that within a few months he would have mislaid or lost it. I never saw it in action.

My last three terms at Rugby went very swiftly. A successor had to be advertised for and selected: the appointee could not take over the duties from me until the term after I was 60, so I stayed on the extra three months to help the Governing Body. My successor who was 52 on appointment was to die within five years after having had to take a whole term off earlier when he had had a coronary thrombosis.

At speech day, Pat Dean, the Chairman, and Jim Woodhouse, the Headmaster, made flattering remarks about me to the assembled boys and their parents, for many of whom I would only have been an official name. The governors present included Sir Robert Birley, an overnight guest of ours for the occasion, Sir Derek Hilton, deputy chairman of the Governing Body and a former president of the Law Society (both he and Birley have been described), Tom Howarth, the historian who had been on Montgomery's staff before becoming High Master of St Paul's, Sir Oliver Chesterton, one of London's most in demand after-dinner speakers, nephew of G. K., whose family name of estate agents is seen on half of the 'for sale' notices in London (I had worked closely with him when he was Chairman of the Rugby's Founder's London Estate in Camden dating from the founder's land there in the seventeenth century), and Sir David Steel (son of Gerald Steel who had been a leading figure in my initial appointment), chairman of the War Memorial trustees and later to be himself as unruffled a chairman of the Governing Body as might be expected of a holder of a DSO and MC. With their wives they joined Patrick

Dean in our garden for the last tea party that for many years Anne and I had been giving the governors after each speech day.

In my last term I had just seen the introduction of girls into Rugby — three of them into the sixth form, but still noticeable and refreshing among the 740 boys who were an unvarying sight dominating the streets and assemblies. They were undoubtedly to bring a civilizing aura to the school: they now number 100 among 640 boys, eventually to increase to half of 740, participating in the whole of the life of the school. Whether it is more to the advantage of the preponderance of boys or to the clever minority of girls has still to be judged over a number of years.

Alan McLintock, specialist in finance in the skilled tradition of Terence Maxwell, had just joined the Governing Body. I had been fortunate with the many members of the Governing Body, the chairmen and the three headmasters, with all of whom I had had to work closely in the span of 25 years, as well as with fellow Governing Body officers such as James Hunt, a real friend as Second Master (followed in this post by Warwick Hele before he went on to become High Master of St Paul's, and Alan Lee), as well as John Sparks, so distinctively qualified as the Medical Officer with an MD degree, and Eric Ingram, the level-headed Assistant Bursar in my last seven years.

There had been excellent colleagues, too, in my time among the teaching staff, with whom I had been in close contact. Without, I hope, being invidious or attempting a comprehensive count, I can readily pick out some former housemasters, Reverend Richard Broxton, Allen Tatham, Norman Hughes, George Keay, Jim Willans, Bill Loughery, Geoff Helliwell, Will Inge, H. J. Harris, Jim Larmour, Jack Baiss, R. H. Walker (too taciturn to be everybody's cup of tea), Donald Bulmer and Brian Richards. Some non-housemasters included C. P. Mortimer, Reverend A. W. V. Mace, E. J. (known as Loony. I can't think why: he was more normal than the norm) Harris, L. E. Godfrey-Jones, F. H. Murray, J. D. Graves, J. W. Toomer, Reverend L. H. Morrison (ex-colonial administration, Malaya, who converted to the Church as a Japanese prisoner of war), R. A. Schlich, H. E. Bland, P. G. Parks and J. P. King. A few left to be headmasters, among them Nigel Creese (Christ's College, Canterbury, New Zealand, and

Melbourne Church of England Grammar School), John Tyson (Thimphu, Bhutan and Kathmandu, Nepal), J. A. E. Evans (Brentwood), P. J. Cheshire (Warwick), J. G. Dewes (Barker College, New South Wales) and D. J. Skipper (Ellesmere and Merchant Taylor's).

Teaching staff tended to change at the rate of five to ten a year out of the 80 odd. I would have known about 300 in my time, so therefore I might be excused if I have overlooked a name or two who have escaped my recollection of their camaraderie. A few stayed after retirement to embody the continuity so important for contacts and records, including Ian Miller and two ex-housemasters, John Marshall and John Inglis (the former was an acting headmaster and the other a registrar after my time).

Some of the non-teaching staff of excellent quality included L. Livingston, the New South Wales and Northants cricketer who was coach for some years before Geary, J. W. Potter, the ebullient marshal and sergeant major of the Combined Cadet Force, Jack Alldis, Geoff Barlow and Doug Truman of the works staff, Basil Norman, head groundsman and, one of the most remarkable of all, Arthur Reece. He had been assistant at 14 to his father as marshal and was the most efficient manager of the school shop imaginable. Now, at 88, he has an unsurpassable record of association with the school, for he is still a neighbour of it and the most loyal of honorary Old Rugbeians. Edna Graham, the model of a headmaster's secretary for so long, is also still a school neighbour. Then there were Enid Simpson, my model secretary through thick and thin with her loyal assistant Margaret Catherall, the two assistant accountants, John Gray and Joan Joiner supported by Vera Grainger, and Harry Gay, the accountant who had started in 1914 and was still attached to the school more than 60 years later. His service and that of Arthur Reece and Jim Boneham, the head porter, had exceeded half a century and they were accordingly greeted by the Queen — records that in today's vastly changed conditions can never be anywhere near exceeded.

All these were known of course to hundreds, running into thousands, of pupils. With an annual intake of about 100 there would have been 2500 passing through during my quarter-century. I knew few of them. The Bursary was better known to parents. But virtually all pupils would inevitably have seen me, most of them wondering (not without reason) what a bursar did. The post didn't carry a Rugby Victorian nickname such as the Bodger for the headmaster. Walter Hamilton was a more suitable recipient of that title than Arthur fforde or Jim Woodhouse.

As an interlude, before I left Rugby I went to the International Cricket Conference, which that year had as its chairman Prince Philip, President of the MCC for the second time. He was a model chairman, the best I had known in my 30 years of attendance — which is about ten years longer than anyone else's in the records (other than the venerable Sir Arthur Sims), so my assessment has some validity. He hardly ever consulted the Secretary of MCC alongside him. He seemed to have all the intricacies at his finger-tips, which he poised with authority above his multiple papers — though it is so easy to lose one's way in such a bundle, he never did. Prince Philip listened carefully to all that was said and replied spot on. He had briefed himself for the really quite technical business, which he put through so smoothly that, unusually, we had time to spare at the end.

Since a county match was being played, Prince Philip, with a gin and tonic, stayed on to watch through the vast committee room window, inviting two or three of us to keep him company for a couple of hours. He was certainly knowledgeable about the game and a professional chairman among professional administrators. With the light from the window full on his face, I noticed how sandy, almost mild auburn, were his eyebrows and the hair on the sides of his head. The Mountbatten–Battenberg nose could of course not be ignored. His voice, which sounds permanently strained, semi-choked, was genial. He did not recognize that his day had been a full, arduous one. As virtual prince consort he has a demanding role but I formed the impression at the conference that there was little he could not have handled and that his abilities and resources could have been more effectively applied.

It is of course in no way original to say this but, along with so many others and as a subscriber to the World Wildlife Fund under his admirable patronage, I do wish he would desist from keeping and then shooting such magnificent creatures as pheasants. In the same context, like a mass of anti-hunting, anti-shooting thinkers, I cannot help hoping that Prince Charles will relinquish such pastimes. Perhaps, like the association between maharajahs and tiger shoots, these pursuits will turn the corner before too long.

The Indian ICC representative this year was P. M. Rungta, large and very square, who liked to be known as Rung, but was not the Maharajah he could sometimes seem. My bag of this breed was now three (properly two, Baroda and Morvi, discounting rare game in Kapurthala: the genuine Gwalior and Sind were to be added 18 years later).

The summer of 1975 was a splendid one and I was sorry I had not retired in July to be able the better to soak in the sun. I felt I had finished my work at Rugby by the end of the academic year and it was with a sense of anticlimax that I returned for a last extra term to Christmas.

Around this time, although I would in theory on retirement from Rugby have had more time available instead of using nights and weekends, I gave up reviewing Pacific books. I had written many for *The Geographical Journal*, the journal of the Royal Geographical Society, and *Man*, the journal of the Royal Anthropological Institute, and some for the *Daily Telegraph*, *The Times*, the *Sunday Times* and other papers. But mostly I had been sent books by the *Times Literary Supplement*. Before I concluded my work for it, the paper had abandoned its policy of anonymity for its reviewers. This in no way affected my decision. Indeed, I would have preferred to have been known for what I had written. The clandestine cover certainly never affected what I expressed as my judgement of a book under review. One was not paid a great deal but the books could be kept. I had more substantial, continuous writing ahead of me and did not want it diverted.

I was now able to survey at the end of the day that I had never missed a meeting of the Governing Body, or its finance committee, appeal committee, estate committee, or War Memorial trustees, for all of which, meeting three times a year, I had written virtually all the papers without a break. In the course of this quarter-century I had been able to study a few prominent profiles. Of course, there were in addition internal school committees such as for grants, housing, works and buildings, similarly attended without missing a single one over the 25 years.

A Time of Renewal

At the end of the year the Governing Body magnanimously gave Anne and me an ambrosial dinner to which former governors (including Sir Edward Lewis) were also invited. It was believed to have been the first occasion this century when the members of the Governing Body were given the opportunity of a meal together, apart from the quatercentenary lunch I had organized eight years previously. Pat Dean presented me with a silver salver (he had consulted Charles about what I would like and I had requested it take that form) and I felt at ease in that company, which I had been addressing for a quarter of a century (Pat Dean was the only active governor surviving from my first meeting), in my reply, which I had nevertheless rehearsed carefully.

A most congenial occasion, it was held at the grand reception headquarters of British Petroleum, formerly the home of the Dowager Duchess of Grafton overlooking Hyde Park, through the arrangement of David Steel, chairman of British Petroleum (with whom I had worked closely all my time at Rugby: he and his wife, Ann, had also taken us to the Theatre Royal, Haymarket to see *The Case in Question*). The food was so excellent and the wine so fortifying (at that stage of my life, with a few hiccups *en route* to it, I liked to think that I knew the safe boundary of indulgence) that my impending speech was not foremost in my mind and I was able to enjoy the occasion fully.

The Governing Body could not have been more generous over my pension, to which I had of course contributed a percentage of my salary from the start. Because I had joined the school so early in my life (the normal age for bursarial appointments was about 50), supplying continuity in itself valuable in their estimation, and because I had served just less than half the severe qualifying period of 30 years for any Colonial Service pension in those times, they took that gap, which had been seriously uncovered for me, into account and again kindly helped. Pat Dean had wanted me to stay on five further years to 65. This was flattering but I felt that on health grounds for Rugby's good as well as my own I should call it a day at 60, plus the extra term for helping the Governing Body.

On the first day of 1976 my retirement took effect. I was glad to leave Rugby in what was acknowledged to be good shape. It was the end of my official life in which awe and iconoclasm (diplomatically kept to myself, by and large, I hope) were mixed inevitably as and when I thought they were due. In those closing 25 years, my profile had been a relatively low one — deliberately so — compared with both the prewar and Pacific years.

7

The Art Millionaire and the Bus Conductor

O n 1 January 1976, the day of my official retirement, I immediately started on *The People from the Horizon: An Illustrated History of the Europeans among the South Sea Islanders* with Stefanie as joint author. Both of us had seen John Calmann of Phaidon Press of Oxford (but about to be taken over by a Dutch firm) in 1974. Sharp and amusing, like a younger Harry Luke with a turned down nose and full red lips, he with his parents had been emigrants from Nazi Germany but he had not relished being at Westminster during Walter Hamilton's head-mastership. With an acknowledged capacity for drawing out the talents of others, Calmann wanted us to concentrate on the theme of the subtitle, when originally our idea had been to produce a beautifully illustrated book on artists in the Pacific, relying heavily on the superb artists on the French expeditions from the beginning to the middle of the nineteenth century. He had been right to persuade us to change our theme. It broadened the canvas immensely — and our research, although something of the idea had been germane in my mind for years.

Soon after, Calmann left Phaidon to set up on his own, only to be murdered in the south of France in 1980 when he offered a hitchhiker a lift in his Bentley. He had been on his way to visit his parents and was passing through forested countryside. A forest guard saw the car being driven off before finding Calmann's body. The car was later found in Nice but I'm not sure whether the murderer was ever caught. He was the second person I had known who had been murdered; the first — in London — had been the daughter of the Rugby School rackets professional. There were to be three more murders among my associates, which are always of course more perturbing even than deaths in war, in transport or other accidents, or from illness: and there had been the near assassination of H. G. R. McAlpine in Fiji.

Stefanie had read French and German at St Andrew's University but, finding its academic curriculum as medieval and archaic as the grim appearance of its granite buildings, had wisely brought it up to modern practical use by transferring to the Regent Street Polytechnic, London, now Westminster University. She quickly became an associate of the Institute of Linguists and, very conveniently, secured a post at the British Museum. This was a real point of advantage for looking at vital sources for the illustrations that were to make or break our book.

But her particular work at the museum had its own intrinsic interest and value. During the Blitz, fire bombs had fallen through the roofs of the wings containing the anthropological specimens. There was nothing that firemen could do but throw them down the stone staircases so that the flames could be drenched with water. In the course of this, vital identification labels had become detached. It was Stefanie's task, with one or two others, including Steven Hooper (then Phelps) — previously mentioned as having collaborated with Jane Roth on a really fine ethnological work after a year of studying customs and artefacts on a remote Lau island in the Fiji archipelago — to attempt to match watermarked labels with artefacts, some whole, some in fragments. A fascinating task which occupied the group for a couple of years when, ironically, on virtual completion, the articles (with their labels) were then put, because of the shortage of space in Bloomsbury, into crates and deposited in warehouses on the edge of the Thames. Stefanie followed up this post with an appointment as librarian at Rugby School, adding to the diversity of her occupations — she had started off by being a model — before settling down domestically and being a translator of French and German.

Because it was a school house, on my retirement Anne and I had to move from Horton House, 6 Hillmorton Road, Rugby. We had hugely enjoyed living in this early Victorian villa. We especially liked its proportions, the size of its rooms, the splendour of the entrance hall with its wide balustraded staircase and gallery, the Lebanon cedar as old as the house itself and set in bracken and crocuses, the home-made fountain (if I could not create botanical gardens then simple fountains were my inclination) and the long lawn leading from it up to the ornamental rear façade. It was always going to be difficult to move to something substantially smaller. The large-scale furniture, which Horton House demanded, had to be retained: we were too fond of it.

I had always decided that any retirement must be to the south, to more sun. Rugby was relatively high up and too near the Welsh rain-attracting mountains with the prevailing cold wind from there and the pall of the Birmingham area. We had been searching for a house for about two or three years and finally, in 1973, selected one at Angmering in Sussex, five miles from Worthing and two miles inland from the closest beach at Rustington. To house the Erard grand piano, dated 1900, which Anne had bought for £19 at an auction 20 years earlier and which neither of us could play, an extension to the drawing room was necessary. Likewise, to accommodate my books and papers, a sun house-cum-library had to be built on an edge of the lawn. It was essential to have my books, quite a turtle shell on one's back, close at hand for the research on *The People from the Horizon*, to which Stefanie was making her separate contributions, after which we would work together in coordinating our chapters and polishing the whole in unison.

When the summer of 1976 came and lasted and lasted, with temperatures of 100°F on the lawn and 140°F in the sun room, I thought that this, our second in Angmering, must always be what a Sussex summer was like. When I had toured it in 1951 for the MCC it was sunnier than other parts of the country seemed to be: this memory had been a determining factor in deciding on Sussex. Sublime as that summer of 1976 was, it was not conducive to the pace at which I wanted work on the book to proceed. It was hard going to force myself on.

On 16 February 1976, Charles wrote saying 'Pam has been gravely ill for some time. We didn't think she would come through.' It had been a dramatic respiratory attack. Hope had been abandoned. Anne and I went to visit her recuperating in King Edward

VII Hospital, Midhurst, not far from Angmering. Charles had been at Texas University at the time. We were hoping that she would be able to break her inhalation of cigarettes and whisky after their interdiction at Midhurst.

She had been intermittently quite ill since the supremely warm summer of 1975, when the garden at the back of Eaton Terrace had been virtually too small and the environment too crowded for the enjoyment of the gentle London air and for affording some sun. The interior of the house was too warm, one thought, to be good for Pam's lungs; and it probably did nothing for Charles if his back trouble was not, as final events showed, anything to do with lumbago. A month after being at Midhurst, Pam was brought by Charles to see our Angmering house, which she judged delightful and 'the garden most enviable', but two months later she was back in hospital with 'muscular collapse' and then went to Brighton to convalesce. I had to tell Charles that the week after their visit to us the robin, which I had trained to feed from his hand so affectionately and always immediately on call, had been killed by the neighbouring cat.

We went to visit a daughter of Sir George Ruthven Le Hunte, whom we found to exist blithely in a dowager duchess manner in her advanced eighties. Her father had been one of Sir Arthur Gordon's protégés in 1874 and Editha was probably the senior surviving child of that period and that pioneering setting.

I also traced another very distant predecessor of mine as District Commissioner Lau, and a valued Pacific contact before she died in 1978. Enid Wise was Sir Basil Thomson's daughter. Thomson was a marginally later protégé of Gordon's than Le Hunte. Enid Wise had been her father's secretary when he and his wife separated and, after marrying an Austrian, Major Weiz, who was an administrator in Somaliland, changed her name in the last war to Wise. She was naturally a positive mine of information on Basil Thomson, as well as on many of his records, with the result that I probably know more about that versatile, distinguished figure — a governor of Northampton, Dartmoor and Wormwood Scrubs prisons and assistant head of Scotland Yard — than anyone.

I was surprised and honoured to be asked by a Lauan I did not know, Filipe (Philip) Bole, to write the foreword to a work he was publishing on Ratu Sir Lala Sukuna. I commended his initiative. It was unexpected that a commoner would make this attempt. Two of the points I made about Ratu Sukuna were that from 1943 to 1946 his national qualities developed international and statesman-like dimensions and that the cultural aspect of him was a rich part of this larger than life Fijian in whom judiciousness and an ability to forgive and forget were paramount. I explained that I could venture an assessment because Sukuna and I had shared many mutual interests, ranging from our government work to sport and literature. Filipe Bole was to become Minister of Education in the 1980s and Deputy Prime Minister in 1992. His idea of a biography was later put out of joint by the committee manœuvring its own. As the published result of the committee's choice falls lamentably short of personal knowledge of Sukuna, Bole's unpublished work cannot be judged as having been superseded.

Jo Rabukawaqa's successor as Fiji's High Commissioner in London was a former director of education, Joe Gibson. Part-European, part-Rotuman (from the leading family of that intriguing group of islands that would like to be independent from Fiji with which they have no linguistic or ethnic links, but with which they are inextricably linked in an economic sense), Joe and his charming, elegant part-European, part-Samoan wife, Emily, came to see us often. They represented the best of Fiji's cross cultures. Joe sadly died in 1992.

A district officer who had gone out to Fiji after me and, disillusioned by some of the European civil service leadership of the 1950s in Fiji, had returned to England to make a life for himself in the City, was David Griffiths. Although he had no time for Christopher Legge's way of going about things as a district commissioner (he, like a few others, thought my friend, I believe, antediluvian), he too became a good friend of mine, for he obviously felt nostalgia for the real Fiji. He married Prince Philip's secretary, Anne, and, tragically, after a term of duty with a firm in Australia, contracted melanoma there from which he died at an early age. After some years of exposure to Fiji's sun, this surprised me, but since I have heard of a number of cases of skin cancer in Australia, there would seem to be something in the sun's rays on that continent against which one needs to be particularly guarded. After his death,

Anne resumed work for Prince Philip, cataloguing his libraries at both Buckingham Palace and Windsor Castle, where she came across my *Cricket in the Fiji Islands*, and was awarded the LVO.

Rosemary Seligman, Sir Arthur Grimble's daughter, came to see us with her husband, Adrian, whose *The Voyage of the Cap Pilar* describing his trip round the world is well known. She has edited her father's works and is an artist of merit. She was especially on guard about the reputation of her father, which seemed to be being sniped at by the Banaban islanders' prolonged action for higher royalties and compensation for the extraction of phosphates from Ocean Island. Only those Europeans who knew Grimble, as did Harry Maude and myself, have been able to refute the modern tendency to denigrate his character. Everyone, just everyone, applauds Grimble's *A Pattern of Islands*. I am not disposed to temper enthusiasm for it — only to advise caution in treating part of the veracity of some of the more colourful episodes.

About ten years previously, when I had been particularly busy at Rugby, Sir Rex de Charembac Nan Kivell, a New Zealander knighted by Australia for his gifts of paintings and books to the Australian National Museum, had asked if I would cooperate with him in producing a synoptic book on the Pacific. I told him that, as I had it in mind to do this myself when I retired, I would prefer to leave it and then go it alone (in the event, Stefanie's coauthorship was vital). I did not know him and unfortunately had no time to visit him in Chelsea and to see what he was doing.

In 1976 a sumptuous volume, *Portraits of the Famous and the Infamous: Australia, New Zealand and the Pacific, 1492–1970*, came out at £50 and I reviewed it enthusiastically. He had found a co-author, Sydney A. Spence. Busy as I was on *The People from the Horizon*, I had to meet them both. The meeting proved to lead to among the most bizarre of my friendships, for each was so palpably individual. Theirs was one of the most improbable of working partnerships.

Rex had asked me to visit him at his Tangier home but that was prevented by my agoraphobia. I went instead to Chelsea and had gin and tonics in a darkened room with him. He had a Moroccan manservant of huge bulk who looked after and chauffeured this frail millionaire bachelor to and from the Bond Street art gallery, one of the sources of his wealth. For a change, he once asked me to meet him there at Bond Street but on the day before I was to do so he died. I was given half a dozen of the folio volumes, inscribed to me. I now needed to obtain the inscription in them of Sydney A. Spence.

He turned out to be living up an open staircase in a very humble wooden first-floor flat on the outskirts of London with his wife, who most generously gave Anne and me a strawberry and cream tea. Sydney was equally generous in his way, giving me a copy of his *Antarctic Bibliography*. Working night shifts as a London bus conductor (by choice so that he could work in the British Museum in the daytime), he specialized in bibliographies and had been able to help Nan Kivell. He astonished me by saying that he had never met him. In addition, he had never been to the countries covered by the joint work. He was also a home printer and binder for his own, now much sought after, bibliographies. But he and his wife obviously lived on a shoestring; she, I imagine, most patiently indulging his expenses on his private work, which would have brought him in nothing.

Nan Kivell had, of course, financed the private appearance of their book, which was loaded with colour illustrations from his lifetime collection, of which he had given me a few duplicates. It is a superbly esoteric production but I honestly have to say that I could have helped substantially with the considerable Pacific portion. Nevertheless, it was a remarkable, quite intriguing combination of two personalities who had nothing in common but their age and research.

When a contestant on *Mastermind* nominated as his subject the life of Captain William Bligh, the BBC invited me to set the questions (thereby entitling me to membership of the Mastermind Club). I was given precise instructions for the form of the 15 questions requiring short, unequivocal answers in a single word (other than yes or no) or simple phrase, and for the 10 questions that required rather more — a descriptive sentence or two. The contestant was allowed to specify what he had read on the subject but the questions did not need be limited to the contents of those works. It took me a long time, aiming for balance between what was not too elementary or too arcane. Watching the programme, I sat on the edge of my chair, agitated in case the victim answered everything, thus indicating I had been too soft, or failed miserably, showing me to be an ogre. To my relief, out of a potential maximum of about 18, he answered 11, just not quite sufficient, with his general knowledge supplement, to qualify for the next round. Charles told me that he thought the questions very fair and claimed that he could have answered three or four.

Two famous cricket names came to us at Angmering. Rev Gilbert Jessop, son of the legendary agoraphobic G. L., had changed little since I had played with him for Christ's in the 1930s (I had not seen him for close on 50 years) when, man of the Church as he was, his demoniac driving was so menacing to the safety of his partner at the other end. He was probably one of the greatest first-class losses to both the game and its spectators when Hampshire, bafflingly, gave him only the barest of opportunities. R. E. S. Wyatt had been having his portrait painted by Juliet Pannett. Living in the village, she would tell me of her sitters, who had included the Queen and, on my suggestion, Pat Dean and Jim Woodhouse. Stefanie and I have also been among her subjects. When she mentioned Wyatt, I was keen to re-meet a famous name of the 1930s. And he was only too ready to talk about Jardine's leg-theory tour of Australia on which he had been vice-captain. We spent some — for me fascinating — hours on the subject, during which he did not fail to remind me that when he played for my MCC team in 1955 he had reluctantly accepted my invitation for him to bowl a number of overs at the age of 54 and had been required to follow this up with his usual batting doggedness. It had been quite a demanding day. He never let me forget it. Of all the distinguished living players of the exciting 1930s, his memoirs and those of Gubby Allen form the most prominent gaps. I never understood why he had not been involved later in MCC administration to become President. Bob Wyatt, living into his nineties and the most senior test player of any country by a clear margin, was, inexcusably, given no honour for his distinguished services to England's cricket.

I remember that at about this time Charles told me that Marshal of the RAF Lord Portal, whom we have met in these reminiscences, had doubts quite late in the day about strategic bombing but could not perform his obvious duty, which was to control Air Marshal Sir Arthur Harris who wanted to bomb German cities when Portal preferred to concentrate on industrial targets. It was a subject on which Charles had always anticipated the view of Portal: he had formed it from what he knew in the war and had learnt later from those closer to the centres of decision-making, such as Blackett and Bernal. But with the devastation of London, Coventry and the Baedeker cities still in acute memory, it must have been almost irresistible not to follow the Harris policy.

It was at this period that he had occasion to reply to a student correspondent (he was punctilious in replying to all but cranks), 'I am sorry that St Andrew's went wrong, but the first-year course at Scottish universities is very unsatisfactory.' Stefanie could echo that from her own experience of its unbending academic starkness.

The draft of *The People from the Horizon: An Illustrated History of the Europeans among the South Sea Islanders* had meanwhile been completed by Stefanie and me. It was overlong, but, try as we might, we simply could not reduce it. I sent it to Christoper Legge in Chicago, imploring him to cut it by 50,000 words: we would not mind what came out, I said in anguish. Excisions to that extent had to be made. Back came a telegram: 'Awfully sorry. Quite excellent. Can't suggest that a single word be omitted. Christopher.' This was complimentary but not helpful in the circumstances. In increased desperation and with some trepidation, I wrote (he did not like the telephone) to Charles to ask if he could do likewise.

I waited anxiously for a rebuff — it was a tall order. He rang up when I happened to be out. That he should telephone was in itself almost without precedent. To Anne's relief, he was all sweetness and light, asking if I really did want him to cut it up. She ratified the request that it had to be reduced to 90,000 words. He said, when she expected that he would suggest somebody else, that he would do it, having checked this point first. Within a fortnight it came back with deletions and, what was more, connections back to the parts where they had been taken out — a most thorough professional job. He commented in his letter that I had caught him in almost the only free fortnight of his life and that, if the words were counted, it would be found to be about right. He had simply guessed as he went along. On counting, it proved almost exactly to be at the 90,000 word limit.

On 28 October I reported to Charles: 'Peter has brought the book back. What a marvellous job you have done.' Stefanie sent Charles a practical gift. A major passion of Charles was Leicestershire pork pies, unprocurable from outside the county. She wrote to him from Clifton-upon-Dunsmore, near Rugby: 'I thought that you might like this as a token of appreciation for your backbreaking work to produce such an excellent effort so promptly. The book was taken by hand to Phaidon today through fog and snow.' Charles replied on 23 December: 'Many, many thanks for your splendid pork pie. There could have been no finer gift.' Anne and I took Charles and Pam to dinner in a restaurant near their Belgravia house on the last but one day of 1976 in inadequate return for the marvellous editing of the book, which had seemed impossible to achieve; it was to be two more years before publication was complete. Many of the illustrations we had selected were deliberately abstruse, yet for that reason the more desirable. But, as can be imagined, the tracing of copyright holders was a formidably elusive task, done conscientiously from our data by the Phaidon Press director, Jean-Claude Peissel, and his staff, notably Simon Lawson. We were honoured to have the assent of Theo Heyerdahl among others.

In 1977 Charles had travelled to the furthest east destination in his life — to Ahmedabad and Baroda for lectures after an earlier cancellation through riots. He relished being treated as a pundit, a role he accorded himself with some justificatory self-regard. Not given to choosing intellectuals in this country for company, he found Indian intellectual society, with its placid reverential manners in academic circles, to be nevertheless home from home. He experienced first hand the loyalty, which friendship with Indians, once established, creates, as I had known at lower thinking levels. He was very much the guru type. Had he lived he would have returned to India as a contrast with his habitual America–Russia rounds.

He had told Pace University in America in 1977: 'Someone once said that clever intellectuals may have their uses. But stupid ones are the bane of my life.' I was to hear him repeat this quite often:

once he had a phrase in mind he did not let it go lightly. No one discriminated more between intellectuals and intelligent people. He once said to me: 'If I had to be isolated with an intelligent colonel or an intellectual scientist I know whom I would choose every time.'

Pam seemed reasonably to have recovered. So Charles decided to write on Bernal, Kapitza and Aldington for a second volume of *Variety of Men*, for which I strongly pressed. He wrote and told me on 24 November 1977 that 'Aldington doesn't really come up to standard as a writer but he was a picturesque character whom I knew well and is a lead to a particular movement and coterie in twentieth-century literature. I shan't be able to include Macmillan and haven't yet settled on the nine or ten.' He had asked me to help in the research for this second series, adding on 7 December that 'almost any piece of odd information is valuable'.

I duly undertook research on Aldington, Kapitza, Bernal, Blackett and Isador Isaac Rabi, the Polish-Russian Nobel prize winner in physics and professor of physics at Columbia University. Charles had warned Peter Kapitza: 'I am now contemplating a second set of people including my own generation. I shall probably do Bernal, Blackett, Rabi, one or two American writers and so on. I should very much like to write something about you. You can trust me to be both warm and discreet.' Aldington was to be included, Charles reminding me for research purposes that his real surname was Godfree and that there was a certain amount of concealment and mystification. I wrote to Charles on 5 December 1977: 'In the New Year I'll keep an eye open for biographical material on Aldington, Kapitza and Bernal.'

He was going to prepare a chapter on Macmillan despite this being likely to hold up the publication, for he was very much alive. Charles had thought of Werner Heisenberg, German Nobel prize-winning physicist (who is considered to have abstained from producing in Germany the atomic bomb with the nightmare belief that others on the opposite side were doing so), as one of the second team for this sequel to *Variety of Men*, together with Ludwig Wittgenstein, the philosopher, of whom I knew absolutely nothing. But he was conscious that, in comparison with *Variety of Men*, it was very much a second team with the exceptions of

Macmillan, Bernal, Aldington and Kapitza. In November 1976, he had told Scribner: 'It is time I did something and I think I can produce some interesting characters, English, American, Russian and even German (I may include Heisenberg). Unfortunately there is no one left as internationally famous as Einstein in any walk of life I can think of.' It will be noted that Charles always eschewed the word 'British'. His studied avoidance was because he insisted that it was the only correct word in its right context. His practice was to treat Britain as a political, not a conversational, term. He said as much in an introduction to *Lands and Peoples: Europe, England*, published by Grolier of New York.

Charles brought out two very different works in 1978. *A Coat of Varnish*, having crime and detection as its *raison d'être*, was almost a reversion full circle in motive to his first book, *Death Under Sail*, very readable, simplistic perhaps but still having its adherents. Like *In Their Wisdom*, it was adapted for the stage by Sir Ronald Millar and, when presented at the Theatre Royal, Haymarket in 1982, he invited Anne, Stefanie, Peter and me to watch it from a box. This was the only time I had been in one of those curious structures situated so much to the side and over the heads of the actors, who seemed to perform not to it but exclusively to the stalls. We were invited to meet the cast backstage in the bar afterwards, among whom were Peter Barkworth, Michael Denison and Dulcie Gray. Others, not in the play but adding celebrity to the occasion, were Katie Boyle, as glamorous as her Camay soap advertisement, and Leonard Rossiter, whom we thought remarkably untheatrical (it perhaps helped that he had not been in the play but was relaxing in the complete normality that must be so hard for professionals to achieve).

Very different from *A Coat of Varnish* was *The Realists: Portraits of Eight Novelists*, for which I corrected the proofs and delivered them to Macmillans while Charles was in America. I welcomed Charles's return to the biographical scene. It is dedicated to me and I cannot withhold my admiration for the vignettes of Balzac, Stendhal, Dickens, Tolstoy, Proust, Dostoevsky, Galdós and Henry James. They were written with almost no research, straight out of his head. His style was astringent, his judgements penetrating, his power of summary commanding.

When I told Charles that I would be pleased to proof-read *The Realists* for him, he wrote on 7 March 1978: 'I shall accept your offer with gratitude ... I have never worked so hard and so continuously since I was 25, and extra reading is a great deal of a strain.'

On Leavis's death, I wrote to Charles and Pam. The latter replied on 20 April 1978: 'Oh, Leavis. Well it doesn't seem to matter much. He had done his ugly worst and damaged Charles quite a bit. I doubt whether he had another shot in his locker.' Then, on 24 April, Charles wrote:

> I have just referred John Halperin to you about books of mine which I do not possess. You may be able to help. He is a good American academic who is writing an unofficial study of me and my work, but I am giving him a certain amount of access. ... Zuckerman has been an enemy of mine for 40 years. He has tried to cut my throat at least four times but fortunately without success on anything that matters to me. If I think it worthwhile I will deal with him in due course.

In 1978 Jack Plumb, having worked for the ambition so long and as slyly as college politics require, inevitably gained the mastership of Christ's after Todd. He had been aiming his sights on this ever since, after a rejection by Christ's which turned him to King's, he returned to the college and its minor offices, time taking its toll of rivals. When he had been a postgraduate at Christ's in the mid-1930s, at the time I was there, one could almost even then sense the jockeying, if not the long-term intrigue, taking shape. He had discovered his *métier*. At that time he was an ally of Charles. Jack Plumb was not too far from the college during the war. At Bletchley on code work, he would turn up at Christ's to test his toe for the temperature and keep his foot in the door.

On his final return to Christ's in 1946, his relationship with Charles was less close and more centred on himself. He had generously given Charles a fiftieth birthday dinner in his room at Christ's in 1960 to which he invited Bert Howard and me but that was a rare occasion and there were long intervals, notably after

Bert Howard's death in Holland in 1964, when there was coolness. A degree of friendship resumed when Plumb (he had not been an observer of the goings-on for elections to fellowships and masterships for nothing) became Master and acquired his deeply coveted knighthood in 1982, the year he retired as Master.

When Jack accommodated Anne and me in the Lodge during the unveiling of the memorial incorporating Charles's ashes on the edge of the swimming pool in the Fellows' garden at Christ's, his hospitality was impressive, as was his superb Sèvres collection in long glass cases. There were imperial features in his refurbishment of the Master's Lodge and his presiding over the Senior Combination Room. From lower middle-class origins, he has been very successful in both his finances and career ambitions. Jack Plumb is richly endowed with social shrewdness and political adroitness.

Rather surprisingly, he was in only one of Charles's novels and then merely as half a character when in life he has been a character and a half. But then Harry Hoff, whom Charles had known for almost as long and had been geographically (and in other ways) closer than Jack, was not even a fraction of one. Both were Charles's longest living friends dating from the mid-1920s in Jack's case and the early 1930s in Harry's. Jack Plumb had written the script, with Sir Huw Wheldon as the commentator, for a much publicized television programme on the Royal collections, which came out in book form as *Royal Heritage* in 1977.

Charles was always surprised at Plumb's comparative lack of prolificacy when he had been a fellow with such long holidays for practically all his life. Charles's suspicions of the sybaritic way of life in universities were deep. When Plumb overlapped the first half of my years at Newton's and my time at Christ's, I would have been endowing myself with preternatural foresight had I picked him out as ultimately likely to make so much of a name for himself — as a historian of professorial status maybe, as an establishment figure at the head of administration never in a month of Sundays. But who has the gifts of prescience to judge one's contemporaries in youth?

About this time Charles gave an interesting summary of his own views of his novels to Robert J. Johnstone:

The neatest novel and most satisfactory in its own right is *The Masters*. I had things which interested me more in *Time of Hope*, *Homecomings* and *Last Things*. I am inclined to think the first hundred pages of *Homecomings* is the deepest writing that I have done. I don't envy his (Powell's) work or that of any writer alive. This is not because I think I am all that good but because, as the Russians say, each has his own word and all one can do is to say it.

He confessed to a professor of English at Minnesota University, where he was delivering a memorial lecture, 'I have no aversion to being interviewed and no particular passion for it either.'

Mention of Powell's name reminds me that, as one of the very few to have gone through Charles's archive (I did so, except for pre-1950 material, in England before it went to Texas), I was aware that Charles had little correspondence with fellow writers. There were Anthony Powell (they exchanged courteous letters), Anthony Burgess signing himself John (he was in fact John Wilson) on an occasionally rather excitable note, and Graham Greene on purely perfunctory matters. Going through the 1950s to 1980 archive absorbed quite a lot of my leisure, for I made notes for use in the books I would be writing. In my *Stranger and Brother: A Portrait of C. P. Snow* I matched (having had them ratified by Charles earlier in his own handwritting) a large number of characters in his novels with the people from whom he had partly (or sometimes wholly) drawn them. Some I did not reveal because the prototypes or partial ones were still alive.

Here are a few others, however, to add to the list. Bidwell is Richardson, his gyp or manservant at Christ's. I was fond of him but Charles, knowing him so much better, saw rascally sides to him. Mr Justice Bosanquet is Brian Gibbens, recorder of Oxford, a QC who presided in the longest trial ever in Britain on a £25 million fraud which ended after 274 days in 1981 costing £3 million. Olive Calvert is Betty Grimes, whom Anne and I liked when we met her at the Christ's May Ball in 1937. Rosalind Calvert is Betty Herbert, a friend who had married a near contemporary of mine at Newton's. She died recently. Adam Cornford is Anthony Storr, the psychiatrist and writer. Margaret Davidson is

The Art Millionaire and the Bus Conductor

Holly Southwell, daughter of Sir Richard Southwell, Rector of Imperial College of Science and Technology, who was deeply fond of him and died early of multiple sclerosis. Dawson-Hill is Alan Pryce-Jones, critic and former editor of the *Times Literary Supplement*, Mr Justice Fane is Mr Justice Stable. Lester Ince is Kingsley Amis. Sir Hector Rose is Hugh (Binkie) Beaumont, the theatre impresario. Azek Schiff is Eric Sosnow. I have omitted about a dozen others directly revealed to me by Charles as being only partial portraits.

There were health worries on our side of the family now. Out of the blue, Anne was struck with a retinal vein thrombosis, practically losing the sight of one eye. Specialists, including Lorimer Fison of Harley Street who had saved Charles's life during his detached retina operation when he had cardiac failure, were sure she would not recover it, but a decade later she has astonishingly done so completely. After it occurred she had a mild coronary thrombosis, a mild ischaemic attack and mild angina. All were found to be connected to undetected high blood pressure, which has most satisfactorily been reduced to an excellent level and controlled, leaving her trail of attacks well behind her.

On 22 June 1978 Charles wrote: 'How are you? How is Anne? I got back from America a couple of weeks ago but in a state of complete exhaustion. I used to think I was as tough as any but I suspect that my days for arduous travel are coming to an end. I have more or less recovered, though I've some pain from lumbago.' His physical condition was now being mentioned in much of his correspondence. To I. Nedev of the Bulgarian embassy he had written on 13 June:

> I have just returned from an exhausting trip in America and am suffering from some physical consequences. It looks to me as though my days of strenuous travelling are coming to an end. It isn't the speeches on the public occasions so much as meeting several hundreds of people whom one will never meet again and having to exert energy all the time.

And to Jacques Barzun, professor of history at Columbia University, he wrote two days after that: 'We returned from

201

America a few days ago, both in a state of extreme fatigue. Pam was worse than me but I too have decided that this sort of arduous travel will now have to be renounced. With me, the chief consequence is persistent lumbago, and I don't like being in more or less constant pain.' All the same he was able to report on other subjects, for instance, on Aldous Huxley as 'a friend of mine, extremely clever and quite abnormally well-informed. But he is one of the most credulous men I have ever met'.

Pam wrote to me on 27 June 1978:

> We are both of us dreadfully distressed about poor Anne. ... We had a really awful American trip and shan't attempt a tour like that again. Charles had dreadful lumbago and I got so weak that I had to be carried around the University of Minnesota in a wheelchair. We both had to have wheel-chairs at Kennedy and Heathrow. ... It isn't the speech-making that is so tiring, it is meeting hundreds of people one is never likely to see again. But all this pales before Anne's misfortune.

Christopher Legge, my somewhat and always delightfully eccentric friend for 41 years — since his never to be forgotten drifting down the Rewa River on a deck chair astride a put-put past my house — died just before *The People from the Horizon* was published in 1979. His correspondence with me on it and long before on a multitude of subjects was unflagging: he was always a wonderful mine of miscellaneous information, not least on the Pacific. His bold handwriting was done virtually upside-down, with the left hand pointing into himself at right angles to his body.

If the post had existed with comparable stipend, Christopher, instead of being an administrative officer with its heavy linguistic demands for work with both Fijians and Indians (of whom he was nevertheless a penetrating judge without their always recognizing his powers of perception), should have been curator of the Fiji Museum and archivist. It would have been his absolute niche in the colony and Fiji would have been immeasurably the richer in its records and memorabilia. An example of his curiosity off the beaten track and of rare value to the country was his encouragement and bringing into real light the precious talent of W. J. Belcher. This humble road foreman on Taveuni was found by Christopher to have an exquisite collection of paintings he himself had done of Fiji birds, some of them no doubt extinct but fortunately all recorded in published form.

Generous to a fault and without an ounce of mordancy in him, his air of absent-mindedness in making his way about, in hardly appearing to listen, was utterly misleading. He took everything in and gave as much and more out. He was 74 when he died. Perhaps he may be said to have lived on borrowed time for 45 years, ever since the spectacular affliction of blackwater fever, which is described in the first of these two volumes.

The publishers of *The People from the Horizon*, which I would dearly have liked Christopher Legge to have seen in published form, set a price far too high, completely against the advice of Stefanie and myself. We implored that it should not be £40 but somehow kept in the £30 range. We realized of course that with the 40 magnificent colour plates and 250 splendid black and white pictures, it had been expensive to produce: printed in Italy, the publication looked quite superb. Owing to inept salesmanship in Australasia, it was rarely seen there — an obvious market unexploited. Priced at £40, it was remaindered at short notice, with copies being snapped up for less than £10.

In 1986 McLaren of London had it reprinted, again magnificently, this time in Singapore — 3000 copies at the absurdly low price of £9.95. There seemed to be no follow-up in the sales department and again it was quickly remaindered. For those who find copies at about £10, it must be one of the best bargains for a coffee table. So again, there had been little luck financially with one's literary output. The reviews in 1979 from all parts of the world were complimentary: it was regarded as an exceptionally fine publication. The mass of pictures had seldom, if at all, been seen before — for that was our policy in Stefanie's diligent search for, and our selection of, them.

On 1 February 1979 Charles wrote, 'I don't like illustrated books and I have always regretted doing the *Trollope* in that form.' But that was before he saw the published version of *The People from the Horizon*, regardless of the fact that it was specifically an illustrated history and that he did not see any of Stefanie's and my pictures until it came out later in the year. He had thought that the text in the draft, to which he had so unselfishly put his masterly editorial touches, stood in merit on its own. *Trollope* was the sole book of his to be produced with pictures in his lifetime.

This same year the first competition for associate members (that is, the non test-playing countries) of the International Cricket Conference took place. For years I had been on the organizing committee, after having conceived the idea for it, supplemented emphatically the following year by Alma Hunt, President of the Bermuda Board of Control. The only Bermudan to have played in a West Indian trial, he is a fine, conscious eccentric (wearing a Sherlock Holmes costume — check caped coat, deerstalker hat and Meerschaum pipe — creating with his Caribbean colouring an indelible impression in London's streets) and a warm, loyal friend of long standing.

Once the concept of associate membership had been established, the question for me now was how to secure the Fijians' participation. They would have to come further by far than the players of any other country, as many as 2000 miles more each way than even the Papua New Guineans. The cost was estimated to be enormous. Fiji could raise nothing. I tried the two richest benefactors of whom I had heard. Sir Jack Hayward, the philanthropist exiled in the Bahamas, expressed willingness in theory but regretted that his trust required that the words 'Great Britain' had to be attached to all projects. In no way could Great Britain–Fiji or Fiji–Great Britain be manœuvred.

Having heard that he was probably the wealthiest man in the world and generous with his money, I then wrote to Adnan Al-Khashoggi and then forgot all about it and abandoned hope rather than anticipate disappointment. To my astonishment and intense pleasure, he replied that if the Fiji cricket team had never been to England before they should certainly come and here was a cheque for £25,000. No strings attached. He had apparently bought an enterprise in Fiji called Pacific Harbour, about 30 miles from Suva, beyond Navua, for tourists and assumedly thought that the publicity must be good as he liked Fijians.

I later sought information about him. Apparently, his father had been a humble Saudi Arabian who had managed to acquire medical qualifications and to be appointed surgeon to the court of the King. He had then been able to educate abroad Adnan, who in turn became a global entrepreneur, dealing, it is said, like other billionaires this century, among other financial interests, like governments themselves, in arms between governments. In Paris, he had met a young Irishwoman accompanied by her mother: their short stay there had been the result of having won a competition. He had then married the young woman who changed her name at 19 from Patricia Jarvis-Daley to Soraya Khashoggi.

She and her mother, a waitress, had lived in a terraced house where Richmond Road, Leicester, joined Lansdowne Road opposite the public library, outside which I used to philander. She would have been too young then, indeed not born, to have caught my eye. But when I revisited Richmond Road occasionally in 1946 and from 1951 onwards, she would have been growing up at No. 90 Lansdowne Road, which in fact looked more like part of Richmond Road at that junction. Her house still exists, whereas there is a gap where No. 40 Richmond Road had stood. On divorce, Soraya claimed she had made Adnan a socially acceptable international figure, sued for $2 billion alimony and received $1 million.

There had therefore been two fortuitous links with Adnan Khashoggi. I hadn't known that he had property in Fiji and he of course had not known that his wife could hardly have been a nearer neighbour of ours in Leicester. His help for Fiji was a lifesaver for its cricket. My gratitude for the start that it gave has been perpetual. If Richmond Road has a claim to fame through the plaque on it for C. P. Snow, Lansdowne Road adjoining it has not been lacking in distinction through Soraya Khashoggi's phenomenal rise from obscurity. As mentioned very early on in the first volume, in the 1930s the road also housed three sisters, all beautiful and all singers — Shirley Lenner, Judy Shirley and Anne Lenner. The last named was outstanding in Carroll Gibbons's Savoy Hotel orchestra before the beginning of the war. I knew the sisters only by sight: perhaps my experience with three other sisters only two roads away imposed its limitations.

Joe Gibson, the Fiji High Commissioner, notified me that he was putting me up for the OBE. When he telephoned later, he said that he had mixed news. An honour was certainly going through but as he himself was getting the CBE in the list it was thought in Fiji — by the Prime Minister — that there could not be two relatively high ones simultaneously accorded to residents in Britain. So an MBE it would be for me. I had to keep quiet for a month until it was in the Queen's birthday honours list. Both Gibson and the Governor-General, Ratu Sir George Cakobau, thought that it should at least be an O and certainly not an M. Jo Rabukawaqa had told me in 1976 that he had put me up then for a C. He showed me his letter — the case that he made was weak and some of it frankly irrelevant. I never had hopes of that. But here was a little something and it *was* My Bloody Effort.

The Fiji cricket team appeared and encountered the wettest June ever known in the Midlands, where the International Cricket Conference trophy competition was being held. Almost everything was washed out: the pavilions were cold, the grounds under water. Yet the team members retained remarkable spirit. In two friendly matches they defeated the USA and Argentina, and in competition matches lost, not unexpectedly to me, to Canada (whose team was almost exclusively West Indian), Denmark (showing immediately strength that has become unmistakable) and Bangladesh very narrowly. They had gained some experience. Sir Josua Rabukawaqa had come over as manager, only to be afflicted immediately on arrival with severely swollen knees and ankles.

These seemed so bad that, on the advice of Dr Theo Waine, Peter's father, an emergency doctor had to be called. It looked as though he would have to be returned to Fiji instantly. I was liaison officer and now carrying out managerial duties. Tablets reduced the swelling and pain for him and, by the end of the month, after having been hobbling about on two crutches at first, then on one, he was ultimately jumping about more vigorously than for years. Apparently, he had similar swelling caused by water retention before leaving. He made a good ambassadorial figure when he had recovered but he was insufficiently expert in the technique or tactics of the game to help the team. I was careful to leave as much as I thought desirable in the hands of the Fijian captain. The team had one European (a New Zealander), two part-Europeans (one the son of Harry Apted) and a Rotuman: all the rest were Fijians. I itched to be 20 years younger and able to play.

The team were great fun to be with and for their part they made it only too clear that I was a legend to them. I had coached, and played with, the fathers of some of them. The pity was that, in the intervening years since my leaving, there had been no coaching and little encouragement from the old players, especially the chiefs. Jo Rabukawaqa had been a leading figure and the shortcomings in his knowledge were patently clear to me. Still it was a start. Anne had helped me with my agoraphobia in my duties as liaison officer-cum-manager. I was able to go to all matches and functions, including a press conference.

About the time of the tour of the Fiji team Charles made what was to be his last visit abroad. He was alone this time and had gone as presidential lecturer to Texas University, where his accumulated papers were housed. The C. P. Snow Fellowship was to be established for readers working on his papers (Donald Dickson, embarking on his large-scale biography of Charles and making frequent visits to Angmering, was to become the first holder of it a decade later). I had of course seen virtually all the papers in England.

He had then gone on to Union College at Schenectady, New York, to receive an honorary degree, his thirtieth and final one (a dizzy total although another was on its way). There he stayed with his new friend Dr Irving S. Cooper, to whom he had become very attached. 'Coop' was to die in the 1980s at a not at all advanced age. They had planned to collaborate on a number of subjects associated with medical psychology and ethics but with the onset of Pam's grave illness and subsequent recurrences in late 1976, Charles had become inhibited about the topic. At that time he had told Scribner: 'This is what I intended to do, and I think that it would make a satisfactory novel, but just at present I shrink from that.' He wrote from New York: 'I have recently had gout and now have backache.' This was supposed to be considered part, however irreconcilable with the true affliction, of the migration of arthritis. On 28 December 1979, he wrote to say that he was on the mend. Pam had written to me on 20 December 1979.

Of course drop in on the 30th. We shall be delighted to see
you both. I do hope Anne's eyes are a little better. Peter,
who called in last night, told me that she had been
depressed, and no wonder ... Charles better at last — touch
wood.

We were both enthralled by the book [*The People from
the Horizon*] which is a beautiful job of work. Alas, we
cannot have it on the drawing room shelves, as none is wide
enough, but it will be put in Charles's special shelves [a
seventieth birthday present] kept specially for him in the
corridor.

Earlier than that, on 2 October 1979, I had had a letter from
Pam containing news I did not like. She had written that 'we had a
disappointing five days at Stratford [where they went most years]
as Charles had crippling lumbago and persistent vomiting. ... He
has lost half a stone. ... Of course we shall be glad to have you
both for the Investiture.' This did not sound like lumbago to me,
and I say this, not with the benefit of hindsight but as it occurred
to me at the time. He had written to Donald Dickson in October
that he had 'been more or less bedridden for a month with acute
lumbago and any irritation is to be avoided'. At the same time he
had written to Anthony Blond: 'I have been having violent kinds
of various rheumatic complaints which have been afflictions of
mine since I was in my mid-twenties. They aren't lethal but
excessively painful and depressing and make ordinary social life
very difficult. In my case, even alcohol becomes repugnant. So I
think I had better stay in seclusion, thinking gloomy thoughts.'
The reaction to alcohol, to my lay mind, made ulcers suspect,
much more than a rheumatic disorder.

Illness apart, to a correspondent he declared: 'Roger Quaife is a
composite character and certainly not Harold Macmillan who is a
personal friend of mine. David Rabin is based largely but not
entirely on an American scientist called I. I. Rabi, a man of great
achievement'. Charles had written to Anthony Burgess (John
Wilson) at Monte Carlo on 18 September 1979: 'When I was
starting to write my elders and betters used to say starkly that you
must never write to give thanks for a review. This didn't prevent

them from doing so themselves ... Your piece [on *The Realists*] gave me intense pleasure.' This is advice I have not myself followed.

A real test for me loomed up — the investiture at Buckingham Palace. In earlier days I would have revelled in it, as to some extent I had when Charles had taken Pam and me to the conferment of his accolade as a knight. Now it was my turn, albeit in the most humble category — in a way that was more of an ordeal for me because MBEs were almost at the end of the hour-long ceremony. Anyway, Anne and I stayed with Charles and Pam the previous night at Eaton Terrace and Stefanie, now living near London (in Welwyn Garden City where she had moved from Rugby in 1977), came along after breakfast to pick us up, me in black morning dress, and to chauffeur us in my car.

I had previously told a most understanding official at the Palace of my predicament. He gave approval for the car to be parked in the forecourt of the Palace near a side entrance where there was a lift straight up to the ballroom, thus saving the climb between shining armour-plated guardsmen flanking the staircase. The official had also arranged for me to sit in the annexe just outside the ballroom door, thus avoiding being in the slow-moving croco-dile headed by knights-designate. Surreptitiously, I supplemented from a hip flask the sweet sherry that I had had straight after breakfast (to Charles's horror: he did not realize that it was a one-off occasion demanding it and that afterwards I would not touch a drop of anything). This had been the main reason for Stefanie driving me to the Palace.

She and Anne were seated towards the end of the ballroom, such was the precedence or lack of it attached to my M. The Queen was ten minutes late in arriving; this was apparently most unusual. The Gurkha orderlies had taken their place like frozen oriental ornamental sentinels and the Lord Chamberlain (Lord Maclean) started announcing for all to hear in the ballroom each name in turn. I recognized a few public faces in the higher orders. Mean-while, the minutes ticked by appallingly slowly, as did the croco-dile. It was fully an hour before an official asked me to take my place in the crocodile — a clasp had previously been fastened on my lapel.

A Time of Renewal

I felt weak in the legs. One of the worst features was that I could see no cloakroom in which to be able to take refuge if unable to go along with the proceedings. There had been one or two (older, I am also ashamed to admit) sitting with me as special cases on the gilt chairs at the side of the annexe through which the crocodile shuffled every minute or two. At last I was within view of the platform where the Gurkhas stood one on each side and two or three aides deftly stepped backwards and forwards from the Queen to the table containing all the decorations. I was now second, then first in the queue, and could see the Queen pinning an MBE on a lapel and also the Lord Chamberlain standing four square in front of the vast seated concourse in the main body of the ballroom.

I thought, as 'Mr Snow' was called out loud and clear by Lord Maclean, 'My God! What happens if I collapse?' I clenched my teeth, walked very conscious of all the eyes behind me (which were of course only idly observing now that they and their relatives had had their minute or so) towards a line at right angles to the Queen, then turned and bowed, as instructed when in the annexe, and took three or four paces up to her. She was of course standing for the duration. I can't remember if she shook hands before or after (or both: I don't think so). She was wearing white gloves but what else, except, I believe, a golden dress, I can't recall. I was anxious not to have everything in too sharp a focus but to have my hyper-sensitivity (sometimes the shortcoming or downside of liking to be a close observer of life) slightly anaesthetized.

As stage performers (and perhaps royalty, although they seem to be trained early on to be inured somehow) must know better than anyone, public nerves are the very devil — they can be the end of careers too easily. It must be so much worse when one has to say some words, or a lot of them, and to be sure to catch the cues. Even so, in the past I had had a number of things to do in full public view before far greater numbers, not least playing in front of crowds exceeding 10,000 for days on end without a moment's misgiving, indeed, with heightened pleasure. The more the merrier.

The Queen, smilingly taking the MBE from an official and hanging it in the clasp, asked to my intense surprise, 'When did you leave Fiji?' (There had been no briefing; Lord Maclean had simply called out 'Mr Snow' and the aides from the table behind had said nothing; nor were there any labels; she had memorized 'Snow' and 'Fiji' among a hundred names.) I had to make a quick calculation (it certainly helped to take my mind off the awful reality of the public moment) and hope that it was right. Deduct 1951 from 1979 went through my head and I came up with '28 years ago, Your Majesty'. I noticed her right eyebrow go up (she has rather prominent eyebrows). This reaction I had seen at Rugby when Jim Woodhouse, next to me and the Queen, had suggested a deviation from the approved and much rehearsed route in 1967. Looking across at him, with the Queen watching us, I had seen that eyebrow go up in surprise when I had unsuccessfully tried to persuade him to keep to the route — Jim had had his way and we had left the red carpet to go across a squelchy lawn.

I half expected her now to ask, 'Have you never wanted to go back?' I would have been ready with my reply: 'My wife and I prefer to remember it the way it was when we left, ma'am,' but the question did not arise. My one and a half or two minutes were nearly up. Now the Queen smiled again and said 'I am pleased to present you with this award for your work,' or words to that effect. This was the key for me to bow and retreat backwards the three or four paces and then to turn in the opposite direction where more officials were waiting to take off the decoration and clasp, putting the former in a black box and handing it to me.

All over successfully, I now walked with a spring in my step down the empty annexe (parallel to the one in which I had been sitting outside the opposite wall of the ballroom) and across the bottom of the ballroom, smiling confidently at Anne and Stefanie to take my seat in front of them in the main part of the ballroom with the other recipients for the short remainder of the ceremony. The band in the gallery over the back of the ballroom where Anne and Stefanie were seated had been playing light music, which was no doubt intended for, and to some extent succeeded in, relieving the weight of the occasion.

I remembered again thinking, as I had when Charles was being knighted, that it would have been amusing if my shaking hands (and Charles doing so on his occasion) with the Queen had coincided with 'When I marry Mr Snow' from *Carousel*. I would have liked a snatch of it for my couple of minutes — if I had had one ear in that direction, which would have been unlikely.

When the Queen had left I felt that I was walking on air and insisted on not returning by the lift but going along the red carpeted corridor, lined with gigantic paintings in elaborate gilt frames, down the staircase between the seemingly seven foot high guards in their scarlet plumes, buckskin riding breeches, resplendent knee-high leggings and gilt breastplates. Outside we were duly photographed with the Order being displayed.

Quite unauthorizedly, I took my camera from the car and went about the inner courtyard taking pictures of it from angles that I had never seen photographed before. It was with reluctance that I returned to the car for Stefanie to drive to Eaton Terrace for a change of dress and lunch. I felt exhilarated with relief and had long forgotten the sherry. I only wanted water to drink at lunch. Such is the psychological absurdity of agoraphobia as I knew it.

I have described the investiture in some detail, not only because it was slightly odd in my case but also because I find there is public curiosity in the procedure and atmosphere of an occasion not too commonly encountered and seldom publicly depicted. A feature of the MBE scroll, which came through the post, was that it was signed at the bottom 'Philip' as Grand Master of the Order of the British Empire and 'Elizabeth R' at the top. It is the only order to bear both the Queen's and Prince Philip's signatures.

Charles seemed well at this time. On 28 December 1979, he wrote that 'he was on the mend'. We visited him and Pam for lunch on the last day of the year as we passed Eaton Terrace from Stefanie's where we had spent Christmas. On 2 January 1980, I wrote:

> In the quick visit, which we enjoyed (please thank Pam for the sustenance for our journey home), I omitted to mention that in addition to the inevitable blue plaque on 40 Richmond Road there will also be one quite nearby — as close as 20 terraced houses away at 90 Lansdowne Road: 'Here was born and lived until the age of 16 Mrs Adnan Khashoggi, the richest woman in the world 20 years later.'

... We were delighted to see you patently so much better than in October.

I would not have proffered this frivolous item had I not thought that he was in a pain-free mood to accept the levity.

He had resumed writing — *The Physicists* was making good progress — and had been awarded the international Dimitrov prize, Bulgaria's highest cultural honour, for his 'outstanding contribution to the better understanding among peoples and intellectuals of different countries'. Not long afterwards, however, there was a postcard from Pam, dated 20 February, saying 'Shall be pleased to see you on 27th. C's back is v[ery] bad.' Charles was clutching a hot water bottle in the small of his back as he deliberately sat at one angle in the chair. But he was otherwise remarkably cheerful when we did see him.

The People from the Horizon had been put in for the first Arts Council of Great Britain's national award (non-fictional part). (When Jack Plumb saw it some years after publication, he said that he wished that a copy had been sent to him from the publishers or me. I hadn't known that he was a judge for the handsome Wolfson award. He was sure that had he known of the book it would have gained that prize.) The next we knew was that it had been short-listed for the final six in the history/biography section. Anne, Stefanie, Peter and I were invited to the prize giving on 24 April 1980 at the Martini Terrace on the top floor but one — the seventeenth floor — of New Zealand House grandiloquently overlooking the lights of London. It is a far, far better building from inside than from its exterior. Charles and Pam were also invited.

In case we were chosen, I had a few words of thanks tucked in my head. I had fortified myself with very sweet sherry in accordance with my policy that I gave myself a party before I went to one and then never drank anything at it. Stefanie had done the driving. The chairman of the Arts Council, Sir Kenneth Robinson, presided. The winners in poetry, children's stories and fiction were announced, received their prizes and uttered their thanks. Now came history and biography. Charles was standing next to me. The name was announced. Not ours but that of Hugh Thomas, a name totally unknown to me.

To the profound surprise of everyone (it made headlines on the front page of the next day's national papers), he made a speech refusing the award and denigrating the system of prizes for literary work, which should not, he asserted, be subsidized by the government. Graciousness was in short supply. Our chagrin was complete. Charles murmured to me the cryptic words: 'Apocalyptic, don't you think?' They were the last words he ever addressed to me except for 'bad luck' as he left.

The crowded room hummed with shock. To have allowed the other short-listed writers to make the unnecessary journey was one thing; to have entered for the award at all if he thought it undesirable and, in his view, unethical, was another. The judge was Dame Veronica Wedgwood, OM, who was present. She was taken aback. There was now an expectation that the award would go to her second choice, Sir Isaiah Berlin, OM, but the Arts Council made no move — a pathetically weak and unfair reaction. The most effective course would have been to ignore Thomas's stance and pass the prize to Berlin. Leaflets were now distributed in the room, describing the short-listed lots of six in each section and showing the judge's order of merit of each within a section.

Berlin was not present: he may have been tipped off. The other four in the history/biography section were there and, although I did not know them by sight, their disgruntlement was ratified when eventually Stefanie and I spoke to Veronica Wedgwood. She thought that the Arts Council ought to have substituted her second choice. We learned from her and the printed leaflet that Stefanie's and my book had been judged the third best: so we were in effect the runners-up. Perhaps if Berlin had not appeared or somehow sided with Thomas, we would have won it. To Thomas, £7500 may have meant nothing: to us it would just about have covered our joint research costs over the three years of preparation. It must have been embarrassing for most of those present.

Soon after, Charles and Pam left the gathering, both nodding to us that they were moving off. They were neither of them given to using the words 'Goodbye' any more than 'Hello'. As they left I remember Charles's broad straight back shuffling through to the exit. I did not of course know at the time but it was to be the last that I saw of him.

8

Close Bereavements and Royalty Near and Far

C harles planned to go to Sofia to receive his Bulgarian medal in mid-1980. After ten years non-stop, he was continuing to write a long review each week for the *Financial Times* of one of the half-dozen books sent to him, usually of a biography, autobiography or history. These columns made wonderful reading. They were so diverse, so kind to the authors (out of the six he was always able to select one to which he could warm) and showed an astonishing range of reading and knowledge.

Letters in the press showed Thomas clearly to be in public disfavour. I could not resist writing to Charles on 5 May 1980: 'What a rum show at the Arts Council function. You will like to see the enclosed judgement of Veronica Wedgwood. It was nice to have seen you there.' Then, on 12 May, in what was to be his last letter to me, Charles wrote:

> I think you are making much too heavy weather of the Thomas episode. You have done extremely well out of the whole business. Running just behind Berlin would be regarded by most people as something of a feat. And, without Thomas's demonstration, there wouldn't have been much in the way of publicity. There never is for any of these literary competitions here or in America. It is, of course, quite different in France.

In a postscript he added: 'By the way, almost everyone in the trade (your publishers are outside the ordinary run) know the winners in advance — largely to make sure they are present. This is standard form.'

On 7 June Pam wrote: 'We shall look forward to seeing you both on the nights of August 13-15 ... How are Anne's eyes? We are always thinking about her. I have finished my novel, which is now with the typist.' I had tried to fix a time for Charles and Pam to see us again at Angmering soon after we would have visited them in August. On 27 June Pam wrote further:

> I'm afraid I can't make a date for our trip to Angmering as Charles is still so bad. Sometimes the pain is savage and the doctor's pills don't seem to do much. He sleeps at any time in the day as so much sleep is lost at night. Perhaps he'll be better in August, certainly not before that. I am so very sorry and disappointed. I'm glad all seems well with Anne's eyes.

On the same day Anne replied to Pam:

> We are most sorry to hear that Charles has had a reversion since he seemed so well on our last seeing you. It really is too bad and we hope that it will not be too long before he gets back to the much improved state that he was in when we last saw you. We trust that you will be able to come in August as we should much like you all (that is, including Doris, the housekeeper) to visit us. Philip has not been out of the house for ten days or so after a very severe attack of giddiness when getting up which worryingly persisted when he was lying down. The doctor could give no explanation but it might be a middle ear infection seriously upsetting the balance. Bending over, standing and, more peculiarly, lying down flat, he occasionally gets a considerable whirling in the head. This has naturally upset his confidence in getting about anywhere but it does seem to have improved in the last two to three days. ... We're hoping that he will be fit enough to be able to go to the International Cricket Conference on August 14-17 and that Charles too will be better and that we therefore would not be a nuisance.

My loss of balance was not due to an infection and remained undiagnosed except that, once my lifetime practice of sleeping absolutely flat with no pillow was abandoned and I started sleeping, as I still do, in a half vertical position on three pillows, it did not recur.

I don't know whether Charles knew of this letter, or whether it reached Pam before his death. There was reported to have been a violent return of Charles's affliction on 13 June and he wrote to the Bulgarian Ambassador on 26 June, saying that he would not be able to go to Bulgaria to collect his medal. His secretary, Janet Nalder, answering some of his mail (part of which he had dictated) on 1 July, wrote: 'I think that he will probably go into hospital very shortly.'

On 1 July 1980 (it was Anne's sixty-first birthday). Pam was on the phone to me at 4.30 p.m. It was just as unusual for her to use it as it was for Charles. In an extraordinarily controlled voice she said bleakly: 'Charles has died.' I was stunned. It was incredible. He had always maintained that his 'migratory lumbago' was not lethal and I had never had doubts that it was (if it was lumbago). I asked Pam how and when. She said, now waveringly and indistinctly: 'About half an hour ago. Haemorrhage.' I could only think that it must have been cerebral to be so sudden, with no history of anything but 'lumbago'. I asked 'cerebral?' And I thought she said 'yes', but she now seemed to be confused. 'It was awful,' she added. I later learnt that it was not what I had assumed. Doris, their admirable cook, had gone out for some aspirins and the evening paper (which, in normal health, Charles unfailingly collected from round the block). Charles had collapsed in bed. It was all over in minutes or less. The death certificate astonished us after the postmortem by declaring: 'Peer of the Realm and writer. 1 July. Haemorrhage from a perforated gastric ulcer.'

With hindsight, that seemed to have been the trouble all along, even, in my view, back to what he had described to me as 'lumbago' in the 1930s. Of course, his was the temperament to be liable to be host to ulcers. That he had them would explain his aversion to tomatoes (which are a favourite of mine), fruit (except tinned) and other acid-bearing foods (which he wholly eschewed) and the ill-effect of the port to which he was led in his last two or three years as an alternative to whisky. Of course, too, aspirins, which he took to alleviate the pain of 'lumbago', were the worst possible thing to take for an ulcer.

His faith in doctors, like mine (I avoided them professionally as if *they* were the plague) was minimal, virtually non-existent, unlike Pam's (their mutual opposition in this respect was almost akin to their respective attitudes to the acceptance of religious faiths). Charles's horror of hospitals, like mine, was consuming. He was 74, approaching 75 in October, and in every other respect active and agile for his size.

I found out later that Rudyard Kipling had died instantaneously from the same cause after a history of nearly 20 years of what was thought to be no more than 'stomach irritation', despite the 1st Viscount Dawson of Penn, King George V's physician, having been among the many medical men he had consulted over that period. But that, of course, was in eras considered to be less clever in diagnoses. Apparently, gastric ulcers can remain dormant or be classified as 'sleeping' and out of range of X-rays. It can only be supposed that this must have been so in Charles's case. What is believed to be certain is that ulcers were not suspected. He was due to have another check the day after he died. His only tendencies to overindulgence were in whisky and again only when he had company: he would, also only in company, practically chain smoke but he never inhaled.

The national papers of 2 July carried the announcement of his death on the front page. *The Times* obituary of that day said, *inter alia*:

> Lord Snow, C. P. Snow, the novelist who died yesterday at the age of 74, occupied a position in English life such as no writer has held since H. G. Wells and Arnold Bennett. ... The quality he most valued in men was magnanimity and he was himself a conspicuously magnanimous man. No one can have had a larger circle of friends and they were drawn from all walks of life and many countries.

At the private cremation at Putney Vale there were Alan Maclean, Harry Hoff and Janet Nalder, in addition to the family in London, Eric and his wife Jess, Anne and myself. On 12 August, *The Times* announced: 'Lady Snow thanks all those who have written to her. She has broken her shoulder and will not be able to finish answering all the letters. They have brought her great comfort.'

I select two letters of condolence to Pam who passed them all to me. On 2 July Anthony Powell (that most courteous of literary figures) wrote:

> Violet and I send our deepest condolences in your loss. I have the most lively memories of the visit Charles and I paid to Bulgaria not so very long ago. ... He [Charles] cannot fail to have been gratified by having added several phrases to the language, an achievement that everyone in a profession would like to be able to congratulate themselves upon.

And this, on the same date, from Vladimir Velchev, the Bulgarian Ambassador in London: 'We, the Bulgarians, will always remember Lord Snow as a great writer and public figure, a distinguished proponent of international peace and cooperation, democracy and social progress.'

I could not face up to the numbers who would be attending the memorial service at St Martin-in-the-Fields. Anne and I were the only close relatives not able to be there. Pam was there but in poor physical shape. Some of those attending were Lord Boothby, Mary Duchess of Roxburghe, Lord and Lady Clanmorris (Madeleine Bingham), Lord Elwyn-Jones, Countess Lloyd George of Dwyfor, Bronwen Viscountess Astor, Lord Vaizey, Baroness Birk, Maurice and Hon Dame Katherine Macmillan, Lady Antonia Fraser, Sir Ronald Millar, the Lord Mayor of Leicester, Sir Norman Lindop, Sir Arthur Vick, Sir Victor Pritchett, Mrs C. P. White (Dame P. D. James), Margaret Drabble, Susan Hill, Robin Lloyd George, John Braine, Kingsley (later Sir) Amis, Elizabeth Jane Howard, Marghanita Laski, Anthony and Catherine Storr, Alexander Macmillan (later Earl of Stockton), Count and Countess Antonini, Alan and Robin Maclean, Michael Rubinstein, Margo Bowden, Paul Scofield and Jack Plumb. Ratu Sir Kamisese Mara, the Prime

Minister, arranged for Fiji to be represented by Taufa Vakatale, the lady Assistant High Commissioner and later Deputy Prime Minister of Fiji.

Harry Hoff gave an address. A particularly close friend of Charles's from his Christ's undergraduate days (just before mine) and a friend of Pam's for the last 30 years (writing under the name William Cooper), he had been secretary to the Civil Service Commission when Charles was a civil service commissioner after the war. He had started teaching at Newton's in my last year and was there up to the war. As a scientist and novelist, he was perhaps Charles's most intimate protégé. Between them they launched Kingsley Amis. As previously stated, Amis never expressed thanks, such is sometimes the reverse side of patronage. Charles once told me: 'Those you help most can be the first to turn round on you.' Philip had been in charge of the arrangements.

Correspondence with Pam was inevitably gloomy: there were only occasional disparate shafts of light. Barely legibly, she wrote on 29 September 1980: 'I am still unwell and have a house companion and wheelchair. Obviously I can't keep on the house and the thought of a move is a nightmare.' On 5 October she wrote to Anne when Anne seemed now to have a detached retina: 'But there is fresh hope for detached retinas with laser beams. ... You know Charles's eye was eventually put right. ... Can't write much more — my shoulder aches too much. ... I think of you constantly and wish you luck with the eye. You poor darling.' And then to me, on 22 October: 'Tell her [Anne] that I shall never be able to type again or to write a book and that my career is at an end. Everything seems to have come to an end since dear Charles died.'

But when we told her that Stefanie was expecting a child she wrote to Anne on 29 October: 'What wonderful news about Stephanie, tell her how delighted I am and how envious. ... I am fair to middling.' And again, on 31 October, to me: 'I too have the excellent news that *Strangers and Brothers* is likely to be done by the BBC as a 12-part serial after all! The remaining seven scripts have been commissioned and a further £3000 is coming to me, so I shall be in no hurry to sell the house, thank God! It's wonderful news about Stephanie.'

On 11 November there was a return to the gloom when Pam wrote to me: 'I was disappointed to realize that the house goes to the estate and I only get the income from it. How Charles expected me to find anywhere else on that I don't know.' On 9 January 1981 she wrote to me again: 'It was lovely to see you ... I'm very glad that Anne's retina is not detached.' I wrote to her on 11 January 1981 to say that 'I'm assembling all the material I have on Charles's early life. What I have is unique and of the utmost interest.'

There were two letters from Pam before she went into hospital. In the first, of 16 January, she wrote that her 'medical bills recently have been appalling. ... I am pretty worried about money. ... Far more seems to go out than comes in.' And in the second, of 23 January 1981, she wrote: 'I am worried stiff about money. ... My weight is only seven stones five pounds. Charles could never have anticipated that I should need a nurse.'

Then, after having returned from the London Clinic, she wrote on 18 April 1981: 'I'm still extremely weak. I am allowed to drink but not to smoke: you can't imagine what hell it is still for me to do without cigarettes.' Being forbidden to smoke (she used to start smoking as soon as she got up in the morning and would continue non-stop through meals until retiring to sleep) gave me some hope — she would go into alarming paroxysms of coughing, any one of which I feared would be fatal. Being permitted to drink whisky (almost neat) as she did from mid-morning to last thing at night was marginally preferable. I was always surprised that, with so strong a mind, she could not renounce both entirely. One could say nothing on a family level. It was frustrating as it could only have one conclusion.

The final communication from her, on 22 May 1981, was a card when Philippa was born, on which she wrote: 'What wonderful news! Warmest congratulations to you, Anne, Peter and Stephanie. I wonder what the name will be. ... Yes, do drop in on your way to Welwyn Garden City. I shall long for your news and will write soon to Stephanie and Peter. ... Best love and warmest congratulations to you all.'

Had it been Pam who had died in 1980 this would not have been unexpected. She had been seriously ill on so many occasions, collapsing frequently in the house. Emphysema was her main trouble, not helped by her chain-smoking and inhaling from which she would not be dissuaded. Her coughing and efforts to regain breath were alarming to witness. She survived little longer with increasing frailty, dying at the age of 69. Her death certificate read: 'Widow of C. P. Snow. Writer. 18th June. Bronchopneumonia. Obstructive airways disease. Congestive cardiac failure. Cerebral infarction.'

She had borne up courageously to the cremation of Charles. At Putney Vale hers was attended only by the immediate family from London, where Stefanie also was, Eric and Jess from Leicester, Anne and me from Sussex (in a car specially sent by young Philip, as for Charles's cremation), Harry and Joyce Hoff, Alan Maclean and Janet Nalder. Father Gerard Irvine, the Anglo-Catholic brother of one of the characters in the *Strangers and Brothers* series and friend in particular of Pam's — and a particular one of John Betjeman's — officiated. I could no more easily attend Pam's memorial service than Charles's. It was at St James's, Piccadilly. Attended by the same close relatives (except Anne and me), it included some of those who had been at the service for Charles — Lady Clanmorris and Bronwen Astor among them — while Harold Macmillan read a lesson and Susan Hill gave an address

Charles had appointed me with Michael Rubinstein, his lawyer, as the executors of his estate and as one of the two literary executors. He left £286,000 net (£312,500 gross), mainly to Pam and Philip. Included in his will was Anne Seagrim, who had been his secretary and confidante. In the 1950s they had resumed their intimate relationship with the epitome of discretion. Apart from one or two confidential letters, whenever an opportunity arose (such as when Pam had retired for the night), Charles would ask me in person to see that she was looked after properly if and when anything happened to him and insisted that I should get in touch with her in the event of any crisis. I had telephoned her only once — in 1964 — after Charles had suffered cardiac arrest during the operation on his eye.

My first task when Pam rang me with the cataclysmic news in 1980 was to telephone her. I did not have a number for her, only her address, and she was ex-directory. I explained my dilemma to the telephone exchange, which could not vary their rules, so I rang the police in her area and they agreed to send someone round. She told me that she wished to be at Charles's cremation but I advised against it.

I was just recovering from the worst effects of the shock when I was able to switch to my other world. We had what could not have been nicer visitors to Angmering to help us forget events momentarily. I had seen Ratu Sir George Cakobau and his attractive wife, Lealea Balekiwai, at a few functions since leaving Fiji in 1951; he had been one of the party 'casing the joint' at the House of Lords in 1970. But now we were to have a whole day together, resuming a close friendship going back to my very first days in Fiji in 1938. His wife, noble in appearance, was the daughter of a fisherman (who was also the ferryman) from the regal island of Bau, whom we have met briefly in the first volume, on a visit to it. Accompanying them were the Governor-General's ADC, Lieutenant Savenaca Draunidalo, who had recently gained the MC in the Fiji peace-keeping force of the United Nations in the Lebanon, and his private secretary. Draunidalo was at the time married to Adi Vuikaba, great-niece of Ratu Sir Lala Sukuna, whose second marriage was to Dr Timoci Bavadra, the short-lived Prime Minister removed by the coup of 1987, which forms the narrative a little later.

George was positively delighted to put aside for hours the cares and duties of Governor-General of Fiji — he was the first Fijian to hold that position — and to chat over incidents of the last 42 years. We had been carefree youths together in 1938, intoxicated as much with life as with liquor and sharing samples of both, as a result of which we came to know each other well. The passage of time and bleaching in the sun had whitened our hair but not dimmed our memories. Lealea explained that there was no one in Fiji with whom he could discard his viceregal status and chat informally and uninhibitedly. I heard later when factions were trying to involve him in the 1987 coups that his memory of yesterday was hazy but his recollections of the 1940s to the last decade were sharp. I certainly found that the past had been etched markedly in his current interests.

We had an absorbing tête-à-tête, in which Lealea and Anne

sometimes joined us. The ADC would come across the lawn from the house to the sunhouse-cum-library to remind him politely of the time. George would nod and disregard visits from him every hour before finally and ruefully acceding to the need to be driven back to London in the limousine bearing the ingenious number-plate FIJ 1 (bought from Ireland on independence: Tonga could only try to approach it with 1 TON).

For Kadavulevu (as George Cakobau had asked me to call him, just as it was Jo with Lala Sukuna, Ted with Edward Cakobau, Peni with Penaia Ganilau and Kamisese with Kamisese Mara) and perhaps for me, the most spirited phase of our exchange of recollections was my team's 1948 tour of New Zealand when he had been my vice-captain. We had a most happy relationship on that tour. I would accompany him quite often after a day's play to cinemas, which he loved, and return him to our hotel. In any case the bars had closed firmly at 6.00 p.m., a barbarous practice since abandoned in New Zealand but a convenient one for helping to control George's predisposition in that era towards a drink.

He had for many years now, in fact since marrying Lealea and forming a new family, been drinking only orange juice. His features had improved and he made a most imposing governor general. On the Queen's last visit to Bau she conferred on him the Royal Victorian Chain, the highest possible Royal gift, one of towering status bestowed only on intimate members of the royal family (limited to the Queen herself and Queen Mother) and eminent foreign sovereigns such as the reigning kings or queens of Norway, Thailand, Jordan, Denmark, Nepal, Sweden, the Netherlands, Spain and Saudi Arabia. It has never been appreciated in Fiji just how exalted was this honour for their leading chief. Its bestowal was an imaginative link with history to acknowledge the gift by George's great grandfather, King Cakobau, and leading chiefs persuaded by him, of the Fiji islands to Queen Victoria, personally making her the Queen and her successors the monarchs of Fiji. Below are excerpts from the obituary I wrote for the *Daily Telegraph* (at least much of it) when George died at the end of 1989:

Ratu Sir George Cakobau, who has died in Suva aged

seventy-seven, was Paramount Chief of Fiji and the first Fijian to hold the post of Governor-General. His great grandfather, Ratu Ebenezer Seru Cakobau, the one and only King of Fiji, arranged for the Cession of the islands to Britain in 1874. That illustrious ancestry gave Ratu Sir George a right to a prime say in Fijian affairs from his youth onwards.

As Vunivalu of Fiji — the country's Paramount Chief — his supremacy had never been dangerously challenged. Ratu George was educated at Queen Victoria School, Fiji, Newington College, Sydney, and Wanganui Technical College, New Zealand — although arguably his status required an English School and University.

Less prepossessing than his father, he made youthful capital out of the inevitability of his succession to the title of Vunivalu. The strength of his impulsiveness did not augur well for a sense of responsibility. In the year of his father's death Ratu George began official life at the bottom, as temporary clerk in training in the Colonial Secretariat ... In 1943 he joined, as a captain, the Fiji Infantry Regiment fighting the Japanese in the Solomon Islands with his cousin, Ratu Edward Cakobau (natural son of King George II of Tonga and Adi Litia Cakobau) about whom — strangely, given his own superior Fijian rank — he had a sense of social inferiority.

After the 1939–45 war he was a police sub-inspector and again a Fijian magistrate and Roko Tui of various provinces. ... On Fiji's independence in 1970 Ratu George was Minister for Fijian Affairs but he had little predisposition to executive posts, except his ultimate one as Governor-General.

Athletically built but not specially tall for an aristocratic Fijian, he was an enthusiastic games player. In 1939 he captained the Fijian rugby team in New Zealand but the tour was somewhat marred by his overindulgence in the bottle; it was officially decided that he should not represent Fiji abroad again. In his youth and up to his mid-thirties Ratu George was often in his cups, though he never drank in his last forty or so years. In 1948 Ratu Sir Lala Sukuna, President of the Fiji Cricket Association, consulted Philip Snow, captain of the Fiji cricket team to tour New Zealand, whether he would take Ratu George. Snow ... insisted that he should go and not only do so but be vice-captain, guaranteeing that he would look after him as a close friend. Ratu George proved to be the most successful all-rounder on the tour — to which the International Cricket Conference in 1987 gave first-class status for the Provincial matches, thus making Ratu Sir George, at 75, the oldest cricketer to be officially given first-class ranking in the history of the game. ... As he aged Ratu George increased strikingly in impressiveness. His judgement, so long tested, was now placid and impeccable. Rank, breeding and poise radiated from his appearance as his hair turned white. He displayed charming affability and total enjoyment of his Vice Regal post, mixing antipodean with English humour. His appointment in 1973 as Governor-General was inevitable and entirely fitting, although he had had to surpass the urbane, cosmopolitan distinctiveness of Ratu Sir Edward Cakobau, who had been the first Deputy Prime Minister. At the centenary in 1974 of the Cession of Britain to Queen Victoria by King Cakobau, the guest of Cakobau's great-grandson as Governor-General was Queen Victoria's great-great-grandson, the Prince of Wales. ... Ratu Sir George was appointed GCMG in 1973 and GCVO in 1977. In 1982, on the Queen's visit to Bau, he was accorded the exceedingly rare honour of the Royal Victorian Chain.

A distinguished Bauan, Ratu Josua Brown Toganivalu, and his part-European wife from Levuka, Alice, succeeded the inestimable Gibsons in the Fiji High Commission in London. Jo, as he was to me (and I Phil to him), was the third high commissioner in succession with that abbreviated name. He had been a minister and I was virtually the last surviving European to have known his grandfather, a distinguished chief on Bau with an unusual penchant for history, even more unusually applied to giving lectures and writing articles. Fijian chiefs know their history orally in a way that could not be bettered but almost never put it down on paper or talk about it publicly.

The more I came to know Jo Toganivalu and his penultimate successor in London, Ratu Epeli, the stronger my conviction that chiefs like these should have been sent to England for education following the examples of Ratu Sukuna, Ratu Mara, Ratu Edward and Ratu Penaia (in the two last cases too briefly and a little late in years). This would have ensured a succession of sophistication valuable to Fijian leadership. There seems to be a void, not necessarily in latent ability but in polish, when Ratu Mara retires as he inexorably and regrettably must some day. Even so, Jo Toganivalu and Epeli would have many years ahead of them, English educated or not, for highest office. Cambridge or Oxford should certainly have been provided for Ratu George.

The obituary in the *Daily Telegraph* testified to my affection and respect for him and hints at what might have further enriched his life and Fiji's history. It is doubtful whether the highly talented and lively commoner, of very distant descent from a shipwrecked Negro on Bau and married into the island's aristocracy (his attractive sister, Ateca Vunivalu, was the first Fijian stenographer in the highly selective Secretariat staff of my time), Ravuama Vunivalu, who died of cirrhosis of the liver, was temperamentally suited to further progress beyond being a district officer and would have benefited from an English university education. In any case he was in the same age group as Ratu Mara. Otherwise, if there were not sufficient chiefs of quality, commoners of ability, like him and the inimitable Uraia Koroi, ought to have been selected for education in this country. Ratu Sukuna did not seem to entertain this idea of a repetition (except for Ratu Mara) of his own Oxford upbringing but then governors and colonial secretaries should have shown the same wisdom for later selections as had been made for Sukuna's own career.

We were pleased to come to know Jo and Alice to the same close extent as their predecessors, Jo and Adi Mei Rabukawaqa, and Joe and Emily Gibson. It might have been thought that it was a prerequisite for Fiji high commissioners all to have the same shortened first name. The next broke the sequence in more ways than one. Fiji was held in high esteem in diplomatic circles in

London and at the court for the distinctive presentability of its representatives.

An interesting visitor to us was Sheila Ramsay Lochhead who, as Sheila MacDonald, had been the widowed Ramsay MacDonald's daughter/hostess during his prime ministership at 10 Downing Street. She had been to Fiji in the 1930s but was hardly known there during her stay in the 1970s with her husband, who was a lecturer at the University of the South Pacific. Clustered in Laucala Bay at Suva Point, this institution still needs to gain the confidence to pursue research into every aspect of Fiji's history. That she, although a reserved person by nature, was not recognized as the daughter of a British prime minister was typical of the Fiji that has lost a number of links with England since the end of the colonial era, from which it had parted as amicably as one would expect from a mutual relationship of cordial enlightenment.

An urn containing Charles's ashes is one of the four monuments round the swimming pool at Christ's; the other three are from centuries ago. I was able to be present with Anne and Stefanie at the unveiling of this by young Philip, which was followed by lunch at the Master's Lodge, with Jack Plumb presiding. The only non-family present were George and Zara Steiner; Eric, Jess and Lindsay, Pam's daughter, were there. Philippa, too, in a carrycot. Philippa Wigmore Waine had been born on 21 May 1981.

Stefanie and Peter had been hoping that Charles and Pam as great uncle and aunt might have been alive so that Philippa might have had some first-hand memories of them. Anne and I could not have been more delighted than to have a granddaughter in whose growing up we have been fascinated. Peter was kind enough to agree to the idea (Stefanie's, I think) that her second name, not especially euphonic but of particular historic relevance to the Snows, should be Wigmore. My maternal grandmother, a Wigmore, had come from Stamford, as had my mother. Charles had entertained the idea of making his title Baron Snow of Stamford, if not of Aylestone, but ultimately opted for Leicester.

We were always pleased to have a proved connection with that family back to at least the seventeenth century and maybe earlier. Research in the belief that it may extend to Edward IV's first son, Edward de Wigmore, born a year after the King's precontract

228

marriage in 1462 to Lady Eleanor Talbot, widow of Lord Boteler (or Butler), daughter of the 1st Earl of Shrewsbury and granddaughter of the Duke of Buckingham, never ceases to occupy us. But we fear that we are up against Richard III and Henry VII and their bludgeoning supporters in our attempts to prove or establish direct links with Edward de Wigmore, who reputedly survived by sanctuary in a convent (where Lady Eleanor died as a recluse) not too far from Stamford and demolished by Henry VIII.

There would have been no one whom those three monarchs would sooner have seen out of their way to the throne than Edward IV's eldest son and any descendants of his, granted the validity at the end of the fifteenth century of precontract marriages. A subsidiary title of Edward IV was Lord of Wigmore. A Wigmore of the mid-eighteenth century living in Stamford where Edward IV frequently stayed — he was also Lord of Stamford — had drawn up a tree showing ancestry back to this first son of Edward IV, Edward de Wigmore, but there are a couple of gaps which so far, not unexpectedly, defy filling in, except perhaps by some determined and diligent pedigree scholar, before achieving something no less than sensational.

Charles was always amused by the thought of our possible descent from Edward IV but when Garter King of Arms was researching all the branches of the family for his baronial coat of arms Charles did not wish to spend the money necessary to have him look into the Plantagenets of around 1460. (I must say that Garter King of Arms did seem reluctant to upturn the stones along that particular path: it might have been more than his job was worth.) This was to the natural disappointment of his relatives who had done as much research as their resources and leisure allowed.

Belonging now to the Order of the British Empire, I was able to arrange for Philippa's christening to take place in the crypt of St Paul's Cathedral, which has its own special connection with the Order. It was an awesome setting in which a number of the most eminent people in the country's history are commemorated. Happily concluded, the function was nearly the *coup de grâce* for me, for, descending the numerous broad steps (up which the 8th Earl Spencer, after a stroke, had such understandable difficulty escorting Lady Diana Spencer for her marriage with the Prince of Wales), I caught my heel and had to jump down five to save myself from crashing on them. I've always thought that, despite possible aesthetic objections, there should be balustrades on to which to hold. The occasion was a pleasant joint one for the Waines and Snows.

Posthumously, *The Physicists*, which Charles had almost finished, came out dedicated, as he had mentioned to me that it would be, to Stefanie. Harry Hoff had completed it. I only wish that it had been the follow-up to *Variety of Men* and contained a wider range of personalities. But, as Harold Macmillan was to be almost the paramount figure in the second team, it could not have been brought out, even if Charles had embarked on it, until after Macmillan's death, which came much later than his physical appearance had seemed to prognosticate for so long.

Alan Maclean of Macmillans wished me to bring out as soon as possible my study of Charles, which Charles had known would one day be forthcoming. Requiring very little research, it was largely written straight from my head. Certainly, it required infinitely less research than anything I had done before — indeed, almost none apart from referring to an occasional note I had made during my arduous perusal of his archives over the previous 30 or so years.

The title, *Stranger and Brother*, was Alan Maclean's choice out of several permutations on that theme. It came out in 1982, with an American and a second edition the following year. Part-serialized lucratively on the whole of the front page of the *Sunday Times Supplement*, it sold well. It was my first literary success financially. To Macmillans' expert knowledge, the 77 reviews of it throughout the world were a near record number for any book, most of all a biography. Of these, 33 appeared in North America where Charles had been almost as well known (he maintained better known) as in this country. One critic of Charles was Auberon Waugh, whom he had sued successfully for libel. Waugh, whose father, Evelyn, Charles could not abide but whose uncle, Alec, was a friend both of Charles's and mine, did spare a word of praise for me: 'An affectionate and readable memoir.'

Some reviewers were so warmly disposed that I was impelled to write and thank them. Pleasant correspondence resulted and I was surprised by how many people from various parts of the world wrote in — and still do over a decade later — to express gratitude and pleasure and in some cases to resume contacts of long ago, always one of the most rewarding results of writing books. (Perhaps the most unexpected of these letters came from Colonel Heinrich Amstütz of the Swiss cavalry; he and I have become good friends over the last 15 years.) This was my seventh book over a span of almost 50 years and my world has been broadened as a result of this writer–reader relationship. The subject matter of *Stranger and Brother* was intimate: I never received an unfavourable letter. And, from having seen all Charles's correspondence, which passed through my hands at his request, neither did he for his own grand score of books. He did receive the occasional lunatic letter: that was to be expected in a lifetime of writing on so many subjects and that would be the only type to which he did not reply. To all the others a short, appreciative, punctilious acknowledgement of their interest would be sent promptly. His correspondence manners could never be faulted.

A warm tribute to him and to my biography was published in the Venice newspaper, *Il Gazettino*. A review from there would have pleased Charles. It was written by an old friend, Count Giacomo Antonini, who, with his delightful wife, Karin, lived close enough, I found, to Angmering for us to have lunch with them —he was too frail to visit us.

As a result of the publication of *Stranger and Brother*, one who resumed contact broken through the years since we were contemporaries and friends at Christ's was Gavin Ewart, a professional poet who should surely have been Poet Laureate. He had liked *Stranger and Brother* with its evocations of Christ's and of the staircase, at the bottom of which he had lived with Charles above him, and felt that he must say so on a personal visit. Such was the tone of so many readers, including some of Charles's American friends, that we gained a whole new circle from among those of his friends whom I had missed meeting.

Professor Joe Maloney, who had been a particular friend of Charles and Anne Seagrim's, has now become a delightful friend of ours and regularly visits us from America. He is the founder of the Snowflakes, an organization of graduates of Louisville University,

Kentucky, where Charles had had a D.Litt. conferred on him. Charles had given the members of this body a conducted tour round Cambridge and the House of Lords to see the background to some of his novels.

Following the eventful year of 1981, 1982 had been no less so, with reviews continuing to appear amidst all the letters. An accolade was bestowed on my *Stranger and Brother* by my being invited to Hatchards' Best Authors of the Year party in the Martini Terrace high up in New Zealand House, where the books were displayed with about half a dozen more, all apparently the very personal choice of the directors of Hatchards.

Among those present were Theo Aronson, whose *The Coburgs of Belgium* I had much enjoyed; Sir Arthur Bryant, to whose saturnine features I had often spoken at Collins's publishing functions; Mark (Lord) Bonham-Carter, with whom I had often played cricket and who had not advanced my *Bronze and Clay* years earlier which had now been cannibalized; Lady Chichester; Leo and Jilly Cooper; Roald Dahl; Clare Francis, diminutive for so intrepid a sailor; Lady Antonia Fraser, whom I had often seen in the British Museum reading room when I was researching there; the 7th Earl of Longford; Michael Bond; the 5th Earl of Lichfield; Angela Rippon, preternaturally bright and highly photogenic on television despite, or because of, her intriguingly inward focusing eyes; Rupert Murdoch; Eric Newby; Nicholas Mosley (3rd Lord Ravensdale) and Philip Ziegler.

I introduced Anne, Peter and Stefanie to Harold and Lady Wilson, the fingernails of the former straight from gardening, it seemed. When reminded of Charles he said: 'Ah yes, Charles Snow, a great man,' and then meandered off in thought and speech on political matters, which entirely failed to hold our attention. Entertainers are renowned for their egos: they depend on them. Perhaps it is unfair to say that we were not impressed by Frankie Howerd, who accompanied us, otherwise on our own, in the lift: he was friendly enough, yet was nothing but his stage self. Anne was an ardent fan of Eric Morecambe, so I introduced her, Stefanie and Peter to him, who in turn introduced us to his wife and son.

Morecambe was the soul of genuine affability and not at all

egocentric. Like Joe E. Brown, whom we had met in 1943, offstage he was unaffectedly amusing because of the mere agility of his wit, often tinged with wryness, his fast repartee with unexpected twists at the end and his basic sense of comedy and realism. We said afterwards that we had never been so spontaneously and continuously entertained for half an hour as by Eric Morecambe. He apparently rehearsed his stage and television performances meticulously, yet still achieved a free and easy, fizzy spontaneity. He seemed the essence of likeableness and was obviously highly intelligent. I read later that he was an atheist and had originally been a miner during his national service under the Bevin scheme.

Meanwhile, I had managed again to raise the money for the second Fijian team to visit England for the second International Cricket Conference trophy competition in the Midlands. There were still no possibilities of sponsorship from within Fiji; so it had all fallen on me again. Adnan Khashoggi had become involved in law suits, including the one by his wife for billions of dollars of alimony, and I could not resume contact with him. It occurred to me to approach the 2nd Earl Jellicoe, chairman of Tate & Lyle sugar company, and Barclays Bank International. Both responded warmly. George Jellicoe, son of Admiral of the Fleet 1st Earl Jellicoe who had been alone but so accurate in prognosticating a soft imperial battle centre in the Solomon Islands for the Second World War and whose career culminated in the governor-generalship of New Zealand, had been a friend of Charles's and I had met him at the House of Lords. He was especially accommodating.

So the team were able to come over and I was able to watch them, making notes on where they could raise their standards. Harry Apted's son was now captain but the whole competition was again overwhelmed by diabolical weather, which made play almost impossible. Fiji defeated Singapore and lost again to Bermuda and, on a first meeting, to Holland (of much underestimated strength). As in 1979, the match with Malaysia was abandoned, as too were matches against Bangladesh and West Africa. The conditions, which created a sense of moroseness among all the players (there were many glum faces), were just not favourable to any team and made it impossible to form any reliable judgements about their true relative strengths.

In 1982 Alice Brewster, widow since 1939 of Adolph Brewster Brewster (formerly Joske), the intrepid district commissioner who had written the classic *The Hill Tribes of Fiji*, died aged 113, the oldest person in the United Kingdom. She had been blind since her nineties. When Anne and I visited her at the age of 97, she could recall being stationed for the last decade of the previous century at Nadarivatu, then the most remote and arguably most hazardous of districts. Asked if she had been anxious about being left by her husband doing his tour of duties in what had been cores of cannibalism 20 years earlier, she told us that the only thing that worried her was the reverberation of the thunder round the mountains and the purple vividness of the lightning as it struck the jagged hills.

At the annual International Cricket Conference the Chairman was Peter May, President of the MCC. In talking to him about his having been coached by Geary, it was evident that he recalled him with warmest gratitude. Not as forceful a personality as he had been a batsman, this gentle man was soon to be faced by a traumatic time as the chairman of selectors for the next six years. My being senior by far in continuous attendance of all of the delegates of every country enabled me to have perspective in judging a wide range of leaders of cricket's principal organization. A wise chairman between Prince Philip and P. B. H. May had been David Clark, former captain of Kent and the only Rugbeian president of the MCC since Sir Pelham Warner.

My brother Eric, who was five years younger than Charles and is five years older than me, persuaded Leicester City Council to have a plaque put up on the site of Charles's birthplace at 40 Richmond Road. Before a small assembly of old friends (including Lucy Wilde, née Parker, who had been our eldest brother Harold's fiancée at the time of his death in 1927) and curious residents of the area, with Stefanie bringing along Philippa to be present at her first public function, the council presented a Wedgwood blue plaque, which Eric then unveiled. The Leicester council had been prompt in taking action: it also published a description written by Eric and me. The plaque reads:

Close Bereavements and Royalty Near and Far

City of Leicester
C. P. SNOW
Author and Scientist
1905–1980
Lord Snow of Leicester was born at
40 Richmond Road opposite this plaque

I was fit for this little ceremony but Eric had arthritic problems, which persist. He had been a successful chairman of a firm of heating and ventilating engineers he had founded after a career in the industry. His principal interest is Leicestershire, markedly its cricket, on which he is the world expert after having published two outstandingly scholarly histories on it. Other publications of his have been *Sir Julien Cahn's XI* and *E. Phillips Oppenheim*, who had resided in Leicester.

Lucy as Harold's fiancée was our last personal link with earliest days at Richmond Road. After the ceremony she rebuked me for not smiling. I told her that in many years as a magistrate I had had to conceal my feelings. When she returned to Grantham in Lincoln-shire she said that she was sorry to have been, as she put it, 'too forward' in her observation. She had been a great favourite of mine as the only female member of the relatively large household apart from my mother. Now 97, she was 88 at the time with a brilliant memory and handsome script. She remembered us as a very amiable family and me as a 'happy and outgoing boy'. With the greatest of blessings — energy — all my life, I was never bored then nor later. That's a sweeping statement. I hasten to make two exceptions.

Church-going was one. The other was when I was confined for six weeks through scarlet fever (now extinct, but in my childhood all too common an affliction, with the peculiar effect of a snake-like sloughing off of the skin) in a bedroom where the only person allowed to see me was my mother. The isolation hospital was full during the epidemic; Eric was there and naturally miserable. Life for me was only tolerated through a bountiful gift of mounds of *Magnet* and *Gem*. They were a gift because they had regretfully to be destroyed when the door was finally opened for my escape, only to be sealed promptly for fumigation. School books were not

235

allowed. My absence from school coincided neatly with the introduction of trigonometry, which I could never subsequently pick
up, with absolutely no detriment whatever to the course of my life.

What Charles had for so long been hoping for now actually
occurred — the televising of *Strangers and Brothers*. The contract
had been signed a year before he died and casting for it in theory
had been much occupying Charles and Pam. They had wanted
Richard Chamberlain as Roy Calvert: there would not have been
too wide a dissimilarity in appearance. Eventually, the part was
taken by Nigel Havers — good casting. Others included in the
various episodes were Anthony Hopkins, Andrew Cruickshank,
Peter Sallis and Cherie Lunghi. By far the most difficult character,
that of Lewis Eliot, absolutely pivotal, was taken by a little known
actor, Shaughan Seymour who, perhaps not surprisingly, never
seemed to look or fit the part.

But the main drawback was that the sequence was taken as
such, that is not broken up into separate, identifiable books. The
chronology and the characters seemed blurred and, with the
exception of only two or three cameos, it never came across distinctively enough to rival other televised programmes of the
period. Thirteen 50-minute scripts were quite inadequate for the
wide range of 11 novels, some of which were not dealt with at all.
I felt that it needed Ronald Millar's skilled hand at adaptation and
perhaps a totally different approach. An attempt of the producer
to change the title of the series to *Corridors of Power* was resisted
by Harry Hoff and myself as literary executors. But, having seen
the televised series, I rather wish that it had not been blessed with
the title *Strangers and Brothers*.

Anne and I were ourselves on the radio in a series of programmes — as ourselves. June Knox-Mawer, with her considerable
broadcasting experience (it is inexplicable that with her youthful
Elizabeth Taylor looks she was never on television), literary ability
and likeable personality — she would have made an ideal first
woman member of the colonial administration — had an excellent
idea of going round to old Pacific hands to gather vignettes of their
recollections before it was too late. Recorded and broadcast by the
BBC and then published as *Tales from Paradise*, they comment
valuably, if in too slender a form, on life in the South Sea Islands,

an area done scant justice in literature, film or television when compared with the intrinsically less attractive India and Africa.

To emphasize Pacific superiority in attractiveness one has to come back time and again to the quintessential charm of Fijians as set off by the beauty of their country. Their names may look forbiddingly centipedal but that does not matter: their impact as individuals or *en masse* (which is rare of any country) is charismatic.

Ratu Meli Vakarewakobau (that is a mouthful but can be limited to Meli, even bypassing the chiefly prefix Ratu) epitomized it. As assistant commissioner of the Royal Fiji Police, that is number two in the force, he was a handsome figure, tall, erect, with an aquiline nose and noble head of hair. His handsomeness was in fact that of his late father, Kitione Lalakomacoi, who had been the leases clerk in my first office in Fiji at Naduruloulou. Meli's mother, a sister of Ratu Sir Lala Sukuna's, had lacked pulchritude. It was his duty and pleasure, he said, to come and visit his father's old friend. The striking feature of Fijians is that they are a race without chips on their shoulders. Their manners are impeccable, their dignity elevates any meeting and their humour is identical to ours. In short, they have style.

People of mixed Fijian–Tongan descent are perhaps even more striking looking than their pure Fijian or Tongan counterparts. Anne and I had been privileged to live among that amalgam in Lau which was a rare experience for a European.

We were both invited in 1983 by the prime minister, Margaret Thatcher, to lunch with the King and Queen of Tonga at 10 Downing Street. I had first met the King when he was still the Crown Prince at a private lunch given by Ratu Sir Lala Sukuna at his Suva house, Rairaiwaqa, and, as previously mentioned, had met him again at a number of other functions. I had not, however, been to 10 Downing Street before and, like so many who see it almost daily on television, had wondered what it was like inside the black door.

My constitution supplemented with a sweet sherry or two, we went by taxi. Anne had been wondering whether to wear a hat; so we stood for a while at the police-manned barrier (since supplanted by a formidable iron gateway) at the bottom of the street observing others who had been invited going through. Anne had some sort of headgear to put on if it was in evidence. It wasn't, so we presented our tickets at the barrier and made our way, bumping into Norman (later Lord) Tebbit, who was crossing over from the other side of Downing Street. He insisted on giving way to us. Inside the black door was a permanently lit, narrow room with a modest fireplace and a range of coat racks. So far, it was not impressive. Then we had to climb up a wrought-iron staircase lined with portraits of all the prime ministers from Walpole (the first) to the present. At the top of the staircase was the small room with a marble fireplace where pictures of prime ministers shaking hands with eminent overseas visitors are invariably taken. Past that, we went into a superb large room. All three previous Tongan high commissioners were there, headed by Baron Va'ea of Houma, whose imposing son was ADC to the King. Va'ea had his usual expansive smile: we had not seen him for a long while as he was now a leading minister in Tonga.

After the King, with his 25-stone frame bent over markedly, and the Queen had passed through the room, we were all ushered into an equally large, splendid room. Here, on my name being announced, Mrs Thatcher shook my hand, turned to the King next to her and, to my surprise (there was no briefing from anyone: she must have memorized 'Snow, writer' among the 60 guests, fewer than the Queen's 100 or so in 1979), said 'Your Majesty will know of Mr Snow's books.' The King politely nodded. It was unlikely that he did, although, along with much about Tonga, *The People from the Horizon* had been sent to him, as had, years before, my *Bibliography of Fiji, Tonga and Rotuma*, which the Tongan government had helped finance. He could not of course possibly have remembered Ratu Sukuna, on presenting me to him (then Crown Prince) in 1950, having made a similar remark to Mrs Thatcher's after my *Cricket in the Fiji Islands* had been published. Reading is not a favourite pastime of people in the Pacific. We then re-met the Queen of Tonga and passed on to Denis Thatcher in the receiving line.

Almost immediately afterwards, all 60 of us (I counted the number on the menu card, which listed the names of those present) were directed into a light-panelled banqueting hall and, once the King, Queen and Prime Minister had taken their chairs at the small high table, we sat down. The lunch was one of the very best I have ever had — quite ambrosial:

Rudesheimer Berg Schlossberg Kabinett, 1979
Chateau Lynch-Bages, 1961
Graham, 1963
Delamain Pale and Dry

Mousse of Avocado with Crayfish Tails
Cognac Sauce

Medallions of Veal
Lemon Sauce
Noisette Potatoes
Selection of Seasonal Vegetables

Grape Pavlova

Coffee

10 Downing Street
26 October 1983

I had Tongan nobility seated on each side of me and some embarrassingly ignorant Members of Parliament opposite, whose opening gambit to the Tongans was predictably: 'Where exactly is Tonga?' They pronounced it of course with a hard 'g', which was enough to send shudders down the spines of Tongans and Tongaphiles alike. I remember having to correct George Formby backstage when remeeting Wallas Eaton, a Newton's and Christ's contemporary of mine who never quite made the acting grade after minor roles as in *Take It From Here*. That was in the London show *Zip Goes a Million* at Cambridge Circus in which the 'g' in one of the main songs, 'Rarotonga', was again not sung silently. As we did not see it a second time, we do not know if our advice was heeded. It would have sounded more musical with a soft 'g'.

The Lord Mayor of London was present at the lunch but most of the non-Tongan guests were an extraordinarily unimpressive collection of MPs doing this country no good in the estimation of the Tongans, who can be exquisitely sensitive, not to say snobbish.

Margaret Thatcher stood up and made an apt and brisk speech, unfortunately marred by 'Tong-qa'. How could the Foreign and Commonwealth Office not have briefed her on this integral key word? But, in the contrary earning of good marks for my self-esteem, who briefed her on my books? That, like the Queen's question when conferring my MBE, never ceases to make me wonder about the feats of some people's memories. How could she — all credit to her — have remembered it when my name came up out of 50 or so visitors in addition to the regular suite? The Prime Minister's speech was felicitous but I did not expect the King, not noted for any loquacity, to respond. And he did so with such a light touch. He reminded, or informed, Mrs Thatcher that before becoming a sovereign he too had been a prime minister. Wryly, he added that the only other person he knew to have been in both offices was a prime minister who later became King of Saudi Arabia and was promptly assassinated. Both speeches were *tours de force*.

We all retired when the high table emptied, the King and Queen back to the Tonga High Commission, Denis to who knows where. But my surprises of the day were added to by the Prime Minister being alone just inside the door leading out into Downing Street to shake us all by the hand. She had to rush off immediately afterwards to make a very important statement to the House of Commons on the Grenada crisis, over which she had been kept up virtually the whole night with telephone calls to the President of the USA. Yet there was not a hair out of place, not a suggestion of being preoccupied with the unforeseeable consequences of an uninvited American invasion of a British colony. Her poise was magnificent. She has commanded my respect ever since, although I'd thought of her highly in her term as Secretary of State for Education and Science.

I had enjoyed every moment of the occasion, which is what one is supposed to do and presumably does in nine cases out of ten. I had now been to functions at, or connected with, nearly all the grand centres in London — Buckingham Palace, the House of Lords, the House of Commons, Westminster Abbey, St Paul's

Cathedral, 10 Downing Street, Marlborough House and Mansion House. But not the Guildhall. When I was invited there in 1988 for the MCC bicentenary, I was unable join the distinguished cricket company from various parts of the world (I was to have sat next to the monumental batsman, Ponsford) because Anne was unwell.

Another outstanding occasion of the year was a dinner given by the Prime Minister of Fiji, Ratu Sir Kamisese Mara, in a marquee in the grounds of the High Commission house at Hampstead. Prince Edward was present: I found him most personable in the allotted quarter of an hour I had with him. He had just returned from a teaching sojourn at Wanganui Technical College, New Zealand, and his first visit to Fiji, with which he was manifestly entranced, so much so that I sent him a copy of *The People from the Horizon*. He was off to Jesus, Cambridge, for his first day next morning and I had a note in rather boyish writing from Second Lieutenant Prince Edward, RM, Jesus College, Cambridge, saying that life was rather hectic but as winter approached his thoughts were often with the islands. Thanking me for what he regarded as a wonderful book, he concluded by saying that it would bring back pleasant memories of charming people.

Tupouto'a, the Crown Prince of Tonga, whom I had met several times previously through my friendship with Ratu Sir Edward Cakobau and Martin and Diane Daly (she being half-Tongan of high rank), invited me to sit next to him. Educated in Switzerland, the Crown Prince was more European than most Europhiles and very cultivated, growing to resemble Ted Cakobau's father and his own great-grandfather, King George II, more closely every year, but no one can explain why at 40 plus he has not married. He speaks as softly as his father, the King, does and with what might be described as a Winchester accent, a little clipped and without any suggestion of being non-English. Cosmopolitan in outlook, his wit is pungent, yet soft-pedalled.

Mara made a superb speech. He said that the dinner was to thank all his friends and former colleagues in the administration and affairs of Fiji, declaring that without the historical goodwill and amiability between Europeans and Fijians the country could never have achieved what it had over a century of official contact. It cannot be often that a prime minister of a newly independent country has lauded the former colonial régime. For its generosity, rarity and graciousness this speech should have hit the headlines, but we know only too well that the press (it would have made no difference if it had been present) tends to have a nose exclusively for the aggressive, back-stabbing and odious side of public affairs.

My good friend the High Commissioner, Jo Toganivalu, told me that the Prime Minister was upgrading my MBE to an OBE, which George Cakobau and Joe Gibson, among a number of others, thought the very least I deserved for my work. I was asked if I would accept it and again I had to keep utterly quiet until it appeared in the Queen's birthday honours list in June.

Now came the crunch. Could I possibly make it to the Palace again in the autumn to collect it? The last occasion had been such an ordeal until it was over. I doubted it. It was causing me so much worry that, although I would in so many ways have loved to have gone through it without a qualm and taken in all the aura I might previously have missed, I resolved that the sensible course was, 'while presenting my humble and loyal duty to HM, to pray that HM may be graciously pleased to hold me excused'. Though I would be slightly earlier in the order this time with not quite so long to wait, bearing in mind where 'S' comes in the alphabet, there would still have been about 60 people ahead of me. About 100-odd are 'done' at a time with the MBEs following the OBEs, and naval, military, air force and conspicuous gallantry medals bringing up the rear — not, it seemed to me, altogether logically in the case of the last named. Back came a letter from Buckingham Palace, signed Elizabeth R, saying: 'I greatly regret that I am unable to give you personally the award which you have so well earned. I now send it to you with my congratulations and my best wishes for your future happiness.'

I comforted myself with the thought that perhaps a letter was in itself uncommon, even more rare than a presence in person. The silver MBE had had to be returned to be replaced with the prettier gilt OBE. Promotion within an order rather surprisingly requires that the previous, lower award cannot be retained; it is understandable that it is of course never used in subsequent address.

From out of the past came Martin Clemens to visit us. We had not seen him for 40 years. He was singularly unchanged but, looking at him now, I thought he would have made a fitting out-post governor had he been induced to stay on in the Colonial Service. After his most eventful stationing in the Western Pacific, he had been transferred at the end of the war to another prime trouble area, Cyprus, as District Commissioner of Nicosia at a time of rampant enosis. Out of sheer bravado he and the Governor, Sir Hugh Foot (later Lord Caradon), had strolled without guards the whole length of the colony's main street known as the Death Mile. With their backs sensitive to snipers, Martin confessed plaintively that it had seemed rather a long mile.

Feeling that he had not been given his due in the Service, on his marriage to an Australian he had retired from it early with a Guadalcanal MC and a final CBE. He had turned down unappealing offers of transfers. His (and my) exact contemporary, David Trench, also with a Solomon Islands MC, had been transferred to Hong Kong and had returned to the Solomon Islands as High Commissioner for the Western Pacific before obtaining a double term as Governor of Hong Kong and a GCMG. He had possibly had more stamina for file-shuffling. Certainly he had no less commanding a presence than Clemens. Both of them had been inspired choices by Major Sir Ralph Furse and C. A. R. Charnaud in the Colonial Office; it was almost as though they had sensed that the Western Pacific, a relative backwater, would be plunged into the maelstrom it became.

I made certain that I derived from Martin the exact details of his heroic diet of scallops on the vitally crucial Solomons island of Guadalcanal in 1942. He had put on weight in the 40 years since our last meeting in 1946 and this had put a heavy strain on his hips. After these were replaced by two metal ones in 1988, he walked with only a hint of a waddle and no sound of a clank. The prominence of the Solomon Islands campaign had been the highlight of his life. For some it would have been hideous, but for Martin Clemens much of his life from then on seemed anti-climactic; flying backwards and forwards regularly from Victoria, where he lives, to his huge sheep farm in Queensland is, in his 80s, merely like commuting from Welwyn Garden City to the City of London.

In 1986 I was again faced with the task of raising alone the

£40,000 necessary for the Fiji cricket team to visit England for the third International Cricket Conference trophy competition. For the only time in the competition's history, this June was perfect, sunny and dry. Cecil Browne was the part-European captain, with New Zealand's Fijian resident representative who, like him, had been on all the tours, as vice-captain. Apart from another Euronesian (mixed Polynesian-European or Melanesian European) and a Eurasian, all the rest were Fijian and, remarkably, all Lauan. Mostly a young side, they did not respond as well as I would have expected to the greater opportunity for play. Gibraltar and Israel were beaten, but Bermuda, Canada (wholly West Indian), the USA, Papua New Guinea (with backing from Australia), Holland and, to my disappointment, Hong Kong all won.

My expectations of the team had been reasonably high, for in Suva in 1984 Fiji had lost by a mere 19 runs to the full England team captained by David Gower (Bob Willis had been resting for the match) during England's first playing visit to Fiji when *en route* to New Zealand and Pakistan.

I had managed to get the Fiji team over by writing to John Paul Getty II who, with Tate & Lyle (George Jellicoe was no longer with the firm), gave the entire amount necessary and would accept only a token of gratitude in return. Paul Getty, soon to be given an honorary KBE, had been touched by the modest Fijian artefact the team had brought for him. (What else can one present to a multi-billionaire?) I had also been touched by the large traditional-style Fijian club presented to me. Now, as a measure of the passage of the seven years since the first tour, the legend had grown: instead of sons, there were one or two grandsons of players whom I had coached. The eldest member of the party, the manager Solomone Wainiqolo, was in fact the son of a man I had picked out to become Buli Lomaloma and then Roko Tui Lau.

As in 1979 (by Joe and Emily Gibson) and 1982 (by Jo and Alice Toganivalu), the members of the 1986 team were given a reception by the current High Commissioner, now a Lau commoner called Sailosi Wai Kepa, and his rivetingly attractive, fine-boned wife, Adi Teimumu Tuisawau, who, as the younger sister of the Prime Minister's wife, Adi Lady Lala Mara, was of the highest rank in Rewa.

Close Bereavements and Royalty Near and Far

After having written the foreword for the competition's souvenir programme, I relinquished my chairmanship of the 18 associate member countries of the conference to which I had been elected annually since being the first incumbent five years earlier. The work had been arduous and I was glad to have it passed on to my most capable deputy, the representative of Gibraltar, Joe Buzaglo, whose strength of character caused general and gratifying surprise.

An outstanding chairman of the International Cricket Conference (and president of the MCC) was Bank of England director J. G. W. Davies. Of Cambridge and Kent, he was a brilliant cover-fielder who became famous for bowling Bradman for 0. Jack Davies was an extremely capable chairman (making the job, far from easy with so many diverse countries involved, look effortless) not only for 1986 but also for the following year when, in the absence through illness of Colin Cowdrey, whom I had often met, he presided over an important meeting for Fiji.

As briefly referred to earlier, ever since the Fiji team had been part way through the 1948 tour of New Zealand, Fiji had repeatedly asked New Zealand to give first-class status to its five three-day matches against the major provinces, two of which it had defeated to the acclaim of all who saw the team.

Indifferently treated by its neighbour Australia on one side, over the years New Zealand was unable to rise to more magnanimous treatment of its neighbour on the other side in the matter of cricket recognition. New Zealand persistently refused to acknowledge the absolute logic of Fiji's case. For 39 years Fiji tried and was rebuffed without any reasons being given. This was until Graham Dowling, the former test captain, became New Zealand's chief executive. As a considerate man, he at last divulged New Zealand's reasons, which had been kept from Fiji and could now be interpreted by us easily as totally illogical pretexts. Fiji then promptly appealed to the International Cricket Conference for correction of New Zealand's glaring injustice concerning the 1948 team's record that was so superior to those of the 1895 and 1954 teams, which had been given first-class status.

Although I had retired from making public speeches (I did not escape having to make them on the spur of the moment at the conference dinners in 1979 and 1986 when I was congratulated on my respective MBE and OBE), I had to address the conference for half an hour. When the turn of the New Zealand number one representative, noted for his unceasing bluff and rugged comment at conferences, came to put up his country's reply, he professed himself to be speechless — much to the surprise and amusement of the delegates. He could summon up no reply. Without releasing anything from the confidentiality of the meeting that is not already known, it can be noted that the chairman put the issue to the vote, which — I dared hardly look at upraised hands or those kept lowered — was 19 for Fiji and 9 for New Zealand. Graham Dowling, the number two New Zealand representative, was the first to congratulate me. It could not have been a more handsome gesture. The following year the habitually voluble number one representative, who had played not very successfully against Fiji in 1948, acknowledged Fiji's first-class status with this comment on the dinner menu card: 'To Philip. My association goes back to your first-class tour. Bob Vance.'

So, after 39 years, the seven surviving members of the fifteen composing the Fiji touring party were at last first class. Most of the team, in fact a surprising proportion, had died. The senior in age was Ratu Sir George Cakobau, who became the oldest player in the game's history to be graded first class, with myself as the second oldest. If it proved nothing else, it demonstrated that tenacity, when the case is straightforward, has its ultimate reward. The main thing is not to be worn down by the process of attrition or too dismayed by the seemingly uncrushable stone face ahead.

Another triumph over the past, this time a minor one but none the less appreciated, was to have tracked down to my disbelief a surviving daughter of a governor of Fiji of as far back as 1910–12, Sir Henry May. Iris Johnston was the third youngest of the four daughters, all of whom had predeceased her. At the age of 87 she travelled from Suffolk to meet us in Sussex, having previously sent for copying the priceless family picture albums of life at Government House in those halcyon days. Not only physically active but mentally alert, she was delighted to have been 'discovered', as she termed it. That particular period covered a gap in my unique private pictorial record of the Pacific dating from the earliest artists' impressions through the beginning of photography to the present, a collection that has been difficult to amass over 50 years. The considerable research has not been helped by having to track down daughters who change their surnames on marriage. I believe they should keep their maiden name and hyphenate it to their married one, as women do, I believe, in one or two Scandinavian countries and in Holland. This would be a bonus for researchers as well as an addition to feminine self-esteem.

9

Paradise Walkabout

These two volumes are neither an autobiography nor memoirs. Neither are they a history. They are more a series of reflections and observations. My having been connected officially and unofficially with the South Sea Islands for close on 60 years, it would represent an odd lacuna (which would be bound to be noticed before this story is rounded off) if a slice of history, albeit a most significant one, were nevertheless neither mentioned nor reflected on, even if only observed second hand and from a vast distance.

The following account is strictly limited to the absolute minimum. While it cannot be first hand, as I have said, and while it remains, perhaps therefore with a modicum of advantage, detached, it attempts to offer a focus on a coherent conclusion — a summary of facts. This was derived from the sometimes disparate views, inevitably amounting now and again to a blurred vista, of observers on the spot, as well as views of one or two central figures on the actual scene expressed to me marginally and in no way officially. Media reports were of varying reliability. There was much general bewilderment, some of it lingering nearly a decade later, not least among those most directly concerned. The official history must be a long way from being written — and then only when perspective has been gained and the dust has settled, if, as one hopes, it will. I needed to have at least some background idea of what had been going on because, until my retirement seven years later, I was still Fiji's representative on an international body, although in the event my work on and for it came in no way to be affected. The Fiji Cricket Association is above politics, which is what it turned out to be all about. And, as a former administrator

248

in the islands, I was and have remained divorced from racial issues and politics, while necessarily keeping an ear to the ground in an attempt to understand what was happening or might happen anywhere at any time.

In 1987 Fiji experienced its greatest disturbance (apart from the Second World War) since its official connection with Britain had begun 113 years earlier. As it has been my habit since retiring from Rugby to stay up writing or reading until 4.00 a.m., I fairly shot up in my seat when a BBC radio news item pierced my subconscious. A laconic statement on the 1.00 a.m. news announced that 'A report of a military coup in Fiji is just coming in. Parliament in session has been surrounded and the Prime Minister taken away. Further details will be in the next bulletin.' But at 2.00 a.m. there was in fact little more detail. Soldiers in Balaclavas had surrounded the Government Buildings, a military coup had been announced by an officer interrupting parliament, and the Prime Minister and members of the Cabinet had been removed in trucks.

At such an hour I did not know whether or not to telephone the High Commissioner in London, Sailosi (Silas) Wai Kepa. His wife, as I have said, was the sister-in-law of Prime Minister Ratu Sir Kamisese Mara, who had recently been defeated in a general election by a new party (with predominantly Indian but some Fijian support) led by Dr Timoci Bavadra, the husband of Adi Kuini Vuikaba. I hesitated but on balance decided that he would wish to know at the earliest opportunity. Sailosi was grateful and said that he would now stay up all night. As it turned out, there was no telephone or radio communication with Fiji; the coup leader had cut all links.

It was some days before even a confused picture emerged. Lieutenant-Colonel Sitiveni Rabuka (under the name of Sitiveni Ligamamada he had visited us in Rugby as a burly forward in the Fiji rugby team touring England in 1970) had organized the coup, while his commanding officer, Brigadier-General (the first Fijian to attain that rank) Ratu Epeli Nailatikau, son of the late Colonel Ratu Sir Edward Cakobau, had been at a conference in Australia waiting for Rabuka to join him. It could not have been described as anything less than a mutiny. The Governor-General, Colonel Ratu Sir Penaia Ganilau, had been virtually isolated in Govern-

249

ment House and some of his staff, a few Indian leaders and out-spoken Europeans, including members of the judiciary and press, had been arrested.

If Epeli (who was married to Ratu Sir Kamisese Mara's daughter, Adi Koila) returned to Fiji, Rabuka would have had to arrest him. If he failed to apprehend him, Rabuka himself would have been arrested for treason. Both Ratu Mara and Ratu Penaia, who ironically and fortuitously happened to be Rabuka's paramount chief (Rabuka was a commoner from a village in Cakaudrove Province), seemed powerless to intervene, despite being of vastly higher rank than anyone else apart from the ailing Ratu Sir George Cakobau. Epeli eventually returned from Australia with an assurance that he would not be maltreated. With news of the coup reported on the front pages of all of England's national newspapers, Fiji had hit the headlines for the first time in its history. For a number of weeks it was also the first item on the English television news, with programmes invariably starting with pictures of Penaia and Rabuka.

It has been contemplated that Rabuka had too large an army, which, apart from contingents in the United Nations' peace-keeping forces in Sinai and the Lebanon (where little peace seems to have prevailed and where they might have learned a thing or two about coups), was insufficiently occupied. It emerged that he himself had been on a course some years before in which he selected as his study — guess what? — military coups. It also became known that Rabuka's alleged motive under the unrelenting pressure of vituperative, extremist Fijian Methodists was to stifle once and for all the possibility of Indian political control of the country. But Indians were now, however, no longer in a majority: in recent years Fijians had caught up dramatically with the Indian birth rate. There was therefore no special logic in the timing.

It was creditable that there was virtually no bloodshed, but then the coup had been remarkably easy to achieve — with 99 per cent of the arms in the country in the hands of the army and police, not much skill had been required to overcome the opposition. Had Australia and New Zealand intervened (their intentions to do so were announced) there would inevitably have been a serious con-flict. A previously clandestine Fijian movement dominated by intolerant, sanctimonious Methodists — the Taukei — expressed support for Rabuka and pushed for impossible measures to be taken against the Indians. When Rabuka, a lay preacher, formed a government its members were mostly drawn from that movement. They were a feckless association. Attempts were made to involve the retired Governor-General, Ratu Sir George Cakobau, at the apex of rank in the country, on one side or another but he was reported diplomatically and veritably to be frail.

Rabuka now required a new constitution (to displace the one agreed on independence in 1970) that guaranteed Fijian dominance of Parliament, the principal offices and all key government positions. The aim to exclude Indians from these was comprehensible — some would say justifiable. There was envy of the Indians' economic success. But how could that be altered without impoverishing the whole country? Fijians are not — and by nature and indigenous custom never could be — a nation of shopkeepers. Those who recalled the Africans' response to the mercantile skill of the Indians in Idi Amin's Uganda were apprehensive.

A first reaction in Fiji was for Indians to leave for Canada, New Zealand and Australia, depriving the country of doctors, dentists, professional men and leaders of commerce. Some of the relatively few Europeans and rather more part-Europeans in the country also decided to leave. It was not frenzy but symptomatic of it. There was a desperate technical and business vacuum.

When the tempo of change did not suit Rabuka, or the Methodist extremists propelling him, he brought about a second, more drastic coup. This resulted in Fiji leaving the Commonwealth. Any attempt to rejoin seemed likely to be blocked by India and Pakistan in one of their sporadic joining of forces. Or so at least I thought until I discussed this five years later in Angmering with Ratu Sir Kamisese Mara, who told me that Rajiv Gandhi, shortly before his assassination, had expressed to him his support for Fiji rejoining. Kamisese astonished me by saying that Canada — and less surprisingly Australia — might be obstacles to any such wish by Fiji. He also told me that leaving the Commonwealth (which had made Fiji something of a pariah in diplomatic circles: since Pakistan's return, South Africa and Ireland were the only former members still out of it) had been such an unnecessary step.

251

A Time of Renewal

Ratu Sir Penaia Ganilau apparently felt that he had no alternative but to grant Rabuka a pardon for his mutiny and then resign from his governor-generalship and become President, thereby at least denying Rabuka supreme nominal control. In a decree laden with religious overtones and clichés, Rabuka proclaimed Fiji a republic. Such a concept was wholly alien to Fiji's rigidly stratified society.

To many admirers of the country and to her indigenous Fijian subjects, the displacement of the Queen of Fiji was perhaps the most distasteful of all the changes. But, as always, Fijians feel a touching and profound allegiance to English royalty and still plaster the interiors of their houses with pictures of them.

If ever Fiji were likely to become a republic it always seemed that this could only happen under the influence of ambitious local Indian politicians. No one foresaw that it would be the result of right-wing extremist action by Fijians, which left Fijian villagers bewildered and the poor Rotumans even more so. This intelligent ethnic group, which staged a brave, pathetic protest with fluttering Union Flags (which the Fiji Army demolished) should not be forgotten. The turn of events was opposed to their way of life — to the placid 'Fijian way' so much publicized since independence by government and businesses alike. The widely recognized and advertised paradise had, to borrow a phrase relating to Australian Aborigines, 'gone walkabout'.

Fijians were split in half. Provinces, tribes and even families were divided. It reminded me of seventeenth-century England and of how, for instance, during the English Civil War the first Earl of Denbigh, whose descendants I knew in Rugby, died for the King while his son and heir fought on the unrelenting opposite side.

A new constitution, with Sailosi Wai Kepa now in Fiji steering it through as Attorney General, was promulgated. It aimed to guarantee Fijian political supremacy (no one but a Fijian could be President or Prime Minister, and there had to be a permanent majority of Fijians in the parliament). One cannot demur over the logic of this, but the outcome could be precariously uncertain. Nothing, it seemed, could prevent another coup or series of coups. The Chief Justice and Puisne Judges had been dismissed: some of them reluctantly accepted reappointment in the interest of national security while others refused out of principle. Ratu Mara saw the imperative need to help steady the country and agreed to be interim Prime Minister: with Ratu Penaia, he retained almost the only semblance of traditional chiefly leadership.

Dr Bavadra, who had been virtually exiled in his village of Viseisei in Vuda District on the northwestern side of Viti Levu and was being kept under close military surveillance, developed cancer of the spine and died in November 1989 at the age of 52. He had almost been a representative cricketer for Fiji (which Mara had actually achieved) and, whatever the views of his political divagations, most people agreed that this medical doctor (which Mara had once nearly become) had considerable personal charisma. Bavadra's widow, Adi Kuini Vuikaba, briefly succeeded him in the leadership of his party.

Ratu Mara had persuaded Ratu Epeli to accept the post of first Ambassador to the United Kingdom (previous incumbents had been high commissioners) and, shortly after his arrival, he and Adi Koila visited us. His mission in the country was to attempt to restore confidence, not least in the economy and in the future of tourism in Fiji. His and his wife's reports put a number of facts in perspective and it was interesting that Rabuka was judged to be no fool and Bavadra a gentle man. All the same, I could not help feeling, at my 12,000-mile distance from Fiji, that it would be as difficult to find a satisfactory solution to Fiji's present difficulties as it had been for most of this century to deal with the potentially explosive points posed by the country's Indian demographic majority. I had always been fascinated, when I had worked at the government's headquarters in Fiji, by the absence of any confidential file on 'the Indian question'.

The evolution of Fiji's relative prosperity up until the coups was primarily due to the Indians' hard work in commerce and industry, along with the Fijians' physical strength in some sectors of the economy. The Fijians' tolerance and good nature also played a part, for their communal system of subsistence, with its lack of personal ambition and competitiveness, was very inexpensive to maintain. It is, however, necessary to acknowledge that Fijians were the beneficiaries, as sitting landlords in some regions, of rents paid by sweating, conscientious Indian lessees.

From the economic angle, at least tourism (a principal source of income) has after a short wobble picked up. So has the main crop, sugar, although this is wholly dependent on Indians. World confidence after the initial radical jolting has been largely regained.

For the first elections to be held since 1987, Rabuka, having secured promotion as the first Fijian to become a major-general, decided to retire from the army and stand for parliament. He gained the key party seat by one vote over the Prime Minister's wife, Adi Lady Lala Mara. He became the Fijian leader of the exclusively Fijian party and, after unpredictably doing a deal with the Indian opposition, secured ultimate power in 1982 as Prime Minister. Ratu Sir Kamisese Mara, who had retired before the elections, was elected as one of the two Fijian Vice-Presidents and immediately became the first acting president of Fiji when Penaia became seriously ill.

While acting President (he so signed our visitors' book in July 1992), Kamisese and Lala, accompanied by Epeli and Koila carrying a fine piece of *tapa*, honoured us with a visit to Angmering (they came by train which Kamisese, who is fitted with a pacemaker, prefers to road travel). They took us out to lunch at an Italian restaurant on the beach and, over it and afternoon tea on our lawn, Kamisese filled me in on epic occurrences since the coups.

It would be a touching gesture of goodwill if Rabuka, now in civilian supremacy, could arrange for Suva's Government Buildings (Fiji's, or indeed the Pacific Islands', finest example of architecture but neglected for 50 years) to be restored to the pristine state of their glistening opening in 1938, when they were as white as driven snow, by water nozzled at high pressure and at little cost.

Allegiance to the Queen of England as Queen of Fiji was the principal factor linking families, tribes and confederacies after the deed of cession of Fiji to Queen Victoria and her successors. Though Sitiveni Rabuka has mellowed and matured with the new experience and weight of civil administration, republicanism might still sit uneasily with Fiji's traditions, which are so strongly upheld. My own personal reflection (I hope I have escaped any accusation of being opinionated about subjects with which I have not been directly concerned), if I may have the temerity to express it, after having been kept in touch with the country and with an advantage that is occasionally conferred by observation from outside, is that should Fiji unfortunately never regain the British monarch as its sovereign, it might consider turning with appropriateness and profit to the system that works in Malaysia.

The monarchy of that country, bicultural with its Malayan/Chinese make-up, as Fiji is with its Fijian/Indian composition, rotates supreme leadership every four years between the handfuls of indigenous sultans who serve during their period in office as the king of Malaysia. This system could be adopted by Fiji's leading native confederacies, especially since their highest chiefs have experience of governing by benevolent autocracy.

For instance, Ratu Sir Kamisese Mara could, as the oldest and as Tui Lau, serve the first period as King of Fiji. Then Adi Lala (his wife) could follow as the Queen representing Lower Rewa (Burebasaga) of which she is paramount chief. After her incumbency for three or four years, the Vunivalu of Bau could serve for a similar period, followed by the Tui Cakau for Cakaudrove (had Ratu Penaia not died in 1994 he could have been the first king as the oldest high chief). Then perhaps the head of a new confederacy of Yasayasa Vakara (northwest Fiji) such as the Tui Vuda or Tui Vitogo and even — to follow — the most chiefly and able leader within a combination of the three Colos (East, West and North), such as a descendant of that fine figure of my time, Tui Noimalu, in Narokorokoyawa. Then, with the circle completed, reversion to the Tui Lau and revolving similarly through the chain of confederacies.

The cycle works for Malaysia. Why not, if necessary, for Fiji? I always remember Kamisese Mara's slight hesitation over the first of the three alternatives he would choose for Fiji's future status — kingdom, republic or dominion? I had put the question to him in Rugby in our very late night discussion that had gone on into the early hours of the morning just before Fiji's independence. He had opted for the last, but that had been disposed of by the coups.

What would Ratu Sir Lala Sukuna and Ratu Sir Edward Cakobau have thought and done about the coups or plans for them? They had always had their eyes ahead and their ears close to the ground, particularly on the vital Indian–Fijian relationships (they were malleable but always firmly turned to indestructible and inalienable standards). Indeed, one of Ratu Sukuna's closest friends in constant attendance was Bramhanand Raghvanand, formerly an Indian assistant to district commissioners and brother of Bhaskaranand Basavanand, my sub-accountant and friend from Nadi days, with whose high-caste Brahmin family Ratu Sukuna had been brought up in Ra.

Meanwhile, beyond the upheaval in what was a small model of a nation the world has continued naturally to turn.

When Charles and Pamela's son, Philip Charles Hansford, married Amanda, daughter of former Permanent Under-Secretary for Home Affairs Sir Clive Whitmore, I was asked to stand in for Charles as a witness at the ceremony in the chapel of Christ's College (where Amanda, her sister, her father, Charles and myself had been; Philip himself had gone to Balliol, Oxford). Again, it was no easy task for me but with Peter driving I was able to have some anaesthetizing sustenance and enjoy the occasion. Philippa was one of the bridesmaids and smiled conspiratorially across the chapel to me. Jack Plumb, Clive Whitmore, Philip and the best man, Robin Lloyd George (a son of Owen, 3rd Earl Lloyd George) made the speeches afterwards in hall.

An imposing visitor to Angmering was Suguna Ramanathan, a high-caste Hindu from India who had written *The Novels of C. P. Snow* in 1978 and whose beauty, intellect and elegance were harmoniously embellished by the orange sari she was wearing.

We were also delighted to have from the outback of Australia the son of the late Wal Warden, JP, the enlightened copra planter on Taveuni. Bill Warden, a sheep farmer in one season and seller of hay in the other was, like his father, interested, composed and dignified. There was good sound stock in that family.

As President of the MCC, John J. Warr was chairman of the 1988 International Cricket Conference. J. J. handled a difficult meeting with the consummate ease of the astringent, witty, urbane man that he is, in addition to being one of the most in demand of after-dinner speakers and the holder of the Binney medal for tackling a criminal on a London street.

John Warr's successor in 1989 was the Lord Lieutenant of Greater London, Field Marshal Lord Bramall. Edwin (shortened to Dwin) Bramall is an affable man, most capable and well able to overcome his deafness in the chair. He ranks very high in all senses among the many ICC chairmen I have known. Prince Philip, Jack Davies, John Warr, Gubby Allen and he have all been outstanding.

At the opening of the 1989 conference, Edwin Bramall complimented me on my 25 years of continuous attendance at annual meetings. This spanned the entire life of the International Cricket Conference, from the year it ceased to be the Imperial Cricket Conference to 1989 when it changed its name again, this time to the International Cricket Council. My attendance was by far the longest. Allen had been some years on the Imperial Cricket Conference and then a further ten years on the International Cricket Conference but no other representative or officer anywhere near approached my span of more than a quarter century. It made me feel that I had seen everything, not least and *ad nauseam* the question of the readmission of South Africa, which left in 1961. I had certainly witnessed or been party to a lot of change in it.

Fiji, Ceylon and the USA were the first members of the non-test playing countries to be elected when my representation started in 1965. The next year Bermuda, Denmark, East and Central Africa and Holland joined, followed by Malaysia (1967), Canada (1968), Gibraltar and Hong Kong (1969), Papua New Guinea (1973), Argentina, Israel and Singapore (1974), West Africa (1976), Bangladesh (1977), Kenya and Zimbabwe (1981), United Arab Emirates (1990) Namibia and Ireland (1993). I was particularly pleased to help Italy achieve associate membership as I retired.

We associate members did not have a truly separate organization until 1982 when I was elected the first chairman and held the office for the next four years. The associate countries sat with the test countries, including Sri Lanka, which had been promoted in 1981. For the initial years, except the baptismal year, 1965, associates were scarcely encouraged to chime in but more recently these countries have been consulted round the table. Each test country has two representatives to an associate's one but the latter can now outvote the former on all but strictly test issues.

After 1965, when the numbers began to swell round the table, I could have done with a Boothbyesque gravel voice to help make audible interjections when one wanted to jump in over the other voices. Allen, England's number one representative, had it to perfection. Indeed, as one knew him and had it ratified by Jim Swanton's superbly readable biography of Allen, in which I am reported as commenting on his mellowing magnanimity, Allen's might have been the ideal life. He died at the end of 1989 almost a millionaire. Although not captain of Eton, Cambridge or Middlesex, but an adroit, universally acknowledged administrator and captain of England when tours were in the grand style by ship, he was privileged until his death at nearly 90 years of age with the singular use of a back gate from his garden behind the Lord's pavilion — all to be envied except his baffling bachelordom.

Had he had some of Allen's affluence, another to envy for his 90 years might have been his patron, Plum Warner, with his captaincy of Rugby, Middlesex and England (but not of Oxford) and all his tours abroad by sea. Inestimable was an amateur's life in cricket, although had I been good enough never to be nagged by worries about holding my place in a first-class team and fortunate enough to have escaped injuries, I would have relished a professional career.

If airships had come in rather than aeroplanes, it is perhaps not too fanciful to think that touring overseas by them might have been tolerable (their very name implies buoyancy and style if not speed: but then if one has to fly it is better to get it over as quickly as possible) and I might have persevered in the air if the trauma of the sight on film of the *Hindenburg* ablaze could have been avoided. Incidentally, towards the top of the list of books giving me greatest enjoyment is an unlikely one (having regard to my disinterest in, or at most dislike of, air travel), *To Ride the Storm: The Story of the Airship R101* by the aviation specialist Sir Peter Masefield. This narrative was fascinating to someone like me who loves detail if it is not too technical and if it adds, as I maintain it does, to a book's interest.

For me no cliché has more basis than that fact is stranger than fiction. The latter can supply for me nothing of the fascination that, for instance, M. R. D. Foot's *SOE in France* presents in so matter of fact a manner. I frankly admit that I read almost no fiction. It is reality I want to know about. Masefield makes in his book the trivialities lucid and tells such a story that for once that other cliché, 'hard to put the book down', applies. Not least the intriguing sideline of the aristocratic-looking brigadier general, Lord Thomson of Cardington, Secretary of State for Air, and his mistress, Princess Marthe Bibesco of Romania.

Thomson virtually smuggled aboard the R101 for its real maiden flight — I had seen the dirigible shortly before on a test flight over Leicester in 1929 — a massive Kurdish carpet for a state banquet in India, which the airship failed to reach. The weight of Lord Thomson's baggage was 254 lbs, of which the carpet was 129 lbs, while the next heaviest for any of the 54 on board was 44 lbs. Of course one knows the end of the story before it begins — I can recall exactly where it was that I saw in 1930 the placard 'R101 Destroyed' — but the detail to one with an aviation phobia is magnificent. Did the carpet fatally upset the balance and control in the airship, causing it to hit the very first hill to be encountered (in northern France) after leaving Cardington's flat base in Bedfordshire, with Thomson not among the eight survivors? This book is such a delight among the vast amount of biography, autobiography, travel and other subjects I cover with anticipation but too rarely with satisfaction. I was impelled to write to the author, congratulating him, something I have done only a handful of times to writers. With Dame Diana Reader Harris, he was to secure my fellowship of the Royal Society of Arts.

After that digression, which I felt I must share with readers, let me now return briefly to the ICC. Fiji always gave me *carte blanche* with respect to the conferences. I have had complete understanding with the honorary secretary Peter Knight, an English solicitor with a Finnish wife in Fiji. Never too diverted by that country's occasional peccadilloes in cricket organization, for which his temperament, tact and touch are absolutely right, he is the embodiment of self-effacement and sympathy, which suits Fiji's laid-back charm.

For years I have believed that the simplest and most effective way of making cricket attractive is to have plenty of slow bowlers. They have largely disappeared since the last war to be supplanted by the most deadly dull seam bowlers of extraordinarily, mesmerizingly boring medium pace. I succeeded in introducing to the agenda of the conference the idea of having only one new ball an innings, thereby making seam bowling effective for only a brief period in it. Although I would raise the item at each annual conference, the conference's recommendation was always deferred to the following year. It was once supported by Australia when its team happened to have one or two good legbreak and googly bowlers. While it was never ruled out, in my view the conferences have shown lack of imagination in not recommending an amendment of the rules to the countries so as to limit balls to one an innings. The press periodically of its own volition reports the idea as if it were a new one, whereas I have advocated and perhaps pioneered it for approaching three decades. Meanwhile, the game remains duller than it need be. When slow bowlers are on something is always happening — sixes or fours or out, often to spectacular boundary catches. Despite the rule allowing so many new balls, it has been stimulating to see the emergence of such class spinners as Shane Warne and Paul Adams.

I enjoyed recently sitting next to two Pakistani representatives, Lieutenant-General G. S. Butt — moustachioed and like a sun-bronzed Englishman but more English than the English and comfortingly serene — and the lively secretary of that country's board (but no relation), Ijaz Butt. Their English was perfect; that of the Indian delegates is customarily the least distinct of all the countries' representatives.

Those whom I have known best, apart from Joe Buzaglo, have been Walter Hadlee, New Zealand's number one representative and a close friend since we were opposing captains on Fiji's 1948 tour of New Zealand; John Warr, captain of Cambridge and Middlesex who was for years Australia's number two; likewise Ben Barnett, the Australian wicketkeeper 'Prince', as the Maharajah of Baroda liked to be known when he was India's delegate; Henry Grijseels (Holland); Gamini Goonesena (Ceylon); the totally inimitable Alma Hunt, uncrowned king of Bermuda cricket; Raman Subba Row, the Northants, Surrey and England player and the most impressive of England representatives since Gubby Allen, being energetic, wise and far ranging in imagination and surely one day to be a worthy chairman of the ICC.

I also knew Graham Dowling (New Zealand test captain and chief executive); Donald King and Ken Bullock (Canada); and Alan Crompton, the Fiji-born chairman of the Australian Board of

Control and a model delegate for Australia in the tradition of Ray Steele, and also surely a future chairman of the ICC. David Richards is a brisk, businesslike chief executive of ICC whom Graham Halbish succeeded as Australia's number two and chief executive. And there was Vic Lewis, a regular broadcasting dance-band leader in England who married a Windmill dancer and became the USA's number two.

Willem van Rossem (of Holland), a naval captain during the war who had to report daily to the Nazi occupying authorities in the Netherlands and who later became ADC to Queen Juliana was succeeded by the diplomatic Hank van Eck. Cecil Cooke, a polished Eurasian former assistant commissioner of police, deputy secretary in the Singapore Ministry of Defence and president of the Singapore Association was followed by a Sikh ally of mine, Harbans Singh.

Another Sikh, Jasmar Singh Gill, represented Kenya with Harilal Shah, who had played for his country, as had Joe Buzaglo in the ICC trophy competitions (Alma Hunt and I were the only others among the associate members to have represented their country — in an earlier era). Charles used to say that if you wanted to be sure of being included in a photograph you should stand talking to a turbaned Sikh, for they are as magnets to a camera. Daljit Singh, though short in stature, made, with Harbans and Jasmar, a colourful and attractive trio with turbans of contrasting hues.

Then there were the fine West Indian opening batsmen of the 1950s, Allan Rae of Jamaica and Jeff Stollmeyer of Trinidad. Their impressively light tanned appearances (they were Creoles descended respectively from Portuguese and Dutch settlers in the Caribbean) and mellifluous voices magically soothed potential abrasiveness in the conference. Were one not to have a gravel voice, one could covet their power to lull the 60 or so people (including occasional observers and officials) in the dignified committee room of the Lord's pavilion with its grand wide window overlooking the sunlit panorama of the ground. No region had a pair of more distinguished and helpful representatives in all my time on the conference. As if they were not impressive enough, they would occasionally be added to by the gentlemanly Lance Murray. These West Indian friends of mine were succeeded by Sir

Clyde Walcott, as amicable as his predecessors with a distinguished presence and competence who, like Sir Frank Worrell (a quiet, dignified gentleman met at a match in Leicester), seemed not un-European in mannerisms and features.

The West Indian cricket figures I have known have always appealed to me, from the time when my opening batting partner at Christ's was a deeply bronzed, handsome Trinidadian, Arnold Kelshall, who would have got a Blue in less strong Cambridge sides than those of the mid-1930s. He was later in the RAF and a prisoner of war. The latest West Indian number one representative as chairman of their board, Captain Peter Short, is imposingly moustachioed (ex-British army) and markedly balanced.

The murder in 1989 of Jeff Stollmeyer in his opulent family mansion in Trinidad by bandits who overcame the bodyguard and also injured his elegant wife Sara (who with Jeff had made such an imposing couple) and his son was a startling end to a gentleman's life. This was not the only murder of an ICC friend. A year earlier, the Malaysian representative, national player and batsman for various states (with one leg three inches shorter than the other as the result of a motorcycle accident) and Supreme Court interpreter, Daljit Singh Gill, a Sikh with whom I had been very friendly and who had always brought sparkle and light mischief to our conferences with his excellent sense of humour, had been set upon and killed in his orchard in Selangor by neighbours with whom he had been involved in a contretemps over land. I had been as fond of him as of the very different, sedate, aristocratic Jeff Stollmeyer, whom I had persuaded to write his autobiography — in the event, a rather disappointing one.

As will have been noticed in these two volumes, having for years been a fellow of the Royal Anthropological Institute I am fascinated by ethnic *mélange*s. The West Indian islands are richly endowed with them and I had asked Jeff to include something about them in his book but he did not do so.

Malaysia also produced another of my friends, Tunku Imran ibni Tuanku Ja'afar, the second son of the Sultan of Negri Sembilan, a state which saw a lot of the Fijians who volunteered to suppress so successfully the terrorists in the jungle warfare of the 1950s. Peter, as the *Tunku* (prince) prefers to be known when not addressed as

His Highness, is very akin to the Crown Prince of Tonga, both in appearance (even to the shape of his ear lobes) and in his smooth wit. His father is currently King of Malaysia under the rotation system.

There was a third murder, after those of Jeff Stollmeyer and Daljit Singh Gill, among my colleagues on the International Cricket Council. Gamini Dissenayake, the leader of the opposition in Sri Lanka, which he represented for cricket — a light-coloured figure of aristocratic demeanour — was blown up when a woman suicide bomber went right up to him at a political meeting. Three murders among the delegates I have known is a high, too high proportion.

What I lacked by not being involved in the internal cricket administration of a country at test level, for which I could never have been anywhere near qualified or to which of course I could never have cherished any aspirations, I to some extent compensated for by having established a record in 1988 of over 50 years' continuous administrative service to cricket, mixed with some playing, which at least included, thanks to the 1987 ICC decision, nine first-class innings. This was a very far cry, however, from the playing experience of some of those representatives of the eight test countries with whom I had established friendships.

When the ICC trophy competition came round in 1990, it was held in Holland, but it was beyond me to be able to get there. To my great relief, Fiji now found the funds from the World Cup competition allocating profits at set intervals. Liking the pitches, Fiji was the surprise team, beating Bermuda for the first time and losing only narrowly to Bangladesh and Kenya. It then beat East Africa, Malaysia, Hong Kong, Argentina and Gibraltar. Cecil Browne, captain for the second time, had almost taken them back to the standard I knew. It was far and away Fiji's most successful tour outside New Zealand.

However, the team was frankly disappointing on going in 1994 to Kenya for the fifth ICC trophy competition. Things, as can happen too easily in cricket, had gone into reverse. It can only be hoped that in 1997, which will be the Fiji team's first opportunity to be able to play nearer (or indeed anywhere near) its own country since the first competition in 1979, it will find the venue of

Malaysia more to its liking, perhaps home from home. Before it leaves for Malaysia, it will first have had a very long mooted first tour of Fiji by the MCC (I had made soundings 50 years ago) — an all too rare chance to meet players other than on the internal circuit.

By 1990 another Indian potentate — a real one, I hasten to add — had crossed my path at the ICC meeting. This was the Maharajah of Gwalior, who became India's number one delegate, to be followed quickly by yet another in my last year on the council, the Maharajah of Sind.

In 1991, the 60 representatives and their wives were all invited to a reception at 10 Downing Street by Prime Minister John Major. This was my and Anne's second visit to that address. We were photographed by his cameraman in the upstairs reception room having our hands shaken by the Prime Minister when we were being introduced by Sir Colin (later Lord) Cowdrey, the chairman of the ICC. The Chairman's term of office was now four years, having been separated from the presidency of the MCC, which itself had been extended to two-year terms. Married to the eldest daughter of Bernard, 16th Duke of Norfolk, Colin lives a couple of miles from me at Angmering Park on the Arundel estate. The Prime Minister could not have been more friendly, saying: 'Hello, Philip. How good of you to have come.' The honour was naturally totally ours and he may have been employing his politician's touch with his constituents but we could not have been made to feel more comfortable.

This was only the fourth time there had been social occasions outside the conferences. The first had been in 1966 when Lieutenant General Leese had invited the then 16 members to his Chelsea flat for a barbecue, followed in later years by the Maharajah of Baroda's reception at Veeraswamy's Restaurant (owned by him), and a buffet dinner by Billy Griffith in his secretary's house behind the grandstand. Thereafter, the numbers attending the conference proliferated, making private hospitality almost impossible.

The Downing Street reception was an auspicious start to a memorable conference able to accept South Africa on the abolition of apartheid after 30 years of exile. This transformation was inexorable of course but F. W. de Klerk seems not to have been given his proper due for a remarkable, quite courageous act of statesmanship. Nelson Mandela, on the other hand, has of course been rightly acclaimed for his share in the achievement and has been duly acknowledged for his demeanour as a chief, which he now clearly relishes. Colin Cowdrey, with his quadruple heart bypass behind him, handled the meeting with a gentle, smooth touch. Lord Griffiths, the President of the MCC and a judge with beetling white eyebrows, let his happily breezy manner govern the dinner (given every year by the MCC) for the ICC, at which I was invited to sit at the top table.

In 1990 Anne and I had our fiftieth wedding anniversary, duly celebrated with a sprinkling of close relatives and nearby friends at the Beach Hotel, Worthing. As I spoke to the 50 present, my eye was on the sea, blue and sparkling on a positively golden day. Had it been Suva Bay rather than the English Channel, this could have been the day of Anne's arrival in May 1940 when her odyssey ended in a whirlwind of wedding activity. In my speech, I parodied Maurice Chevalier's *I Remember it Well* from the film *Gigi* and Anne duly made interruptions parodying Hermione Gingold. It took some time for those present to realize that her interventions were a put-up job. Jane Roth was the only person still alive who had attended our wedding in Fiji but she had been unable to make the journey from Cambridge. The ambassadors Ratu Epeli and Adi Koila were held back from the golden occasion at the eleventh hour. But there were links with Fiji, including two retired administrative officers of sterling quality, Brian Davies and Ted Jones, who had gone to the colony the year we left.

It has been a pleasure to know some of my successors in the Fiji administration — Jack Takala, Raman Nair, Robert Strick, Carl Hughes, Aubrey Parke (from correspondence only) and John Deverell, son of a governor of Mauritius and rising remarkably from being District Officer, Nausori, to be deputy head of MI5, only to be killed in the helicopter crash into the Mull of Kintyre hillside in 1995. With scarcely an exception, the standard among Fiji's administrative officers has patiently been upheld for nearly a century of colonial contact. Each of the other departments, such as audit, police, medical, agriculture and public works, of course also had a memorable tradition.

For my eightieth birthday in 1995, nearby relations and friends were invited to a champagne party on our lawn in the setting sun of the sunniest summer since records began in the eighteenth century. Epeli and Koila had been invited but Koila had telephoned to say that Epeli, who was accredited to Egypt, Israel, Denmark and the Vatican (an esoteric enough assortment) in addition to the United Kingdom, would be in Cairo and that she would telephone greetings to me on the day. To our intense surprise, Epeli, with his personable 12-year-old son Ratu Kamisese Mara, already six foot tall and manifestly taking after his namesake grandfather, appeared on the lawn, beaming hugely at the effect of his unannounced presence. My great friend, his late father Ratu Sir Edward Cakobau, would have delighted in just such a ploy. It had all been a put-up job. Koila's telephoning me had been worked out with Epeli and it had been intended all along that he would come. Koila herself would have come but for a bad throat. She did telephone me after Epeli and Kamisese had left to return to London. My day, introduced by a felicitous speech by Peter, had been made. It had also been marked by an iced cake in the form of an open book, thought of by Anne.

When I retired from representing Fiji on the International Cricket Council, the President of MCC, Dennis Silk, as host, invited me to speak at the annual dinner given by the MCC for the ICC in the Lord's committee dining room. Anticipating this (in 30 years I had heard many valedictions), I had prepared what from long experience I knew to be likely to be right for post-prandial conviviality. What I was not prepared for in the slightest, however, as it had never happened before, was the eight-minute standing ovation I was given by the 60 or so present. It was unique, led, I think, by the four representatives of Australia and New Zealand. In thanking me, Dennis Silk, the Somerset amateur who had captained the MCC team on the same kind of tour of New Zealand as my team had made there 20 years earlier, said that he now knew to whom to turn for the speechifying that dominated his term of office.

The next day, ICC chairman Sir Clyde Walcott presented me with a painting of the Lord's pavilion, where I had been on so many unforgettable occasions. It was a nicer finale than I could possibly have expected. In my wildest dreams I might have hoped some day to have a standing ovation returning from the wicket on the wonderful spongy turf to the pavilion at Lord's. In fact, I was never given that chance, but perhaps would have been if Fiji's promised tour of England with a match at Lord's against the MCC had materialized in 1959. The next best thing, coming down to earth, was such a kind ovation inside the pavilion.

In true Fiji nepotic manner, Peter Waine, my son-in-law, who had known the 1979, 1982 and 1986 teams from that country, succeeded me as Fiji's representative on the ICC. He had stood for Parliament in 1979 and halved the majority of the long-sitting Labour member for Nottingham North, but was never called upon again by the Conservative Office or by any constituency, once more displaying little imagination and judgement. He is now the chairman of a London head-hunting company, a sideline never gone in for by Fijian cannibals.

This brings us towards the end of 1995 in this panorama of reflections and observations. Sir Oliver Popplewell, a judge, was the new President of the MCC, but not of course the Chairman of the ICC. Sir Ewen Fergusson, formerly an ambassador to South Africa and finally to France, became Chairman of the Rugby School Governing Body, thus perpetuating a line of most distinguished holders of this office. I recalled that when his vivacious mother, Lady Bobbie Fergusson (married to a Singapore merchant, also a Sir Ewen), stayed with Anne and me at Horton House, Rugby, he had appeared from Germany, where he had been posted early in his diplomatic service career, with the largest imaginable tin of caviar as a present for us. I lived on it daily for a matter of months.

Also bringing continued distinction to the Governing Body was 3rd Viscount Daventry, Lord Lieutenant of Warwickshire who, as Hon Francis Humphrey Maurice FitzRoy-Newdegate, had played for my MCC team against Rugby Town. I introduced him of necessity in the dressing room as Humphrey Newdegate: he was ineffably modest. He had been ADC to the Viceroy of India before

267

its independence. His father had been captain of Northants under the less arresting name of Hon J. M. Fitzroy, no doubt more convenient for meeting the requests of autograph collectors.

I have had opportunities to observe more of the world and its people than I have been able to reflect upon. Just before I retired from Rugby School, the Hong Kong police needed evidence of a bulk payment of fees at the school by one of its officers on a corruption charge. I could not possibly have coped with that colony's bustle and cramped ambience. Eight or more years earlier I might have weighed dislike of flying with this all-paid opportunity. As it was, I was able to give one of my assistant accountants the chance of her lifetime.

Had I not been circumscribed for the last quarter of a century by becoming an agoraphobic aerophobe — I don't think I have any other phobias (except the one about to be mentioned) and, now allied with arthritis, they are sufficient to be going on with, I would only have wanted, as an almost unrestrainable sun devotee, to have gone to countries where it shone long and strong.

In 1979 I had been invited to be one of five members of an investigatory committee into apartheid in South Africa and its relationship to cricket (separation of spectators, players and so on). In some ways I would have liked to have taken that up, for only man seemed vile in that presumably otherwise attractive country. As an unswerving Japanophobe, I would have put that nation at the bottom of my list of places and persons to see in the world. Not the least of my aversions to it would be its teeming masses. That aspect would apply also, of course, to China.

With regrets that I have about places not visited I reflect on disappointments about not having met certain, but really quite few, celebrated individuals. Indeed, improbably I shared with V. I. Lenin his expressed wish: 'Chaplin is the only man in the world I want to meet.' Or at least much of that wish, for there would in fact also have been the Anglophobe Fleet Admiral Ernest J. King, if only to thank him for his tenacious insistence, against the most obdurate opposition of Churchill, on priority of strategy that purposefully saved Fiji from the Japanese. And there would be Fleet Admiral Chester W. Nimitz whose tactics skilfully implemented that strategy.

There were of course many others of my time whom I would have given much to have met. They included Marshal Tito, Kings Albert I and Leopold III of Belgium, 1st Earl Lloyd George, Ronald Colman, that most handsome of men in full face and profile with a superb clipped English accent, Malcolm MacDonald, the refreshingly unorthodox proconsul with whom I had some correspondence before he died and whose sister, Sheila, had visited us at Angmering, both with what must have been their father Ramsay's lively mind. Then there were coquettish Claudette Colbert and, naturally, the Marilyn Monroe, Sophia Loren, Brigitte Bardot and Elizabeth Taylor quartet, at their peak but of course beyond any reasonable expectations.

I would also have liked to have met Mikhail Gorbachev and Eduard Shevardnadze, with their welcoming open faces in such short supply among Russian public figures, Rajah Sir Charles Vyner Brooke of Sarawak, Victor Borge, with his dry, astringent, poker-faced wit, and the Duke of Windsor, if only to establish my own opinion, having seen him at the apex of his scintillating public appeal as Prince of Wales before his apparently disappointing decline that included too great an interest in Hitler. But I would not have chosen to meet his hot-and-cold friend, Admiral of the Fleet 1st Earl Mountbatten, who was too self-confident in the knowledge of his physical impressiveness, equine though it later became, and not aware enough of his proneness to mistakes as in his supreme command of the utterly pointless and therefore more poignantly disastrous Dieppe raid.

Earlier figures such as King George V, Field Marshal 1st Earl Haig, and Marshals Joffre and Foch would have been fascinating to judge — as would Admirals of the Fleet 1st Earl Jellicoe and 1st Earl Beatty. There also come to mind Maurice Chevalier (whom Ratu Sir Edward Cakobau seemed sometimes to resemble), Adlai Stevenson and Eugene Macarthy, Jawaharlal Nehru, Fred Perry, Jean Borotra, René Lacoste, Sir Robert Menzies, Sir Max Beerbohm (so narrowly missed in 1951), Sir Austen Chamberlain (as mentioned earlier), F. W. de Klerk and, if given an incredible choice, Ingrid Bergman rather than fellow Scandinavian, Greta Garbo. Willy Brandt and Field Marshal 1st Viscount Alanbrooke would have been of interest to me, but not the US army general Douglas MacArthur; he was too vain and imperious.

Disenchantment with most writers I had met did not incline me to wish to meet others. And, like Charles, I preferred the intelligent to the intellectual. But I had met, sometimes too briefly, quite a few diverse characters both high and low in profile — by chance more often than by desire, not leaving many others for my curiosity.

I have myself tried to be as much of an individual as possible in my life. Crowds and the dangerous hysteria they generate and for which they have been responsible historically to such a serious extent are abhorred. In addition to being non-political and non-religious, I have been anti-masonic and against anything cliquish like that. But having recently been given a list of members of the Grand Lodge of Fiji, I am taken aback to find a number of my warmest friends such as Reg Caten, Sir Robert Munro, and auditor and tennis mentor Harry Stanley contained there, some attaining principal rank. But being Masons cannot have helped my friends Reg Caten and Harry Stanley as much as one might have expected, for they both remained under-placed in their working careers, deserving far better if merit, intrinsic worth and excellence of character had their true places in life. So I cannot be anti-Masons as such but simply against the movement, which evokes a peculiar juvenility and inevitably includes some people for whom I have no time, as well as friends in the ironic way in which life takes its meandering course.

For me, individuality is the most precious quality in a person's style. Individuals should be judged as such, separately, in the round and divorced from their environment. Whatever their origins and race, which they can neither help nor do much to change, individuals come above all other considerations.

As these reflections are drawn to a conclusion up to date, I am reminded that I summarized in my *Stranger and Brother: A Portrait of C. P. Snow* the three main male and female influences in Charles's life as respectively G. H. Hardy, Bert Howard and Charles Allberry, our mother, Pam and Anne Seagrim. I find it more difficult to do the same exercise for myself and cannot confine myself to the same numbers in each sex.

Paradise Walkabout

I suppose that the men who have made most impact on me have been Charles (his persistent presence in these recollections will serve as testimony to his outstanding place in my affection and respect), Bert Howard (only until I was about 19 and only from 11), Humphrey Evans and two Fijian chiefs, Ratu Sir Lala Sukuna and Ratu Sir Edward Cakobau. The reasons for the selection of this quintet will be apparent from the way I have written about them.

Of women, it must of course be my mother, Anne and Stefanie, with Philippa intuitively knowing that she is coming up automatically fast in that bracket. Others have had their impact over shorter spans in different ways and cannot be embraced within the domestic triumvirate (or quadrumvirate).

Compared with so many, I have at least made it as far beyond the horizon as it is possible to go on the globe and to have lived there for a reckonable period of my life, only to return home and be thankful about what I have summarily described. It has been, one trusts, not overmuch of an ego trip.

I only hope that I emerge with candour free from all prejudice of class and colour. Indeed, variety of class and colour come high in the ingredients of spice and happiness that I have found.

Not that it matters, but I can't make up my mind whether or not I am a sentimentalist. Readers will have to judge that for themselves. If I am, then I hope I am not a chauvinistic one. In any case, sentimentalists with a sense of balance are a subspecies of the human race, which I trust will never become extinct in our not altogether soft or gracious world.

Bibliography

Allen, David Rayvern (1994) *Arlott: The Authorised Biography*, London, Harper Collins

Amos, William (1985) *The Originals: Who's Really Who in Fiction*, London, Jonathan Cape

Bates, Sir Julian Darrell (1972) *A Gust of Plumes: A Biography of Lord Twining of Godalming and Tanganyika*, London, Hodder & Stoughton

Berwick, Samuel Lawrence (ed.) (1990) *Who's Who in Fiji*, Suva, Berwick Publishing House

Birkenhead, Frederick Winston Furneaux Smith (1978) *Rudyard Kipling*, London, Weidenfeld & Nicolson

Bold, Alan and Robert Giddings (1987) *Who Was Really Who in Fiction*, London, Longman

Boothby, Robert John Graham (1962) *My Yesterday Your Tomorrow*, London, Hutchinson

Bowen, Rowland (1970) *Cricket: A History of its Growth and Development throughout the World*, London, Eyre & Spottiswoode

Braddon, Russell (1952) *The Naked Island*, London, Werner Laurie

Brewster, Adolph Brewster (Joske) (1922) *The Hill Tribes of Fiji*, London, Seeley, Service

— (1937) *King of the Cannibal Isles*, London, Robert Hale

Brown, Antony Cave (1976) *Bodyguard of Lies*, London, W. H. Allen

Carmichael, Peter and June Knox-Mawer (1968) *A World of Islands*, London, Collins

Caten, Reginald Robert Cecil (1997) *Vosalevu: Memories of Life in Fiji during Four Decades 1924–1953*, Carlisle, Western Australia, Hesperian Press

Chamberlain, Walter and Herbert Chamberlain (n.d.) 'Journal of Travel from January 1875 to July 1879', unpublished manuscript

Clunie, Fergus Gourlay Anderson Urquhart and Philip Albert Snow, translated by Stefanie Vuikaba Snow Waine (1986) 'Notes on Travels in Interior of Viti Levu by Edouard Graeffe', *Domodomo: Fiji Museum Journal*

273

Bibliography

Cooper, William (1959) *C. P. Snow*, London, Longmans, Green

Corner, Edred John Henry (1981) *The Marquis*, Singapore, Heinemann

Daily Telegraph (London) Obituaries by Philip Snow of Ratu Sir George Cakobau, Dr Timoci Bavadra, Sir Ronald Garvey and Sir David Trench

De la Mothe, John (1992) *C. P. Snow and the Struggle of Modernity*, Austin, University of Texas Press

Foot, Michael Richard Daniel (1960) *SOE in France*, London, HMSO

Freyberg, Paul Richard (1991) *Bernard Freyberg, VC: Soldier of Two Nations*, London, Hodder & Stoughton

Garvey, Sir Ronald Herbert (1983) *Gentleman Pauper*, Bognor Regis, New Horizon

Grimble, Sir Arthur Francis (1952) *A Pattern of Islands*, London, John Murray

— (1957) *Return to the Islands*, London, John Murray

Hadlee, Walter Arnold (1993) *The Innings of a Lifetime*, Auckland, David Bateman

Halperin, John (1983) *C. P. Snow: An Oral Biography*, Brighton, Harvester Press

Heald, Tim (1994) *Denis Compton: The Authorised Biography of the Incomparable*, London, Pavilion

Hill, Alan (1990) *Herbert Sutcliffe: Cricket Maestro*, London, Simon & Schuster

Holmes, Lowell D. (1984) *Samoan Islands Bibliography*, Kansas, Wichita, Poly Concepts

Horne, Alastair (1989) *Macmillan*, London, Macmillan

Howat, Gerald (1987) *Plum Warner*, London, Unwin Hyman

— (1988) *Len Hutton*, London, Heinemann Kingswood

International Authors' and Writers' Who's Who, The (1989) Cambridge, Melrose Press

International Cricket Conference (1979) *The ICC Trophy 1979: International World Cup Cricket*, Birmingham, ICC

— (1982) *The ICC Trophy 1982*, Birmingham, ICC

— (1994) *ICC Trophy 1994*, Nairobi, Kenya, ICC

James, Robert Rhodes (1991) *Bob Boothby*, London, Hodder & Stoughton

Johnson, Pamela Hansford (1952) *Catherine Carter*, London, Macmillan

— (1974) *Important to Me: Personalia*, London, Macmillan

Kay, John (ed.) (1959) *Cricket Heroes*, London, Phoenix

Knox-Mawer, June (1986) *Tales from Paradise*, London, BBC Ariel

Maddocks, Kenneth Phipson (1988) *Of No Fixed Abode*, Ipswich, Wolsey

Maeyer, Edward A. de (1967) *Who's Who in Europe*, Brussels Editions de Feniks

Marquand, David (1977) *Ramsay MacDonald*, London, Jonathan Cape

Bibliography

Martin-Jenkins, Christopher (ed.) (1992) *A Cricketer's Companion*, Harpenden, Smallmead

— (1996) *World Cricketers: A Biographical Dictionary*, Oxford, Oxford University Press

Masefield, Peter Gordon (1982) *To Ride the Storm: The Story of the Airship R101*, London, William Kimber

May, Hal and James G. Lesniak (eds) (1990) *Contemporary Authors*, Detroit, Gale Research

Millar, Ronald (1962) *The Affair: A Play*, adapted from the novel of C. P. Snow, New York, Scribner/London, S. French

— (1964) *The Affair: The New Men and the Masters*, three plays based on the novels of and with a preface by C. P. Snow, London, Macmillan

— (1975) *The Case in Question: A Play*, based on C. P. Snow's novel *In Their Wisdom*, London, S. French

— (1982) *A Coat of Varnish: A Play in Two Acts*, suggested by the novel of C. P. Snow, London, Scripts Ltd

— (1993) *A View from the Wings: West End, West Coast, Westminster*, London, Weidenfeld

Nan Kivell, Rex de Charembac and Sydney Alfred Spence (n.d.) *Portraits of the Famous and Infamous 1492–1970*, London

O'Reilly, Père Patrick Georges Farell and Edouard Reitman (1967) *Bibliographie de Tahiti et de la Polynésie française*, Paris, Musée de l'Homme

Padwick, Ernest William (1977) *A Bibliography of Cricket*, London, Library Association

Pawle, Gerald (1985) *R. E. S. Wyatt: Fighting Cricketer*, London, George Allen & Unwin

Pope-Hennessy, James (1964) *Verandah: Some Episodes in the Crown Colonies: 1867–1889*, New York, Alfred A. Knopf

Ramanathan, Suguna (1978) *The Novels of C. P. Snow*, London, Macmillan

Ranchhod, Harry (ed.) (1984) *Fiji Cricket Association: Souvenir Programme England Cricket Team Tour 1983/4*, Fiji Cricket Association, Suva

— (1986) *Fiji Cricket Association: Souvenir Programme ICC Trophy Competition, Birmingham, UK 1986*, Fiji Cricket Association, Suva

Robertson-Glasgow, Raymond Charles (1943) *Cricket Prints: Some Batsmen and Bowlers 1920–1940*, London, T. Werner Laurie

Rose, Kenneth Vivian (1983) *King George V*, London, Weidenfeld & Nicolson

Roth, George Kingsley (1973) *Fijian Way of Life* (second edition with introduction by G. B. Milner), Melbourne, Oxford University Press

Roth, Jane F. Violet and Steven Hooper (eds) (1990) *The Fiji Journals of Baron Anatole von Hügel 1875–1877*, Suva, Fiji Museum

Bibliography

Rouse, William Henry Denham (1898) *A History of Rugby School*, London, Duckworth

Shusterman, David (1991) *C. P. Snow*, Boston, Mass., Twayne, G. K. Hall

Snow, Charles Percy (1932) *Death Under Sail*, London, Heinemann

— (1933) (anonymously) *New Lives for Old*, London, Gollancz

— (1934) *The Search*, London, Gollancz

— (1938) *Richard Aldington: An Appreciation*, London, Heinemann

— (1941) *Strangers and Brothers* (retitled *George Passant*), London, Faber & Faber

— (1947) *The Light and the Dark*, London, Faber & Faber

— (1948) 'The Mathematician on Cricket', *The Saturday Book*, 8th Year, pp. 65–73

— (1949) *Time of Hope*, London, Faber & Faber

— (1951) *The Masters*, London, Macmillan

— (1954) *The New Men*, London, Macmillan

— (1956) *Homecomings*, London, Macmillan

— (1958) *The Conscience of the Rich*, London, Macmillan

— (1959) *The Two Cultures and the Scientific Revolution*, Cambridge, Cambridge University Press

— (1960) *The Affair*, London, Macmillan

— (1961) *Science and Government*, Cambridge, Mass., Harvard University Press

— (1962) *A Postscript to Science and Government*, Cambridge, Mass., Harvard University Press

— (1962) *On Magnanimity*, London, University of St Andrews

— (1964) *The Two Cultures: And a Second Look*, Cambridge, Cambridge University Press

— (1964) *Corridors of Power*, London, Macmillan

— (1967) *Variety of Men: Rutherford, G. H. Hardy, H. G. Wells, Einstein, Lloyd-George, Winston Churchill, Robert Frost, Dag Hammarskjöld, Stalin*, London, Macmillan

— (1968) *The Sleep of Reason*, London, Macmillan

— (1969) *The State of Siege*, New York, Scribner

— (1970) *Last Things*, London, Macmillan

— (1970) 'The Case of Leavis — and the Serious Case', *Times Literary Supplement*, 9 July

— (1971) *Public Affairs*, London, Macmillan

— (1972) *The Malcontents*, London, Macmillan

— (1974) *In Their Wisdom*, London, Macmillan

— (1975) *Trollope: His Life and Art*, London, Macmillan

— (1978) *A Coat of Varnish*, London, Macmillan

— (1978) *The Realists: Portraits of Eight Novelists. Stendhal, Balzac, Dickens, Dostoevsky, Tolstoy, Galdós, Henry James, Proust*, London, Macmillan

Bibliography

— (1981) *The Physisists: A Generation that Changed the World*, London, Macmillan

Snow, Edward Eric (1949) *A History of Leicestershire Cricket*, Leicester, Backus

— (1964) *Sir Julien Cahn's XI*, Leicester, E. E. Snow

— (1977) *Leicestershire Cricket 1949 to 1977*, London, Stanley Paul

— (1985) *E. Phillips Oppenheim: Storyteller 1866 to 1946*, Evington, E. E. Snow

Snow, Philip Albert (1940–50) 'Diaries and Annual Reports of District Commissioner, Lau 1940–1941, Nadi 1941–1943, Lautoka 1943–1944 and Taveuni and Nasavusavu 1947–1950', typescript in National Archives of Fiji

— (1943) *Civil Defence Services, Lautoka*, Suva, Government Printer

— (1943) *Important Notice: Air Raids*, Lautoka, Lautoka Print

— (1943) *Mo Ni Kila: Na Kaba ni Meca mai Macawa*, Lautoka, Lautoka Print

— (1945) 'Bronze and Clay' or 'The Thin Edge of the World', typescript

— (1946–51) 'Diaries of Ocean Voyages 1946, 1947, 1951', unpublished manuscript

— (1948) 'Diary of Fiji Cricket Team's New Zealand Tour, 1948', manuscript

— (1949) *Cricket in the Fiji Islands*, Christchurch and Dunedin, Whitcombe & Tombs

— (1951) 'Cricket in Fiji', *Go*, October/November, pp. 49–51, 95

— (1952) 'Cricket op de Zuidzee-eilanden', *Cricket*, Leiden, 23 May, pp. 8–10

— (1953) 'Rock Carvings in Fiji', *Fiji Society Transactions for 1950*, New Plymouth, New Zealand, Avery Press

— (1953) 'The Friendly Isles', *Go*, September/October, pp. 56–8

— (1954) 'The Nature of Fiji and Tonga', *Discovery*, February, pp. 67–9

— (1964) Diary of Visit to United States of America and Canada, 1964', typescript

— (1964) *Report on the Visit of Three Bursars to the United States of America and Canada, 1964* (with D. M. Sherwood and F. J. Walesby), Bristol, Public Schools' Bursars' Association

— (1967) *Best Stories of the South Seas*, London, Faber & Faber

— (1967) *Visit of Her Majesty the Queen and His Royal Highness Prince Philip, Duke of Edinburgh on the Occasion of the Quatercentenary Year, Friday, 12 May 1967*, Rugby, Rugby School

— (1969) *Bibliography of Fiji, Tonga and Rotuma Vol. 1*, Canberra, Australian National University Press, and Coral Gables, Miami University Press

— (1971) Introduction to George Palmer, *Kidnapping in the South Seas*, London, Dawsons of Pall Mall

Bibliography

— (1973) Introduction to Berthold Seeman, *Viti: An Account of a Government Mission to the Vitian or Fijian Islands 1860–1861*, London, Dawsons of Pall Mall

— (1974) 'A Century in the Fiji Islands', *Wisden Cricketers' Almanack*, London, Sporting Handbooks, pp. 123–9

— (1978) Foreword to Filipe Bole, The Life and Times of Ratu Sir Lala Sukuna, Suva

— (1982) *Stranger and Brother: A Portrait of C. P. Snow*, London, Macmillan/New York, Scribner, 1983

— (1983) 'The ICC Trophy 1982', *Wisden Cricketers' Almanack*, London

— (1986) Foreword to *The ICC Trophy 1986*, Birmingham, International Cricket Conference

— (1988) 'The Rarest Printed Work on the Pacific? A Bibliographer's Proposition', *Domodomo: Fiji Museum Journal*, vol. 1, no. 4, pp. 30–43

— (1989) Foreword to *ICC Trophy Competitions 1979, 1982, 1986*, Nottingham, Association of Cricket Statisticians

— (1991) Introduction to Anne Gittins, *Tales of the Fiji Islands*, Salisbury, Lavenham Press

— (1994) *Origin and Development of International Cricket Council Associates and ICC Trophy Competition*, Nairobi, Karibu Kenya ICC Trophy

— (1997) Preface to Reginald Robert Cecil Caten, *Vosalevu: Memories of Life in Fiji During Four Decades 1924–1953*, Carlisle, Western Australia, Hesperian Press

Snow, Philip Albert and Stefanie Vuikaba Snow Waine (1979) *The People from the Horizon: An Illustrated History of the Europeans among the South Sea Islanders*, Oxford, Phaidon/ New York, E. P. Dutton (reprint London, McLaren, 1986)

Stanmore, Arthur Charles Hamilton Gordon (1897-1912) *Fiji: Records of Public and Private Life 1875–1880*, Edinburgh, R. & R. Clark

Sukuna, Ratu Sir Josefa Lalabalavu Vanaaliali (1932–40) 'Diaries and Annual Reports of District Commissioner, Lau', typescript in National Archives of Fiji

— (1939) 'The Fijian's View of the European', speech to Defence Club, Suva

— (1948–51) *Reports of the Secretary for Fijian Affairs 1948–1951*, Suva, Government Printer

Swanton, Ernest William (ed.) (1966) *The World of Cricket*, London, Michael Joseph

— (1977) *Follow On*, London, Collins

— (1985) *Gubby Allen: Man of Cricket*, London, Hutchinson & Stanley Paul

Swanton, Ernest William and John Woodcock (eds) (1980) *Barclays' World of Cricket*, London, Collins

Bibliography

Swanton, Ernest William, George Plumptre and John Woodcock (eds) (1986) *Barclays' World of Cricket*, London, Willow

Tarte, Daryl (1993) *Turaga: The Life and Times and Chiefly Authority of Ratu Sir Penaia Ganilau, GCMG, KCVO, KBE, DSO*, Suva, Fiji Times

Thomson, Sir Basil Home (1888) 'New Guinea 1888', manuscript

— (1894) *South Sea Yarns*, London, William Blackwood

— (1894) *The Diversions of a Prime Minister*, London, William Blackwood

— (1900) 'Journal (Tonga and Niue) 1900', manuscript

— (1902) *Savage Island*, London, John Murray

— (1908) *The Fijians: A Study of the Decay of Custom*, London, William Heinemann

— (1939) *The Scene Changes*, London, Collins

Times, The (London) Obituaries by Philip Snow of George Geary, Sir John Nicoll, George Kingsley Roth, Sir Ronald Garvey, Sir Jacob Vouza, Dr Timoci Bavadra

Tudor, Judy (ed.) (1968) *Pacific Islands Year Book and Who's Who*, Sydney, Pacific Publications, tenth edition

Unibond-ICC Trophy 1990 (1990) The Hague, Unibond

Waine, Stefanie Vuikaba Snow (trans.) (1984) 'Theodor Kleinschmidt's Notes on the Hill Tribes of Viti Levu 1877–1878', *Domodomo: Fiji Museum Journal*, vol. 2, no. 4, pp. 138–96

Who's Who (n.d.) London, A. & C. Black

Who's Who in the World (n.d.) Chicago, Marquis

Who Was Who (n.d.) London, A. & C. Black

Williams, Sir Edgar Trevor (ed.) (1951–60 and 1961–70) *Dictionary of National Biography*, Oxford, Oxford University Press

Wisden Cricketers' Almanack, London

Index

281

Index

Index

Index

Index

Index

124, 133, 138, 149–51, 158–9, 163–4, 168–9, 181, 193, 204–6, 226, 232–5, 241, 244–5, 248, 253, 257–60, 262–3, 266, 268; *see also* Cricket Writers' Club; Fiji Cricket Association; Imperial Cricket Conference; International Cricket Conference; International Cricket Council; Rugby Town Cricket Club

Cricket in the Fiji Islands, 21, 49, 52, 69, 191, 238

Cricket Writers' Club, 21, 31, 58, 72, 80

Cricket Heroes, 59

Cricket Quarterly, 69

Cricket: A History of its Growth and Development, 69

Cricketer, 34

Cromwell Mansions, 43

Cromwell Road, London, 43–4, 47, 57, 82, 101, 113, 116, 132–4, 176

Crook, Arthur, 114

Cross, Leslie, 68

Cruickshank, Andrew, 236

Cumberland Hotel, London, 53

Cunard Lines, 58

Cunningham, Admiral of the Fleet Viscount, 107

Curtis, Anthony, 115

Curtis Brown, 176, 177

Cyprus, 243

Dahl, Roald, 232

Daily Telegraph, 1–2, 75, 171, 183, 227

Dalmeny, *see* Rosebery, 6th Earl, Lord Dalmeny

dalo, 3, 101

Daly, Diane, 241

Daly, Martin, 241

Dandenongs, 31

Dane, Carl, 165

Dartmoor Prison, 16, 189

Daventry, 3rd Viscount, Honourable Francis Humphrey Maurice FitzRoy-Newdegate, 45, 267

Davidson, J. W., 156

Davidson, Margaret, 200

Davies, Brian, 265

Davies, Dai, 20

Davies, J. G. W., 245, 257

Davies, Lord Llewellyn, 178

Davis, Fred, 168

Davis, Joe, 168

Davis Cup, 35

Dawson, Edward W., 48, 151–2

Dawson of Penn, 1st Viscount, 218

Dawson-Hill, 201

de Broke, Lord Willoughby, 11–12, 100, 121, 131

de Gaulle, General, 159

de Klerk, F. W., 265, 269

De La Warr, 9th Earl, 50

De Montfort Hall, 44–5

Dean, Sir Patrick, 8–9, 86, 157, 158, 179–80, 184, 193

Death Under Sail, 197

Decca, 82

Deep South, 85

Denbigh, Earl of, 252

Denison, Michael, 197

Denmark, 111, 206, 224, 257, 266

Desert Island Discs, 173–4

Deverell, John, 265

Devon, 16

Devon and Somerset Staghounds, 69

Devonshire, 11th Duke of, 103

Dewes, John, 48, 181

Dewey, Reverend Meredith, 70, 89

Dickens, Charles John Huffam (1812–70), 197

Dickson, Donald Harold Wauchope, 135, 207–8

Dictionary of National Biography, 5, 23

Dieppe, 269

Dobuni, 18

Don, The Very Reverend Alan C., Dean of Westminster, 7, 30, 89

Dorchester Hotel, London, 134

Dostoevsky, Fyodor Mikhailovich (1821–81), 197

Dowding, Air Marshal Sir Hugh, 11, 37

Index

Index

Index

Index

Index

Index

Index

Legislative Council, 55

Leicester, 1, 41–2, 65, 113, 117–18, 146, 150, 172, 179, 205, 222, 228, 234–5, 259, 262

Leicester, Lord Mayor of, 219

Leicester City Council, 42, 234

Leicestershire, 17, 48, 113, 117, 133, 150–2, 195, 235

Leigh, Vivien, 44

Lenin, Vladimir Ilyich (1870–1924), 268

Lenner, Anne, 205

Lenner, Shirley, 205

Leofric Hotel, Coventry, 94

Leopold III, King of the Belgians (1901–83), 269

Lesuma, Inoke, 93

Levuka, 104, 226

Lewis, Sir Edward Roberts, 82, 184

Lewis, Vic, 261

Leyland, Maurice, 48, 59

Library Association, 64

Lichfield, 5th Earl of, 232

Life, 105

Life of Jesus, 156

Ligamamada, Sitiveni, 147, 249; *see also* Rabuka, Lieutenant-Colonel Sitiveni

Light and the Dark, The, 153

Liku, Adi Maca, 50

Lille, 173

Limelight, 174

Lindemann, Frederick Alexander; *see* Cherwell, Frederick Alexander Lindemann, 1st Viscount

Lindop, Sir Norman, 219

Lindrum, Walter, 168

Lini, Father Walter, 93–4

Linklaters & Paines, 11

Lipton, Sidney, 125–7

Livingston, L., 181

Lloyd George of Dwyfor, Countess, 219

Lloyd George of Dwyfor, David, 1st Earl (1863–1945), 108, 170, 269

Lloyd George of Dwyfor, Owen, 3rd Earl, 256

Lloyd George of Dwyfor, Robin, 219, 256

Local Government Boundaries Commission, 140

Lochhead, Sheila Ramsay (*née* MacDonald), 228, 269

Lomaloma, 90, 93, 244

London, 10, 25, 31–3, 37, 39, 43–4, 50, 52–5, 58, 64, 74, 94, 99, 101, 106, 113, 116–17, 119, 125, 136, 146, 157–8, 160, 162, 164–5, 169, 179, 186–7, 189–90, 192, 194, 203–4, 209, 213, 219, 221–2, 224, 226–8, 239–40, 243, 249, 256, 266–7

London Clinic, 221

London University, 9

Longford, Countess of, 114, 178

Longford, 7th Earl of, 114, 178, 232

Lord's, 2, 14–15, 22, 33–5, 45, 48–9, 52, 56, 69, 81, 101, 158, 258, 261, 266–7

Lord Lieutenants,

of Greater London, *see* Bramall, Field Marshal Baron Edwin

of Herefordshire, 9, *see* Cilcennin of Hereford, 1st Viscount, James P. L. Thomas

of Midlothian; *see* Rosebery, 6th Earl, Lord Dalmeny

of Warwickshire; *see* Daventry, 3rd Viscount, Honourable Francis Humphrey Maurice FitzRoy-Newdegate; de Broke, Lord Willoughby

Loren, Sophia (1934–), 269

Loretto, 63

Los Angeles, 161

Loughery, Bill, 180

Loughton, Essex, 14

Louisville University, 231

Lourie, John, 169

Lower Rewa (Burebasaga), 255

Lubbock, *see* Avebury, 4th Lord, Eric Lubbock

Lucky Jim, 114

Luke, Sir Harry Charles, 1884–1969), 7, 51, 126, 186

Lunghi, Cherie, 236

Lutyens, Sir Edwin Landseer (1869–1944), 80

Lyttelton, *see* Cobham, 10th Viscount, Charles J. Lyttelton

McAlpine, H. G. R., 187

293

Index

Index

Index

Index

Index

Redgrave, Sir Michael Scudamore (1908–85), 41

Reece, Arthur, 123, 181

Rees Mogg, Lord, 178

Regent Street Polytechnic, 187

Renan, Joseph Ernest, 156

Report on the Visit of Three Bursars to the United States of America in 1964, 84–5

Repton, 35

Return to Cambridge, 65

Rewa, 149, 244; *see also* Lower Rewa

Rewa River, 104, 141, 202

Ricardo, Sir Harry, 9, 70

Richard III, King, 229

Richards, Sir Arthur, *see* Milverton, Lord

Richards, Brian, 180

Richards, David, 261

Richards, Frank; *see* St John Hamilton, Charles

Richardson, Sir Ralph David (1902–83), 34

Richardson, Victor York, 133

Richmond Road, Leicester, 42, 205, 212, 234–5

Riot Act, 19

Rippon, Angela, 232

Ritchie, General Sir Neil, 67

Robbins of Clare Market, Lionel Charles, Baron (1898–1984), 178

Robert and Elizabeth, 79

Robertson, Arnot, 44

Robertson-Glasgow, Raymond Charles, 83

Robins, Walter, 110–11

Robinson, Kenneth, 213

Robotham, Alderman W. A., 128

Rodgers, Richard (1902–79), 24

Rogers, Richard, 80

Romeo and Juliet, 40

Rose, Kenneth, 115

Rose, Sir Hector, 201

Rosebery, 6th Earl, 36

Rossiter, Leonard, 197

Roth, Jane F. Violet, 162, 187, 265

Roth, Kingsley, 50, 68

Rotuma(ns), 90, 92, 144, 190, 207, 252

Rouen, 173

Row, Raman Subba, 260

Rowan, Athol, 19

Rowan brothers, 21

Rowley Green, 15

Rowse, A. L., 178

Roxburghe, Mary Duchess of, 115, 178, 219

Royal Anthropological Institute, 64, 161, 183, 262

Royal College of Surgeons, 91

Royal Commonwealth Society, 50, 52

Royal Fiji Police, 237

Royal Geographical Society, 183

Royal Heritage, 173, 199

Royal Institution, 78

Royal Scottish Academy, 6

Royal Society, 9, 64, 70

Royal Society of Arts, 259

Royle, Anthony, Baron of Fanshawe, 149

Rubinstein, Michael, 219, 222

Rugby, 14, 18, 22, 38–9, 41, 48–9, 53, 60–1, 71, 74, 86, 113, 127, 139, 142, 146–8, 151, 157, 161, 163, 165, 167, 187, 188, 195, 209, 249, 252, 255, 267

Rugby College of Engineering Technology, 95

rugby football, 40, 122, 146–7, 225, 249

Rugby Rotary Club, 30

Rugby School, 1–4, 6, 11–13, 17, 21, 24–5, 27–9, 35–8, 45–6, 52–5, 59–61, 64, 68, 70, 76, 78, 82, 84, 86–7, 89, 94–5, 97, 99–100, 103, 106, 110, 120, 126–7, 140, 142–3, 149–50, 157–8, 160, 167, 169, 172, 177, 179–80, 182–4, 187, 191, 211, 249, 268

Old Rugbeian Society, 121

Rugby Town Cricket Club, 17, 45–6, 56, 110, 258, 267

Rungta, P. M., 183

Rushdie, Ahmed Salman, 99

Ruskin College, Oxford, 39

Russia, 61, 152, 156, 174, 195

Russian(s), 43, 106, 116, 132, 151, 196–7, 200, 269

Rustington, 188

Rutherford of Nelson, Ernest, 1st Baron (1871–1937), 170

Rutland, 13, 140

298

Index

Index

Index

Index

Index

Index